PLATONISM

The task of philosophy, the French philosopher Gilles Deleuze once wrote, is to 'overturn Platonism'. This might be true, if only we could define what Platonism is. In this clear and accessible book, Mauro Bonazzi provides the first comprehensive introduction to ancient Platonism. He begins his story with Plato's Academy before moving on to the sceptical turn which occurred during the Hellenistic centuries. He then explains the theologically oriented interpretation of Plato typical of Middle Platonists, and concludes with the metaphysical systems of the Neoplatonists. Platonism has often been regarded as no more than a trivial repetition of the same doctrines. This book, however, demonstrates how the attempts of Platonists over the centuries to engage with Plato's thought constitute one of the most philosophically challenging moments in the history of ancient philosophy.

MAURO BONAZZI is Professor of Ancient and Medieval Philosophy at Utrecht University. His books include *The Sophists* (Cambridge, 2020) and *En quête des Idées. Platonisme et philosophie hellénistique* (2015). He is currently completing a monograph on the uses and abuses of Greek thought in Modern philosophy.

CLASSICAL SCHOLARSHIP IN TRANSLATION

Series editors
RENAUD GAGNÉ, *University of Cambridge*
JONAS GRETHLEIN, *Ruprecht-Karls-Universität Heidelberg*

Classical Scholarship in Translation provides English translations of some particularly notable and significant scholarship on the ancient Greek and Roman worlds and their reception written in other languages in order to make it better known and appreciated. All areas of classical scholarship are considered.

Recent titles in the series:

Platonism: A Concise History from the Early Academy to Late Antiquity
MAURO BONAZZI

The Greeks and their Histories: Myth, History and Society
HANS-JOACHIM GEHRKE

The Hera of Zeus: Intimate Enemy, Ultimate Spouse
VINCIANE PIRENNE-DELFORGE AND GABRIELLA PIRONTI

PLATONISM

A Concise History from the Early Academy to Late Antiquity

MAURO BONAZZI
Utrecht University, the Netherlands

Translated by Sergio Knipe

CAMBRIDGE
UNIVERSITY PRESS

Shaftesbury Road, Cambridge CB2 8EA, United Kingdom

One Liberty Plaza, 20th Floor, New York, NY 10006, USA

477 Williamstown Road, Port Melbourne, VIC 3207, Australia

314–321, 3rd Floor, Plot 3, Splendor Forum, Jasola District Centre, New Delhi – 110025, India

103 Penang Road, #05–06/07, Visioncrest Commercial, Singapore 238467

Cambridge University Press is part of Cambridge University Press & Assessment, a department of the University of Cambridge.

We share the University's mission to contribute to society through the pursuit of education, learning and research at the highest international levels of excellence.

www.cambridge.org
Information on this title: www.cambridge.org/9781009253420

DOI: 10.1017/9781009253413

First published in 2015 as *Il platonismo*. Copyright © 2015
Giulio Einaudi editore s.p.a., Torino
English translation © Mauro Bonazzi 2023

First published 2023

Printed in the United Kingdom by CPI Group Ltd, Croydon CR0 4YY

A catalogue record for this publication is available from the British Library

Library of Congress Cataloging-in-Publication Data
NAMES: Bonazzi, Mauro, 1973– author.
TITLE: Platonism : a concise history from the early academy to late
antiquity / Mauro Bonazzi, Universiteit Utrecht, The Netherlands.
DESCRIPTION: Cambridge, United Kingdom ; New York, NY, USA : Cambridge
University Press, 2023. | Series: Classical scholarship in translation |
Includes bibliographical references and index.
IDENTIFIERS: LCCN 2022033348 | ISBN 9781009253420 (hardback) |
ISBN 9781009253413 (ebook)
SUBJECTS: LCSH: Platonists – History.
CLASSIFICATION: LCC B395 .B596 2023 | DDC 184–dc23/eng/20230105
LC record available at https://lccn.loc.gov/2022033348

ISBN 978-1-009-25342-0 Hardback

CONTENTS

Contents

FIGURE

FOREWORD

David Sedley

Readers of this book know, or are about to learn under Mauro Bonazzi's expert guidance, how continuous and yet at the same time how diverse was the ancient philosophical movement known to us as Platonism. How can there have been so many Platonisms, or, if you prefer, so many competing versions of Plato's philosophy? After all, every published word of Plato, the school's iconic founder, survived and was, as indeed it remains today, open to direct scrutiny? Why wasn't that enough to make Plato's philosophical meaning transparent? In other words, why was Plato not himself the ultimate authority on his own philosophy?

The Platonic *corpus* is a large, diverse and brilliant collection of writings, nearly all of them purporting to be or to include reports of dialogues. But Plato himself is never named as taking part in these conversations. The figure who is virtually always present, and more often than not asks the questions, is Plato's revered master Socrates. Does this literary figure Socrates, then, tend to speak for Plato? So it has generally, and very plausibly, been thought. Yet across the corpus, Socrates himself varies widely in the opinions he seems to favour – when, at any rate, he favours any, and is not simply interrogating others, perhaps in order to expose their assumptions and test these for mutual coherence.

To pick just one example out of many, is knowledge humanly attainable? Socrates makes few substantive knowledge claims on his own behalf in any Platonic dialogue, and repeatedly refutes others' pretensions to knowledge. Indeed, in the *Phaedo*, Socrates seems at times to go so far as to treat knowledge as unattainable by the soul until it leaves bodily incarnation behind altogether. Yet this same character Socrates is also the lead speaker of the Republic, where he argues that human happiness depends on the remote but real prospect of living under the governance of highly trained philosophers who possess comprehensive knowledge of the Forms, all the way up to the ultimate explanatory principle, identified as the Form of the Good.

In the course of two-and-a-half millennia, Plato's readers have adopted a variety of strategies for dealing with this kind of problem. Perhaps Socrates does not always speak for Plato, for example. Perhaps when he disavows knowledge he is speaking 'ironically', with his own articulated philosophical knowledge lying just below the surface. Perhaps Plato used Socrates only to puncture others' epistemic vanity. Or perhaps Plato's own views changed over the years, and these developments were reflected by philosophical shifts of position in the dialogues.

We may start with this last hypothesis. Today, it is very widely assumed that Plato's writings fall into three main phases, albeit with some works classed as 'transitional' between one phase and the next. The three postulated phases are as follows:

- An 'early' period, in which he was still working out the meaning of Socrates' philosophical legacy;
- a 'middle' period, dominated by the immortality of the soul, and by a dualistic metaphysics of intelligibles and sensibles, or of Forms and their participants; and
- a 'late' period critically readdressing major political and analytic themes, but also including the *Timaeus*, Plato's one dialogue devoted to physics.

It would indeed be hard for today's readers to set aside the whole of this chronological matrix, which has the additional merit of seeming to correspond to stylistic changes in Plato's writing, with the philosophically earlier dialogues prone to mimic the natural flow of conversation, whereas the philosophically later ones seem like self-conscious literary constructs, often thereby placing much greater demands on the reader.

It is therefore of utmost importance to appreciate that the task of dating Plato's individual works relative to each other, a major priority in modern scholarship, was of little concern to ancient Platonists. Of course, the dialogues must have been written in some order, and the *Laws* was explicitly recognised to have been the last. Since, however, it was inconceivable to his followers that the 'divine' Plato should ever have been forced to change his mind, developmental assumptions were not invoked to resolve apparent contradictions between earlier and later dialogues.

Was there not a much easier way for Platonists to establish a global interpretation? Surely they simply had to ask Plato! By 'they' I mean the many distinguished intellectuals (see Bonazzi's Chapter 1) who had joined Plato's celebrated Athenian school, the Academy, during the roughly four decades from its foundation to his death in 347 BC. These included not only Aristotle, but also Plato's nephew and chosen successor Speusippus, and the latter's own eventual successor as school-head, Xenocrates. Who, it might be asked, could have been better placed than Plato's own long-time close associates to preserve for future generations his full philosophical system?

What actually happened, however, fell far short of that. True, a set of 'unwritten doctrines' attributed to Plato circulated after his death (Bonazzi's Chapter 1). But consider how Plato's most iconic doctrine, the theory of Forms, fared in the school. Aristotle, before departing to set up his own rival school in the Lyceum, wrote a refutation of the theory, entitled On Forms. The theory was likewise disputed by both Speusippus and the mathematician and moral philosopher Eudoxus, himself a member of the Academy. Most significant of all, one critique of the theory was written by none other than Plato himself, in the opening part of his Parmenides.

We should infer that the educational agenda of the school in Plato's lifetime was one in which critical independence was strongly encouraged, orthodoxy discouraged. Even the decision to bequeath the school-headship to Speusippus, to all intents and purposes a non-Platonist, may reflect a fear on Plato's part that in future generations reverence for his own authority might lead the Academy into a hagiographic search of the *corpus* for his own ultimate principles, thereby stifling open-ended philosophical inquiry in a way he had expressly warned against in the *Phaedrus* (275d–e). At all events, by 339 BC, when Speusippus was in turn succeeded as school-head by Xenocrates, the reconstruction of such a Platonist orthodoxy was already under way. And so it would remain for most of the movement's history, with just one significant exception, recounted by Mauro Bonazzi in Chapter 2.

Foreword

The difficulty of extracting a full-blooded Platonism from the corpus can be appreciated by asking how we ourselves would fare if, without the benefits of an established reading, order, we were presented with those same scrolls and invited to give a conspectus of their underlying philosophy, paying no attention to the contributions made by literary virtuosity, genre-switching, the interplay of diversely motivated speakers, or (other than in the Letters, which are of disputed authenticity) the author's apparently almost exceptionless avoidance of any personal presence in the narrative or self-reference in the interplay of arguments.

We certainly would not make much headway if we gave equal weight to all the dialogues, nor if we picked one of them at random, be it *Phaedo*, *Phaedrus*, *Philebus*, or *Protagoras*, if only because different initial choices might bring in their wake radically differing perspectives on the author's entire philosophical orientation.

This vicious circle could however be plausibly broken by concentrating initially on one specially privileged text, the *Timaeus*. Today comparatively few students of Plato ever even reach the *Timaeus*, let alone study it in depth. In antiquity, from Plato's death onwards, this dialogue was on the contrary treated by both Platonists and their opponents as if it were a semi-official manifesto for his system.

Why so? What has come down to us as the *Timaeus* is evidently the first part of an unfinished trilogy of speeches, in which Timaeus' speech on the creation of the world was evidently the only one of the dialogue's three intended speeches to have been completed by the time of Plato's death. At the end of the preserved text, the speech of Critias breaks off in mid sentence (*Critias* 121c). Although various of the *Timaeus*' innovative ideas (for instance that of the 'receptacle of becoming') are likely to have been already familiar to Plato's close associates through school discussions, the fact that he had still been at work on it when he died may have helped spotlight it for his successors as potentially the most authoritative account of his system. (No similar canonisation could credibly have been proposed regarding his late and not fully revised political-theological masterpiece the *Laws*.)

When finally published, the *Timaeus* quickly became the focus of a millennia-long debate, still unresolved today, about

xii

the meaning of *Timaeus'* very first doctrinal assertion: the world, he maintains, 'has come to be' (28b7). Could Plato really have believed that something destined to exist for infinite future time, as the world was agreed to be, might nevertheless have a merely finite past existence, starting from a dateable act of creation? Most Platonists, thinking such a temporal asymmetry incoherent, tried to show that Timaeus' grammatically past-perfect tense, 'it has come to be', had been intended by Plato not as a literal truth claim, but in the spirit of an epexegetic creation myth. Most anti-Platonists, including Aristotle, for the same reason insisted on reading it literally.

Why, it might be wondered, did the early Platonists did not simply ask Plato which of the two he meant, and thereby settle the dispute? The question is readily answered, however, if we accept, as suggested above, that it was only as part of Plato's posthumous legacy that the *Timaeus* came to prominence. By the time this great interpretative schism emerged, Plato was dead.

But the value of Timaeus' speech as an entry route to Plato's philosophy could in any case not, by any stretch of the imagination, be exhausted by disambiguating this single verb. Although the speech's theme is physics, his cosmic creation narrative embodies (from a physical point of view) a whole network of metaphysical, ethical, psychological, epistemological, and even logical theses that had been individually defended in other dialogues, usually by Socrates but on occasion by another main speaker. This constitutes very strong evidence that Plato already had a structured philosophical system, into which paradigmatic Forms, the tripartite soul, the epistemological dualism of intelligibles and sensibles, the immortality of the rational soul, the explanation of false belief, and much else besides, had been integrated.

I have already mentioned Plato's restraint in absenting himself from his own dialogues. Even that remark now needs qualifying, however. The *corpus* contains many anonymous references which, tantalisingly, could be to Plato. Some of these are predictive, as when in the *Charmides* 168e–169a Socrates' remarks that we will have to await the arrival of a 'great man' to solve the problem whether there can be a self-moving motion; and when Parmenides (*Parmenides* 135-b) similarly expects a 'great man' one day to resolve his own criticisms of the theory of Forms. Others have an implicit but clear present reference, notably *Republic* 4.427c–d and 9.580c, where the dialogue's two major conclusions are celebrated, with each in turn attributed by Socrates to 'the son of Ariston'. Within the economy of the dialogue these are Socrates' two main interlocutors, respectively, Adeimantus and Glaucon. But their half-brother, Plato, was a third 'son of Ariston'. Readers are surely being challenged to notice how, in the double deployment of Plato's patronymic, the *Republic* conceals within itself its author's indelible signature.

With this in mind, we may return now to the *Timaeus*, which I have characterised as conveying to its future readers the basic tenets of Plato's proprietary philosophical system. There of all places we might expect to find his authorial fingerprint. And so we do! In the opening lines we learn that, since one of the expected speakers has failed to turn up, Timaeus will be speaking on his behalf. That is to say, the teachings imparted by Timaeus in his speech will be those of the missing person.

Who then is this anonymous absentee? It is Plato. The clue lies in Timaeus' explanation of his absence: 'Some kind of sickness has befallen him, Socrates. For this is a gathering that he would not have missed willingly.' The words are calculated to remind us of the opening pages of the *Phaedo*, where we learn to our mild surprise that Plato was too ill to attend that most important of all philosophical gatherings, Socrates' final conversation and ensuing execution. The sicknote story may not reveal Plato in a very heroic light, but its very banality allowed the all-important identity-clue to pass almost unnoticed, awaiting eventual rediscovery, much like its counterpart in the *Republic*.

Did any of Plato's followers or readers in antiquity arrive at this same decipherment? Yes, according to Proclus (who does not himself find it credible) the covert allusion to Plato was pointed out by one Dercyllides – of uncertain date and identity, but in all probability a Middle Platonist. By the Middle Platonist era (Bonazzi chapter 3), the *Timaeus* was widely believed to be a Pythagorean work, and Timaeus, its presumed author, an authentic Pythagorean. If Dercyllides was the first reader to discover Plato's indelible signature in the *Timaeus*, he was probably concerned above all to reclaim this dialogue from the Pythagoreans. But if, intentionally or not, he was also making available to future generations Plato's concealed certification of the *Timaeus* as his own philosophical testament, his is truly a name to celebrate.

It becomes ever clearer that, almost throughout the near-millennium during which ancient Platonism thrived, the *Timaeus* not only exerted a unique influence on the reception of the Platonic *corpus*, but in doing so may well have been fulfilling Plato's goals more faithfully than it has done in any modern reconstruction of his philosophy.

Pushing that heretical thought to one side, I shall stand no longer between the reader and Mauro Bonazzi's rich and absorbing monograph.

ACKNOWLEDGEMENTS

This volume, a revised and updated edition of *Il platonismo* (Turin: Einaudi 2015), was made possible by the generous support of the Department of Philosophy and Religious Studies at Utrecht University to which I am extremely grateful. For further comments, conversations, access to unpublished material, and feedback that have improved the content of this book, I especially thank Thomas Bénatouïl, George Boys-Stones, Riccardo Chiaradonna, Giulia de Cesaris, Federico Petrucci, and Jan Opsomer. I also thank David Sedley for generously writing the Foreword, Sergio Knipe for the translation, and all the teams at Cambridge University Press for their extremely competent and collaborative support.
This volume is dedicated to the memory of Pierluigi Donini.

THE EARLY ACADEMY

Plato, Platonists, and Platonism

Writing a history of Platonism is difficult for one very simple reason: it is not clear what being a Platonist means. This might seem like nit-picking: one might object that tracing a Platonist's profile is not hard at all. A Platonist is someone who believes in the truth of Plato's philosophy and aims to defend it against opponents' criticism and against alternative philosophical theories. More specifically, as some have argued, it might be noted that Plato's philosophy, as it emerges from the dialogues and other testimonies, is a complete and perfect philosophical system: the Platonist's task is to explain this system; and, in doing so, to show its intrinsic worth and superiority.

The problem with a reconstruction of this kind is that it takes for granted some theses that are far from obvious, starting from the underlying assumption that there exists a philosophical system developed by Plato which is self-evident and indisputable – a system that can either be accepted or rejected, but whose fundamental outline cannot be doubted. This is precisely where the real difficulty lies because it is not at all evident what Plato's alleged system consists of. There are countless variations on this theme and – as we shall see in Chapter 2 – there are even thinkers who regard themselves as Platonists precisely because they believe that philosophy cannot be enclosed in any one system. We will discuss these issues in due course. What is clear for now is that tracing a profile of a true Platonist is more complex than it might seem at first sight.

In order to correctly frame the problem, then, it is necessary to acknowledge this complexity. In other words, it is best to take account of the potential difference between Plato, on the one hand, and Platonism, on the other, as well as of the intrinsic ambiguity of the adjective 'Platonist'. A parallel with Karl Marx, one of the few philosophers to enjoy a reputation comparable to Plato's, might help clarify the problem. By now it has become clear – and not just to scholars either – that Marx and Marxism do not wholly overlap. The distinction between 'Marxian' and 'Marxist' has become current: the former term applies to those seeking to reconstruct Marx's thought, and the latter to those who draw upon his thought more freely in order to adapt it to new historical, cultural, and doctrinal contexts. The problem with Plato and Platonism is that, although the situation is much the same, a distinction of this kind is lacking, potentially giving rise to much confusion.[1] All in all, the problem is that there never was a single and indisputable Platonism in antiquity, to be either accepted or rejected – the very term 'Platonism' only entered into use in the eighteenth century.[2] Rather, what we have are a series of 'Platonisms' competing not only, as one would expect, with the other philosophical schools, but also with one another. This variety is what makes Platonism a worthwhile subject from a historical and philosophical standpoint. The multiplicity and originality of the attempts made to reconstruct Plato's ancient thought and his most genuine message is what makes Platonism interesting: clearly, to be a Platonist is to believe in the superiority of Plato's philosophy; but the problem – and the interest – lies entirely in the fact that to be a Platonist means many things. This is why reconstructing the history of ancient Platonism, a history spanning almost a millennium, is so difficult yet at the same time so stimulating.

Dropping the assumption that there exists a single and indisputable Platonic philosophy, it is worth taking a more discreet route, by identifying the point of departure of the various Platonists, which is to say of those philosophers who openly drew upon Plato's teaching. This is an easier task and the answer is twofold:

[1] In English – but not in many other modern languages – there exists of course a distinction between 'Platonic' and 'Platonist', but these terms are often used as synonyms, without any real awareness of the problem.
[2] The first attestation of the term 'Platonism' would appear to come from the famous *Encyclopédie raisonnée des sciences, des arts et des métiers*, and more specifically from the twenty-sixth volume, which features the entry 'Platonisme', written by Louis de Jaucourt: see Neschke-Hentske 1995: 2–7, offering some very interesting observations on the problematic relationship between Plato and Platonism.

a first and obvious starting point is Plato's own texts, his dialogues. Yet there is more to this, particularly at the initial stages of the long history of Platonism: no less important is adherence to the school Plato had founded, the Academy. Starting in the first century BC, by which time the Academy had closed down, the importance reserved to Plato's texts was the criterion by which to tell a Platonist; in earlier times, affiliation to his school was just as important, if not more so. This distinction is also clearly illustrated by the use of different terms: initially, a follower of Plato was called an *akademaikos*; only in the first centuries of the imperial era did this adjective come to be replaced by *platonikos*.[3] It is from this institution, therefore, that we should set out in order to reconstruct the history of ancient Platonism.

The Early Academy and Its Leading Figures

In 387 BC Plato travelled to Sicily. The ruler of Syracuse, Dionysius the Elder, appeared to be interested in philosophical teachings. But things soon went askew. When discussing power, Plato argued that it belonged to the most just, not to the strongest; this irritated Dionysus, who retorted that these sounded like the words of a dotard. Plato's answer was brilliant, but not very judicious: the sovereign's words smacked of tyranny. And the sovereign behaved like a tyrant, handing the philosopher over to a Spartan merchant, that he might sell him off as a slave. At the market of Aegina, however, Plato was fortunately redeemed by Anniceris, who also purchased a plot of land for him inside the Academy's garden, to allow him to live and teach there.[4]

It is difficult to tell how much of this anecdote – or other similar ones circulating in antiquity – is true: probably, not much. But at least it gives us a date and place where to start. Plato used to frequent the Academy, a park dedicated to the local hero Academus. It was located outside the walls of Athens and also housed a gymnasium popular among sophists and orators (Socrates visits it in the *Lysis*).[5]

---

[3] See Glucker 1978: 206–25; Bonazzi 2003b: 52–8.
[4] D.L. 3.17–20; a slightly different version is found in Philod. *Acad. ind.* III.
[5] Plat. *Lys.* 203a–b: along with a passage from the *Axiochus* (367a, but this text is most probably spurious), this is the only mention of the Academy in the dialogues.

In this garden, between 390 and 380 BC, Plato acquired a small plot of land, where in all likelihood he lived and – for sure – established his school of philosophy. This much is certain, whereas the exact location of Plato's school and house is still a matter of debate, as are numerous other details.[6] In particular, it would be important to know whether there was also a library in which Plato's works were stored, and where the altar dedicated to the Muses and *exedra* were located (the latter being the teaching venue probably depicted in the famous mosaic preserved in the Archaeological Museum of Naples (Figure 1.1), the so-called philosophers' school).[7] What was also located in the area is the philosopher's tomb, a pilgrimage site where ritual celebrations (purifications, libations, and symposia) took place over the centuries (it was still visible in the fourth century AD). The presence of the inscription ἀγεωμέτρητος μηδεὶς εἰσίτω ('Let no one ignorant of geometry enter') above the door of the school is instead a late invention.[8]

Be that as it may, the Academy soon acquired fame and prestige, drawing people from every corner of Greece and beyond – so much so that once a Chaldaean standing by Plato's bedside was told off for singing songs that were too barbarian for the philosopher's liking.[9] It is within this school that we find the first 'Platonists', who soon came to be referred to as 'Academics', after the place in which they operated, and who were immortalised in the famous mosaic in Naples. Upon the founder's death, in 347 BC, Plato's nephew Speusippus (the son of his sister Potone) became scholarch. He continued to lead the school until 339 BC, when he passed away.[10]

---

[6] An extensive overview of the various problems and hypotheses can be found in the exhaustive study by Caruso 2013 (see however Verde 2014) and in the essays collected by Kalligas et al. 2020; useful information is also provided by Billot 1989 and Baltes 1993.

[7] Gaiser 1980; Rashed 2012; Sedley 2021b.

[8] Saffrey 1968.

[9] Philod. *Acad. ind.* V. Diogenes Laertius (3.25) reports that a Persian by the name of Mithridates had a statue of Plato installed in the Academy, which he dedicated to the Muses. While it is difficult to tell how reliable this testimony might be, it is noteworthy that most of the Academy's pupils came from outside Athens. It is also worth recalling that precisely in this period, and on the initiative of several Academics (especially Hermodorus and Philip of Opus), the idea started circulating of an affinity between Zoroaster and Plato: see Horky 2009.

[10] For editions and collections of the testimonies and fragments, see Isnardi Parente 1980 (all fragments are cited following this edition) and Tarán 1981. Cherniss 1974, Isnardi

Figure 1.1 *The Mosaic of the Philosophers*. Museo Archeologico Nazionale di Napoli 124545. Photo by Giorgio Albana. Reproduced by permission of Ministero per i Beni e le Attività Culturali – Museo Archeologico di Napoli

A solution of this kind was probably due to the desire to keep the property within the family, but it also depended on the age of Speusippus, who at the time was one of the most senior and authoritative members (significantly, the mosaic shows him sitting next to Plato, second and third from the left). Besides, we should not underestimate the importance of his contributions to

Parente 1979, and Krämer 1983 remain fundamental studies on the early Academy in general. More recently, see Lévy 2000; Dillon 2003; Berti 2010; Dancy 2011 and 2012; Trabattoni 2016; El Murr 2018.

the philosophical debate and research conducted in the Academy: Diogenes Laertius reports that Speusippus was the author of numerous works on a wide variety of topics. As we shall see, Speusippus certainly comes across as a thinker with many original insights, although not all of them, perhaps, are equally convincing. His appointment, therefore, is hardly surprising. What proved more complex was the choice of his successor: voting took place and Xenocrates of Chalcedon (396–314 BC) defeated Menedemus of Pyrrha and Heraclides of Pontus by a few votes,[11] while another great representative of the Academy, Aristotle of Stagira, was missing. In all likelihood, Aristotle too was a potential candidate; however, it is difficult to give credit to the rumours that he definitely abandoned the Academy in protest against this election.[12] But the fact remains that he expressed some scornful opinions about his colleague. These contemptuous statements do not do justice to the complexity, standing, and thought of Xenocrates, who was a man much admired by his contemporaries for his moral qualities, as well as the author of numerous treatises.[13] Over time, as the historical, philosophical, and cultural context changed (we are now entering the so-called Hellenistic centuries), the Academy's interests also changed. The two successive scholarchs, Polemo of Athens and Crates of Athens, were in charge, respectively, from 314/313 to 270/269 BC and from 270/269 to 268–264 BC (unfortunately, the dates are uncertain) and are chiefly known for their practical-moral reflection, whereas their contribution to other fields is more questionable.[14]

However important they may have been, scholarchs were not the only notable figures in the first century and a half of the Academy's life: the roughly 150 people we know about include

---

[11] Philod. *Acad. ind.* VI–VII; it is noteworthy that none of the candidates was Athenian.
[12] In support of the historical reliability of this episode, Watts (2007: 115–16) has noted a parallel with the other two candidates, who in turn would appear to have quit the Academy (cf. Philod. *Acad. ind.* VII). One reasonable hypothesis is that Xenocrates' moral rectitude was the decisive factor behind his election.
[13] For an edition of the testimonies and fragments, see Heinze 1892 and Isnardi Parente 1982a (new ed. by T. Dorandi, 2012; all fragments are cited following this edition).
[14] For a first collection of the testimonies and fragments, see Gigante 1976 (Polemo) and Mette 1984 (Crantor); collections of testimonies and fragments by other Academics can be found in Lasserre 1987.

some thinkers who are just as interesting. For the first phase, mention must be made of at least the names of Philip of Opus, Heraclides of Pontus, and Eudoxus of Cnidus. Philip helped Plato with the final drafting of the *Laws* and is the presumed author of the *Epinomis*, the dialogue intended to complete the *Laws* by introducing a sort of astral theology. Heraclides was a multifaceted and often eccentric figure at the crossroads between the Academy (which he apparently directed during one of Plato's voyages to Syracuse) and the Aristotelian Peripatos (which he seems to have joined late in life). He chiefly focused on physical problems, championing some form of atomism and arguing that the soul, while immortal, is not immaterial but composed of light. Eudoxus instead is one of the most important Greek mathematicians and astronomers. Another figure who came to enjoy particular repute, at a later date, is Crantor of Soli, who is presented by some sources as the first commentator on the dialogues and who was highly regarded as the author of a treatise *On Pain*.[15]

There is then another 'Academic' whom we should take into account, namely Aristotle of Stagira (384–323 BC). This statement might seem surprising at first: was Aristotle not Plato's great opponent, as in Raphael's fresco *The School of Athens*? Actually, it is simply a matter of acknowledging a historical fact: for twenty years, from 367 to 347 BC (and beyond, since in 339 BC Aristotle was still a potential candidate to be head of the school), during the years of his intellectual training (between the ages of seventeen and thirty-seven), Aristotle was a full member of the Academy, taking part in the discussions and defending it against polemical attacks by its opponents.[16] This simple biographical information

---

[15] In addition to the aforementioned studies, see also Alesse and Ferrari 2012; Aronadio 2013 provides a new edition, translation and commentary of the *Epinomis*; Gottschalk 1980 is a detailed reconstruction of Heraclides (whose fragments have been collected in Wehrli 1969 and more recently in Schütrumpf 2008; see also Fortenbaugh and Pender 2009); see Lasserre 1966 for a collection of testimonies on Eudoxus, and Puech 2000 for an introductory overview. As for Crantor, see the presentation at the end of this chapter. It seems that two women, Lastheneia of Mantinea and Axiothea of Phlius, were also active in the Academy, although they used to dress up in male clothes (D.L. 4.2, with the commentary in Dorandi 1989).

[16] One might mention for instance the *Gryllus*, in which Aristotle polemically attacked Isocrates, or the *Protrepticus*, an exhortation to philosophy celebrating the lifestyle upheld by the Academy.

is enough to prove that Aristotle's relationship with Plato and the Academy is a complex one, which certainly cannot be reduced to a simple opposition.[17] Aristotle's philosophical programme does not always necessarily coincide with that of Plato or the other Academics, yet there is no doubt that he embarked on his research within the Academy, by setting out from Plato's philosophical project: a project that Aristotle never tired of discussing and criticising, but also of taking up and developing further. With all his questions, objections and suggestions, Aristotle de facto provided an essential stimulus not just for Plato and the first Academics, with whom he constantly engaged and polemicised,[18] but for the whole Platonist tradition, down to late antiquity. In other words, it is not so much Raphael's fresco as, once again, the 'mosaic of the philosophers' in Naples – which features Aristotle the last on the right, in a more inconspicuous position, yet still within the group – that offers the most appropriate description of the complex relationship between Aristotle, Plato, and the Platonists: he was an awkward, at times even annoying, figure, yet one that could not be ignored.[19]

The Academy and Plato

As Aristotle used always to relate, such was what befell most of those who listened to Plato's lecture on the Good. For, he said, they came, each expecting to find out one of those things that people think good, such as wealth, health, or strength – in general, some kind of wonderful happiness. But when the discourse was manifestly concerned with mathematics and numbers, and geometry and

[17] See Gerson 2005.

[18] As further confirmation of Aristotle's importance, it may be recalled that he is our primary source for reconstructing the thought of the two leading Academics, Speusippus and Xenocrates: as scholars have shown, although he hardly ever mentions them by name, in several texts he discusses their doctrines in detail. Without Aristotle's crucial testimony, our knowledge of the early history of the Academy would amount to very little, since the other sources at our disposal are mainly useful from a biographical standpoint (Philodemus, Diogenes Laertius) or are likely to be distorted by interpretative prejudices even more than Aristotle (the Neoplatonists: cf. *infra*, The Doctrine of Principles and the Abandonment of the Theory of Forms, n. 45 on Speusippus; an interesting overview, with regard to Proclus, may be found in Tarán 1987).

[19] What need not be discussed here in detail is Aristotle's life and thought. I will be talking about Aristotle either as a source (in the present chapter) or in relation to what various Platonists have to say about him (in the following chapters).

astronomy, and the end result was that the Good is one,[20] it seemed to them, I think, to be quite contrary to their expectations; some of them either derided the subject matter, while others found fault with it.[21]

A: What are Plato and Speusippus and Menedemus up to? On what subjects are they discoursing (*diatribousin*) today? What weighty idea, what line of argument (*logos*) is currently being investigated by them? Tell me this accurately, in Earth's name, if you've come with any knowledge of it.

B: Why yes, I can tell you about these fellows with certainty. For at the Panathenaea I saw a troop of lads in the exercise-grounds of the Academy, and heard utterances indescribable, astonishing! For they were propounding definitions about nature (*peri physeōs aphorizomenoi*), and separating into categories the ways of life of animals, the nature of trees, and the classes of vegetables. And in this connection they were investigating to what genus one should assign the pumpkin.

A: And what definition (*horos*) did they arrive at, and of what genus is the plant?

B: Well now, first of all they all took up their places, and with heads bowed they reflected a long time. Then suddenly, while they were still bent low in study, one of the lads said it was a round vegetable, another that it was a grass, another that it was a tree. When a doctor from Sicily heard this, he dismissed them contemptuously, as talking rubbish.

B: No doubt they got very angry at that, and protested against such insults? For it is unseemly to behave thus in such public gatherings.

A: No, in fact the lads didn't seem to mind at all. And Plato, who was present, very mildly, and without irritation, told them to try again to define the genus to which the pumpkin belongs. And they started once again to attempt a division (*diairesis*).[22]

The events surrounding the first Academy are a real riddle for us:[23] the sources we have are few and rather inconsistent, so that many different hypotheses have been put forward, without scholars having reached any consensus. For a long time, the dominant thesis was the one developed by the great philologist Ulrich von Wilamowitz-Möllendorf, according to whom the School was to be regarded as a sort of *thiasus*, a religious brotherhood devoted to the cult of

---

[20] This is the meaning of the Greek here according to Hans Joachim Krämer's translation, followed by Levin 2009: 97 (whom I am quoting here). An alternative translation, proposed by Margherita Isnardi Parente, would be 'that there is only one Good'. Clearly, these are not trifle variations, but this is not the place in which to discuss them.
[21] Aristox. *Elem. harm.* 2.39–40.
[22] Athen. *Deipn.* 2.59d–f (= Speus. fr. 33); trans. Dillon 2003: 7–8.
[23] As expressed by the title of Cherniss 1974.

the Muses.[24] Accordingly, the hallmark of the Academy was seen to be a sort of mystical cult rather than any real teaching activity, in the modern sense of the term.[25] Equally authoritative, however, have been those interpretations stressing the political objectives of the institution, based on those ancient sources presenting it as either a school of freedom or as a breeding ground for tyrants – depending on whether their attitude was a favourable one or not.[26] It is difficult to come up with a coherent reconstruction of the contrasting testimonies from antiquity; hence, it is hardly surprising that, faced with such a daunting task, many scholars have – either unconsciously or not – yielded to the temptation of back-projecting images and models typical of later ages onto the Platonic School.[27]

These apparently secondary historical problems pose significant obstacles to any attempt to correctly reconstruct the philosophical debates taking place within the Academy.[28] The identification of the Platonic School with modern institutions has often gone hand in hand with the assumption that its philosophical activity exclusively revolved around the endorsement and defence of Plato's philosophy. The first passage quoted in this chapter has often been used to support such a claim, as if to suggest that the Academy's main activity was to expound Plato's thought (the topic of the lecture), to which the other members of the Academy were expected to conform.[29] Recently, however, there has been

---

[24] Von Wilamowitz-Möllendorf 1881. This thesis fell into disrepute after the criticism levelled by Lynch 1972: 108–27 and Glucker 1978: 226–55. However, it has been newly defended by Caruso 2013: 38–42.

[25] Howald 1921.

[26] On the Academy in Athenian politics and society, see now Haake 2020. A collection of sources and discussion is in Isnardi Parente 1989: 63–78; more generally, on political activities within the Academy, see Appendix 1.

[27] See Cherniss 1974: 72–3; on the institutional and educational structure of the Early Academy, see now Horky 2018.

[28] As for teaching, it seems that the members of the Academy were divided into two groups: the *presbyteroi*, Plato's peers and collaborators, and the younger students, the *neaniskoi* (consider for instance Aristotle, who entered the Academy at the age of 17); see Baltes 1993: 10 and D. Frede 2018: 80–2.

[29] Interpretations of this kind found particularly fertile soil in the Tübingen-Milan school, which identified the conceptual heart of Plato's philosophy with a series of 'unwritten doctrines' that could be reconstructed on the basis of Aristotle's testimony (cf. *infra*, n. 33). According to these scholars, a philosopher's endorsement of these doctrines is the measure of his adherence to the Platonic School: see, among others, Krämer 1964 and, more recently, Thiel 2006.

a shift in perspective, through a suitable reassessment of other sources, such as the aforementioned passage by the comic playwright Epicrates. Scholars have noted that it would be rash to speak of any kind of orthodoxy within the School. As we shall see, Aristotle was not the only philosopher to critically discuss Plato's theses: they all did so. However, this should not lead us to go too far in the opposite direction, as though the Academy were a centre in which people could pursue any kind of research whatsoever. More likely, the truth lies in the middle. In its final years, Plato's philosophy focused on a series of specific problems, and it is interesting to note that according to most surviving testimonies it was with these problems that the Academics were most concerned. So Plato's centrality remains indisputable. Yet, his centrality does not imply strict adherence to his theses; rather, it should be thought of in terms of an attempt to engage with and defend or reject these theses. Borrowing a Greek term, scholars have spoken of *boetheia*, aid:[30] the most important Academics would appear to have conceived their pursuit as an attempt to follow in Plato's footsteps and to test the strength of his theses, an attempt that nonetheless did not rule out the possibility of significantly distancing themselves from Plato. It is this combination of discussions focusing on the same problems and conducted with absolute freedom that makes the early Academy one of the high points in the history of philosophy.

The Doctrine of Principles and the Abandonment of the Theory of Forms

According to Diogenes Laertius, Speusippus 'maintained to the same doctrine as Plato'.[31] However, Aristotle informs us that Speusippus abandoned the theory of Forms.[32] These two apparently incompatible testimonies are not actually too far apart, if

---

[30] Isnardi Parente 1998: 216 on the basis of Arist. *De caelo* 1.10.279a32–280a11 and *Scholia in Arist. De caelo* 489a9–12 Brandis (= Speus. frs. 94–5). See now D. Frede 2018: 93–100 for a convincing reconstruction of how debates and investigations were freely conducted under Plato's headship.

[31] D.L. 4.1 = Speus. fr. 2.

[32] Arist. *Met.* 13.9.1086a2–4 = Speus. fr. 77.

we consider the philosophical project which Plato was attending to with his fellows in the Academy. The theory of Forms, important as it is, did not enjoy the kind of absolute prominence which modern scholars generally assign to it, particularly in the light of Plato's later writings and his so-called 'unwritten doctrines'.[33] What seems truly central for Plato is the underlying metaphysical assumption, namely the distinction between the sensible (corruptible) dimension and the intelligible (incorruptible) one: the task to be pursued is precisely to explain and justify the need for and meaning of this distinction.[34] The theory of Forms was conceived in order to fulfil this very task; but already in the dialogues – especially the *Parmenides* – Plato had shown himself aware of the difficulties to which the doctrine in question gives rise. Speusippus' thesis, not unlike those of Xenocrates and Eudoxus, was developed as an alternative solution, capable of providing a more adequate foundation for the same metaphysical distinction; and it is in this sense that we can speak of the philosophical reflection of these men as a *boetheia*, an aid to Plato's philosophy. Loyalty to its basic tenets did not translate into slavish repetition.

More specifically, Speusippus' solution took the form of a marked mathematisation of reality which drastically developed a line of research already present in Plato in the light of certain distinctive aspects of the Pythagorean tradition:[35] he argued that

---

[33] Very briefly, a fair number of ancient sources, starting with Aristotle, inform us that, in addition to what is expounded in the dialogues, Plato orally developed and discussed a metaphysical doctrine of principles. This doctrine apparently entailed a pair of principles called the 'One' and the 'big and small', or 'infinite dyad', from which all ideal entities (ideal numbers, Forms, and numbers) stem; interaction with such entities would then give rise to all other entities, from the soul to sensible things. Rivers of ink have been poured out over the problem of Plato's unwritten doctrines, which have given rise to heated polemics. But this is not the place to discuss them. No doubt, such doctrines played some role in Plato's philosophy, and they also crop up again in the theories of some Platonists: I will be noting when this is the case, without entering the debate about Plato.

[34] See Trabattoni 2016 and Lévy 2000: 801, according to whom the problem for the Academy was to find a 'substitutive transcendence', which is to say: a theory capable of justifying transcendence more effectively than the theory of Forms.

[35] One truly important aspect of the early Academics' activity is their adoption of many Pythagorean insights and doctrines. However, it is important to bear in mind that the relationship between Pythagoreanism and the Academy went both ways. In the Academy's case, the Pythagorean influence is chiefly reflected in the increasing importance assigned to mathematics. As regards Pythagoreanism, it progressively came to be identified with Academic doctrines: in the doxographical and philosophical tradition

first of all 'the objects of mathematics exist and the numbers are the first of real things, and the ideal 1 is the principle'.[36] In other words, as the foundation of reality Speusippus posited a first principle that, by interacting with the opposite principle of multiplicity (*plethos*) and ordering its infinite divisibility, has given rise to numbers (which are always complex units) and all other realities:

> some do not think there is anything substantial besides sensible things, but others think there are eternal substances which are more in number and more real, e.g. Plato posited two kinds of substance—the Forms and the objects of mathematics—as well as a third kind, viz. the substance of sensible bodies. And Speusippus made still more kinds of substance, beginning with the One, and making principles for each kind of substance, one for numbers, another for spatial magnitudes, and then another for the soul; and in this way he multiplies the kinds of substance.[37]

Despite the silence of the sources, it is possible to reconstruct in what sense a doctrine of this sort could find a place within a Platonic framework. Plato – particularly the late Plato – would appear to have wavered between Forms and Principles when it comes to the ultimate foundation of reality. Speusippus staunchly chooses the latter option, discarding the first possibility;[38] reality, in his view, stems from these two principles, which are envisaged as seeds.[39] In other words, as rightly noted by Margherita Isnardi Parente,

developed over the following centuries, eminently Academic doctrines – such as that of principles – erroneously came to be regarded as an expression of early, original Pythagoreanism. Burkert 1972a: 83–96 remains a fundamental study on this topic; more recently, see Horky 2013; Zhmud 2013 and 2016.

[36] Arist. *Met.* 13.8.1083a20–35 = Speus. fr. 76.

[37] Arist. *Met.* 7.2.1028b18–24 = Speus. fr. 48; Iambl. *De comm. math. scientia* 4.15.6 = fr. 72. This kind of generation or derivation should not be understood in terms of a temporal process; rather, as we shall see with regard to the eternity of the universe in the following chapter, we should think of it as a process of mathematical construction. This process unfolds in time, but what is constructed is an eternal structure (whose principles are not 'first' in a temporal sense, but rather in the sense that what follows depends on them): in other words, the construction helps discover what already exists; the succession is a logical, not chronological, one. See Bénatouïl and El Murr 2010: 64–5 (with many references to ancient sources); Dancy 2011; Bénatouïl 2017; and *infra*, The Academy and the Sciences: Cosmogony, Cosmology, and Mathematics, p. 23.

[38] Dillon 2003: 51–2 has argued that Speusippus did not abandon Forms, but simply confined them to the level of the World Soul discussed in the *Timaeus*. However, there is no explicit textual evidence in support of this suggestion; hence, there is no reason not to follow Aristotle's clear statements on the matter.

[39] Arist. *Met.* 12.7.20172b30–4 = Speus. fr. 53.

13

Speusippus believed 'that the One and Multiplicity are principles that in themselves adequately encapsulate the ultimate roots of reality; but that, given such premises, the hypothesis of Forms is useless, and that the rational perfection of numbers is enough to constitute the weft on which sensible things are woven'.[40]

While the underlying framework is clear, it is harder to establish why Forms were completely abandoned in favour of numbers: one reasonable solution is that Speusippus believed Forms to be incapable of fulfilling the function for which Plato had introduced them. The main issue would seem to concern epistemological problems. Knowledge, in order to be truly knowledge, requires stable and immutable objects, which can be fully understood. Forms had been introduced precisely in order to fulfil such a purpose. But this assumption risked being undermined by Plato's dialectical method,[41] according to which in order to truly know a Form, one must be fully cognisant of its positive and negative relations with all other Forms: a view which de facto risked entailing a potentially infinite task, thereby undermining the epistemological usefulness of Forms. Numbers and mathematical entities displayed a very different potential, insofar as they could be fully encompassed within adequate definitions and therefore were perfectly suited to their epistemological role.[42] In addition, numbers seemed capable of better explaining the nature and properties of other realities. This function too had been reserved for Forms, yet it remained difficult to explain how they could fulfil such a purpose. By contrast, numbers and geometric magnitudes could pythagorically[43] be understood as the basic constituents of all other realities.

Speusippus' theory, then, emerges as an attempt to lay out in more correct terms that metaphysical dualism which lies at the basis of the Platonic project. However, we can hardly fail to notice that, as a whole, this theory also led to a misrepresentation of

---

[40] Isnardi Parente 1998: 218.
[41] Cherniss 1974: 46–7.
[42] Arist. *Met.* 14.2.1090a3–b5 = Speus. fr. 80. We shall be returning to these epistemological problems later on: see *infra*, Epistemology and Dialectic, p. 28.
[43] Note, however, that according to the Pythagoreans, numbers were the immanent, not transcendent, elements of reality: see Arist. *Met.* 13.6.1080b14–35 and 14.2.1090a20–35 = Speus. frs. 75 and 80.

Plato's philosophy: Plato no doubt acknowledged the importance of numbers, yet never to the detriment of Forms. Even more significant is what emerges with regard to the first principle. At first, the emphasis on this principle might seem fully 'Platonic', particularly if we also consider the so-called 'unwritten doctrines' mentioned by Aristotle and other ancient sources. But in this case too, the way in which Speusippus develops his theory introduces some substantial changes. One of the main problems with Platonic Forms was the fact that, insofar as they maintain a relation of similarity with sensible realities, they risk giving rise to an infinite regress.[44] By presenting the first principle as a seed – which is to say, by resorting to an analogy with plants and animals – Speusippus could claim to have found a brilliant solution to the problem, since in this case the principle does not possess that of which it is the cause (or, at any rate, only possesses it potentially);[45] for the seed is different from the plant, even though it is its cause. But a solution of this sort also came at a heavy cost, because it deprived the first principle of any positive axiological connotation: for the reasons just outlined, the first principle cannot even be called good (so much so that the principle of multiplicity would be evil). Speusippus' theory takes

---

[44] This is the so-called problem of the Third Man, or of Forms' self-predication, already found in Plato's *Parmenides* (132b–c) and later made famous by Aristotle. In brief, the problem goes as follows: if the reasoning that leads us to posit the existence of a Form is based on the acknowledgement of the presence of the same property in a range of distinct entities (e.g. beauty in a painting and in a person), and if even the Form in question possesses the same property (e.g. the Form itself can be said to be beautiful in some way, like a painting or a person), then the outcome will be an infinite regress, because it will be necessary to posit the existence of a further principle that holds together the beauty of the painting and that of the person, on the one hand, and the beauty of the Form, on the other – and so on (the example adduced by Aristotle concerns the property of being a man, hence the name by which the problem is known).

[45] See Speus. frs. 52–9; this is what Dancy 1991: 98 calls the 'principle of alien causality'. A controversial testimony from Proclus' commentary in the *Parmenides* (38.32–40.5 = Speus. fr. 62) has recently been used to support the thesis that, according to Speusippus, the transcendence of the One, which radically differs from everything else, also entails transcendence with respect to being; if this were the case, Speusippus would already display the distinguishing feature of post-Plotinian Neoplatonism: Dancy 1991: 86–96; Halfwassen 1993: 372–3; Dillon 2003: 56–9; Brisson 2010. Interesting as it may be, this hypothesis does not take the peculiarity of Proclus' testimony into due account, as rightly shown – among others – by Steel 2002a, following in the footsteps of Tarán 1981: 354–6: interesting analogies are to be found between Speusippus and Plotinus as regards the 'Third Man' problem, although this does not justify a Neoplatonic reading of Speusippus: see Chapter 4, The Doctrine of Principles: The One and the Hierarchical Structure of Reality, p. 135–136.

the form of an ontology, without leaving any room for an axiology
(i.e. a theory also capable of accounting for values such as goodness and beauty): the doctrine of principles explains reality as it is,
not its value. This entails a radical difference compared to Plato,
for whom axiological requirements come before ontological ones:
we can argue as to whether there is such a thing as a Platonic ontology, but no one could ever deny the axiological concerns underlying his philosophy. In Plato's case, the investigation of reality is
also intended to identify some guiding values by which to govern
one's actions; in Speusippus' case, theory is set apart from *praxis*,
much as it is with Aristotle. To put it differently, Speusippus' principles are conceived as the causes and elements of things, and no
longer as models: Speusippus offers a conceptual simplification of
Platonic doctrine, which may have the merit of attaining a greater
degree of coherence, but which also forced him to abandon certain
aspects that Plato had deemed crucial.

Speusippus' doctrine is also open to a series of theoretical objections, which Aristotle did not miss the opportunity to highlight.
Aristotle agrees with Speusippus that Forms are basically useless, and in principle he is not averse to a theory of elements. The
problem with Speusippus is that, insofar as he continues to defend
the transcendent character of these first principles, he makes them
useless as a means to explain the reality that surrounds us: if numbers are transcendent, it is difficult to understand how they might
make up the elements of things, nor is it clear how mathematics might be a science capable of explaining sensible reality.[46]
As for the One, insofar as Speusippus is opposed to Forms and
to ideal numbers, it is difficult to understand what it might be,
since everything suggests that it is a sort of ideal principle (and
not a simple number).[47] Finally, an even more complex picture
surfaces from the doctrine taken as a whole: if the causal process
does not depend on the first principle but newly emerges at every
level (that of numbers, of geometric magnitudes, of the soul, and
of sensible things), as the elements are only principles of the
realities of which they are elements, we risk having an 'episodic'

[46] Berti 2010: 110.
[47] Arist. *Met.* 13.8.1083a20–b1 = Speus. fr. 76.

16

The Doctrine of Principles and the Theory of Forms

universe, made up of unconnected elements like 'a poor tragedy', to quote Aristotle.[48] Not all these criticisms are equally pertinent, perhaps, and Aristotle himself was to draw upon some of Speusippus' insights, as scholars have rightly noted.[49] However, it is true that Speusippus' attempt apparently failed to solve all difficulties, starting from the fundamental one: ultimately, for Aristotle (and others too), the real problem remains the metaphysical-transcendentist assumption, and it is difficult to understand how Speusippus' theory might prove better than the Platonic one.

Compared to Speusippus, Xenocrates stands out for his greater conservatism, which translates into an attempt to save the Forms within the doctrine of principles. At the origin of everything there remains a duality of principles: on the one hand, the One, also called the Monad or Intellect, identified with Zeus; on the other hand, the (indefinite) Dyad, the principle of multiplicity which comes into play at different levels of reality and is identified with matter and with Hera.[50] These two principles give rise to ideal numbers, from which everything else is produced via a process of derivation: the line from the ideal two, the surface from the ideal three, the solid from the ideal four, and so on down to the soul, the heavens, and all sensible things.[51]

Xenocrates – and this is a first significant difference compared to his predecessor (who had stopped at the soul) – aims to offer a complete systematisation of all realities, starting from the first two principles: 'with Xenocrates, then, we would have a doctrine of universal derivation of reality from the principles, without the kind of discontinuity that Aristotle imputed to Speusippus, but at the same time we would have a sort of cosmologisation of reality as a whole, which is to say a conception of it as one big cosmos,

---

[48] Arist. *Met.* 12.10.1075b37–1076a4 and 14.3.1090b13–20 = Speus. frs. 52 and 86. Cf. Trabattoni 2016: 152: 'given that the principles coincide with numbers […] and given that a number does not have any causative effect on the one that follows it, the realities whose principles numbers are will inevitably be interrelated, precisely to the same extent that numbers themselves are interrelated'.
[49] Cherniss 1974: 97; Berti 2010: 150.
[50] See Arist. *Met.* 14.1.1088b28–35 = Xenocr. fr. 19; Aët. Plac. 1.3.23 = Xenocr. fr. 21, and esp. Aët. Plac. 1.7.30 = Xenocr. fr. 133.
[51] Arist. Met. 7.2.1028b24–6 = Xenocr. fr. 23: 'And some say Forms and numbers have the same nature, and other things come after them, e.g. lines and planes, until we come to the substance of the heavens and to sensible bodies.'

17

or orderly universe, culminating with the principles, understood as deities, which is to say gods'.[52]

Whereas the adoption of the first two principles would appear to differ from Speusippus' conceptual schema only by virtue of its more systematic nature, divergences become far more marked when it comes to the theory of ideal numbers, which implies a defence of Forms: here Xenocrates departs from his predecessor in order to return to Plato. The latter had spoken of (ideal and mathematical) numbers and Forms. Speusippus – as we have seen – had tried to simplify the system by preserving only mathematical numbers (which were nevertheless regarded as separate entities existing beyond sensible things). Xenocrates instead sets out to find a place also for the Forms, which he identifies with numbers; in such a way, he stresses the importance of ideal numbers, which is to say indivisible and eternal units (de facto, these are the Forms of numbers: the dyad, the triad, etc. – for each ideal number there is only one exemplar),[53] very different from real numbers (which exist in many specimens and can be combined insofar as they are divisible).[54] No doubt, this identification between Forms and numbers presented one significant advantage, since it guaranteed the principles' role as both elements and models: as numbers, these principles are the constitutive elements of reality (as already noted by Speusippus: Xenocrates too is strongly indebted to the Pythagorean tradition); as ideal entities, they also serve as paradigmatic models.

Xenocrates' aim, in other words, was to preserve this twofold function that Plato had assigned to his ideal principles and which Speusippus had instead dropped (in favour of their function as constitutive elements).

It is hardly a coincidence, therefore, that we owe to Xenocrates a definition of Forms that was destined to remain normative for

[52] Berti 2010: 152–3, following Theophr. *Met.* 6a23 = Xenocr. fr. 20. This tendency is further confirmed by the centrality of the *Timaeus* as the reference text in these debates (Sedley 2021a: 18–37 also underlines the importance of the *Phaedrus*); see *infra*, The Academy and the Sciences: Cosmogony, Cosmology, and Mathematics, p. 21.

[53] Cf. Plat. *Phaed.* 101b–c.

[54] In general, see Arist. *Met.* 12.6.1080a12–35; on Xenocrates, see Arist. *Met.* 12.1.1069a34–35 and 13.1.1076a10–11 = Xenocr. frs. 26–7. Plato too apparently identified Forms with ideal numbers, at least according to Arist., *Met.* 13.4.1078b9–12; cf. Theophr. *Met.* 6b12–14.

Platonists throughout the centuries, and which stresses precisely their function as models: according to Xenocrates, Forms are 'the paradigmatic cause of whatever is composed continually in accordance with nature'.[55] What Forms are, and what they are Forms of, was a much-debated question within the Academy. In the context of these discussions (destined to come to the fore once more in the Imperial period), Xenocrates' definition constitutes an enlightening example of the scholasticising quality which characterises his thought. This definition not only confirms the exemplary role of the Forms, thereby underlining their function as models (this being the most important point, as we have just seen), but it also aims to define the field of application of Forms: the doctrine of Forms is an eminently ontological doctrine, yet it does not indiscriminately apply to all entities in our world; rather, it only concerns natural entities (as opposed to artefacts), and in particular natural species (plants, animals, human beings), and not individuals (since, unlike species, they are not eternal).[56]

While no doubt interesting, not even Xenocrates' theory was able to solve all difficulties, as Aristotle was keen to note, going so far as to argue that it was by far the worst of the three theories: the 'third way' – as Aristotle speaks of Xenocrates without mentioning him by name – far from improving his predecessors' theories, inherits their limits. Xenocrates made a twofold error: by juxtaposing ideal numbers and mathematical numbers, he risked destroying mathematics (for mathematical operations cannot be applied to ideal numbers); as regards the alleged identification of Forms with numbers, it is unclear in what way it is possible to group together such distinct entities, which fulfil such different functions (since Forms serve as models, and numbers as elements).[57] Xenocrates' philosophy is not devoid of interest, and his attempt to develop a theory capable of holding together the intelligible and the sensible level shows that he had clearly grasped the main problem with

[55] Procl. *In Parm.* 4.888.9–31 = Xenocr. fr. 14.
[56] See Berti 2010: 114. For a defence of the validity of the Proclus passage as a testimony about Xenocrates, see Dancy 2011.
[57] Arist. *Met.* 13.8.1083b1–8 and 13.9.1086a6–11 = Xenocr. frs. 29–30; Arist. *Met.* 1090b31–32 = fr. 38.

Plato's philosophy.[58] But, however harsh, Aristotle's objections are not unreasonable, and find a vivid description in Margherita Isnardi Parente's words: 'the Academics attempted to eliminate the aporias; of course, in doing so, they often created more serious ones'.[59]

Speusippus' and Xenocrates' doctrines are the most important ones within the Academy, but they are hardly the only doctrines.[60] Before proceeding any further, it is worth recalling another attempt made to 'aid' the Platonic doctrines, by the great scientist Eudoxus of Cnidus.

One of the main criticisms levelled against Forms – already in the *Parmenides* and then, even more staunchly, by Aristotle – concerns their transcendence with respect to the sensible things of which they are meant to be the principle. This assumption, which neither Speusippus nor Xenocrates ever questioned, was instead jettisoned by Eudoxus, who spoke of a mingling of Forms and things, similarly to what can 'occur between "white", understood as the colour white, and "white", understood as white things'.[61] In this case too, Aristotle did not miss the opportunity to criticise the many impossible consequences of this thesis (e.g. if Forms mix with things, they ought to be bodies, as only bodies can mix; and if they mix, how can they mix in several things simultaneously?).[62] However, it is worth noting that the Aristotelian doctrine of form as the essential immanent principle of things was based on an awareness of the difficulties involved not unlike that displayed by Eudoxus: like the latter, Aristotle maintained that the only way to save the distinction between the sensible and the intelligible was to deny the transcendence and separateness of ideal and formal

---

[58] In this regard, it is worth briefly mentioning the anonymous treatise *On Invisible Lines*: just after Forms we find the line which, by introducing extension, marks the transition from the intelligible to the sensible level. Now, if a line were infinitely divisible, we would witness the dissolution of the sensible into non-being, hence the need to posit the existence of indivisible lines; see Sedley 2021a: 19–20.

[59] Isnardi Parente 1998: 217.

[60] Another interesting testimony concerns Hermodorus of Syracuse and the issue of what stands in opposition to the first principle: Hermodorus called this matter, and questioned its status as a principle. Cf. frs. 7–8 and the commentaries by Isnardi Parente 1982b: 439–44 and Dillon 2003: 200–4.

[61] Berti 2010: 102, on Arist. *Met.* 1.9.991a8–19 = Eudox. D 1.

[62] See Arist. *De ideis* fr. 5 = Eudox. D 2.

principles. Aristotle's doctrine is interesting and certainly original, 'but it would not have been possible without the debate on Forms which had occurred in the Academy'.[63]

The Academy and the Sciences: Cosmogony, Cosmology, and Mathematics

The debate on the principles was not an end to itself, but rather part of a broader research project, designed to account for reality in all of its complexity. In other words, it was not a matter of elucidating only the metaphysical structure of the intelligible reality on which everything depends; it was also important to account for what depends on such principles, namely sensible reality. An equally ambitious aim for the Academics was to 'save the phenomena', as they themselves put it, which is to say to formulate hypotheses capable of providing the most reasonable and economic explanations for what occurs around us (*phainomena*, which in Greek means 'the things that appear').[64]

As with the discussions about principles, in this case too, the research followed a particular direction, established by Plato: it is Plato who lay out the problems and defined the possible solutions, which the Academics were then free to develop, correct, or modify. More specifically, in this case it was a text that played a normative role: the *Timaeus*, a dialogue destined to exercise a remarkable influence on Platonism throughout the following centuries, and especially in the Imperial age.[65] In practice, the dialogue addressed two main issues: cosmogony and cosmology. On the one hand, what was at stake was the alleged eternity of the universe – the problem of establishing whether the universe was eternal or created; on the other hand, it was a matter of reconstructing models capable of explaining the current functioning of the universe. Both these issues gave rise to rich and lively discussions, which in themselves prove what a remarkable moment in the history of human thought the Early Academy represents.

[63] Berti 2010: 122. On Eudoxus and the parallels between his suggestion and Aristotle's theses, see Dancy 1991: 23–52.
[64] See e.g. Simpl. *In De cael.* 488.22–25; Zhmud 2005.
[65] On the reception of the *Timaeus* in the Early Academy, see Centrone 2012; Bénatouïl 2017.

It is useful to analyse cosmological debates not just because they are intrinsically interesting, but also because they help us better understand certain dynamics within the Academy, and hence to better define the role played by two of the greatest philosophers operating within it, Plato and Aristotle. I have already repeatedly emphasised Plato's distinctive role in promoting philosophical research; with regard to the question of the creation of the universe, it is possible to appreciate his great freedom of thought, which makes him a true teacher, always careful not to impose his views on others.

As far as Plato's pupil Aristotle is concerned, in the previous section I noted how he did not refrain from criticising his inter-locutors (albeit without ever really abandoning the conceptual coordinates within which the research was being conducted). However, the lack of testimonies makes it impossible to understand whether the development of new theses by philosophers such as Speusippus, Xenocrates, and Eudoxus also reflects a desire on their part to defend Plato against Aristotelian criticism.[66] At the present state of our knowledge, it seems as though everyone was discussing everything. The debate on the creation of the universe was to bring out a slightly different and more interesting situation.

The *Timaeus*, then, constituted the starting point and point of reference. But the guidelines it provided were remarkably elusive. The most real entities of all are the intelligible principles, whereas sensible things are at most images, devoid of any real ontological consistency, and dependent on the ideal principles for their existence. Because of this dependence, it is possible to speak of the sensible universe as something 'generated': the *raison d'être* of the universe derives from something else (the intelligible principles).[67] But how exactly are we to understand this generation? Is it to be understood in real terms, as a temporal creation, or rather as a logical creation, as a way of expressing the universe's dependence on the first principles? Plato expounds his view in such succinct terms that he comes across as (purposely) reticent: in the *Timaeus* we only read that the universe *gegone*, which may be roughly translated as 'it has come to be' (28b).

---

[66] As suggested, for instance, by Lévy 2000: 801.

[67] Plat. *Tim.* 28b–c.

What this generation means is precisely what Plato does not say; nor does the rest of the dialogue help clear our doubts and perplexities. Certainly, the *Timaeus* speaks of the Demiurge, the divine craftsman, and this might imply a temporal creation: by contemplating the ever-existent ideal model, the Demiurge gave order to what was in a state of disorder, and this is the universe, which the Demiurge himself will keep alive forever after having crafted it. But what the *Timaeus* recounts is only an *eikos mythos*, a 'likely tale' (29d): are we really to take it literally? The discussion on the *Timaeus*, in other words, shows that the exegesis of the dialogues and the discussion of philosophical issues are not two separate problems: as we shall see again and again, this is a recurrent feature in the history of Platonism.

The surviving testimonies appear to suggest that, at least as far as this specific problem is concerned, Speusippus' and Xenocrates' theses truly represent an attempt to come to Plato's aid, against Aristotle's criticism. As may be inferred from *De caelo* and the surviving fragments of *De philosophia*, Aristotle had no doubts: the text of the *Timaeus* could hardly have been any clearer; and it defended a thesis that was wrong. According to Aristotle, the *Timaeus* upholds the thesis of creation in time, and this is wrong because the universe is eternal (besides, Plato's claim that what has been created can endure forever is equally fallacious).[68] The Academics' response is primarily a lesson on how to read Plato. In their view, the myth of the Demiurge must not be taken literally: for it is a teaching device used to explain issues that would otherwise be almost impossible to understand. Once we have grasped this, we can also understand that the *Timaeus'* 'creation' must be taken in an allegorical sense: it is not a creation in time, but a logical creation; in other words, the creationist language is only used to emphasise the ontological priority of the intelligible principles over the sensible entities.[69]

---

[68] Arist. *De caelo* 1.10.
[69] Speus. frs. 54 and 94; Xenocr. frs. 153, 154, 159. The same thesis was also upheld by Crant. fr. 10. As regards this debate, Baltes 1976: 5–22 remains fundamental; see also Bénatouïl and El Murr 2010: 63–8, and Sedley 2021a: 18–22, who rightly underlines the importance of the *Phaedrus* (see 246b6–c2) in support of the eternalist view. Another two problems of the *Timaeus* that constituted an object of heated debate were the World Soul and the relation between the four elements and the five geometrical bodies. The solution which Xenocrates offers to the first problem clearly reveals the

This thesis, which was largely forgotten in the Hellenistic centuries, later became immensely popular, and came to dominate the whole Imperial age.[70] It constitutes one of the most defining doctrines of the Platonic tradition. But was it really a Platonic doctrine? As we have seen, this is far from certain, and remains a matter of debate. What *is* certain is the fact that the thesis of an eternal universe is an Aristotelian thesis, and it is also likely that the Academics themselves adopted it (and attributed it to Plato) precisely because they were persuaded by the Aristotelian arguments. But if this is the case, we cannot fail to notice the irony in the whole story: what for centuries has been perceived as one of the most distinctive doctrines of Platonism is first of all an Aristotelian thesis. In other words, it is tempting at times to define Platonism as the outcome of an Aristotelisation of Plato: as an attempt to read Aristotelian doctrines into the dialogues in order to defend Plato against Aristotle. As we shall see, situations of this sort crop up again and again in the Imperial centuries, when engagement with Aristotle was constant (and, from the third century, systematic). By contrast, it is difficult to say whether this was also the case in the Early Academy, given the dearth of testimonies. Certainly, Aristotle is a weighty presence in the history of Platonism.

Alongside the cosmogonic problem, there was the cosmological one: it was a matter of correctly describing the universe by developing a model capable of correctly explaining how it worked. Plato had described a universe essentially divided into

significance of his interpretation of Plato, which is designed to keep together the doctrine of principles and the philosophy of the dialogues: the soul is a self-moving number (Xenocr. fr. 108), where the reference to number points to the doctrine of principles (numbers – obviously to be understood as ideal numbers – derive from the interaction between the Monad and the Dyad), while the notion of self-movement refers to a famous passage from the *Phaedrus* (245c). By stressing the coexistence between the soul and the world, Speusippus instead apparently spoke of the soul as the form (*idea*) of what is generally extended (Speus. fr. 96). Again interpreting Plato, Xenocrates further defended the immortality of the soul in all of its components, the rational and the irrational: see Schibli 1993 and Sedley 2021a, underlining the importance of the *Phaedrus*. As regards the second problem, Xenocrates would appear to have simply established the dodecahedron as a fifth basic body that makes up the heavens, the noblest part of the universe (Xenocr. frs. 182–4), whereas Speusippus reportedly questioned this relation between elements and bodies by identifying the original components of the universe in the tetradic pyramid (Speus. fr. 122).

[70] See Chapter 3, Cosmological Issues: The Debate on the Eternity of the Universe, p. 95.

various spheres: at the centre was the Earth, enclosed within a larger sphere, the 'heavenly vault', to which the stars were fixed and which rotated around smaller spheres; in the middle there were the Sun, the Moon, and five planets (Venus, Mercury, Mars, Jupiter, and Saturn) with their own orbits. But was this really how things stood, and did this model correctly represent the universe? In order to prove it, adequate explanations were required, because the model worked in general, but astronomers had detected many irregularities in planetary motions. Eudoxus of Cnidus came up with the most brilliant solution to these difficulties (and his pupil Callippus of Cyzicus later perfected it): he suggested that the planets move according to the resultant of the motions of several spheres, the so-called homocentric spheres, which all have the same centre but different sizes and axes with different inclinations with respect to the outermost sphere, as well as different speeds (hence, the number of spheres was significantly increased).[71] This solution explained some of the apparent irregularities in the motions of the various heavenly bodies, which sometimes seemed to slow down in their course or even to move backwards, growing closer to or further away from the Earth.[72] There is no need to illustrate Eudoxus' theory in detail, not least because it is unclear to what extent the more technical aspects of his astronomic research were connected to the debates held within the Academy. But in its general outline, this was a crucial problem for Academics seeking to make sense of the universe by revealing its intrinsic order and rationality: significantly, the 'mosaic of the philosophers' in Naples shows them discussing cosmological problems, with a heavenly sphere and a solar quadrant in front and behind them respectively. It is important to recall that the model developed through these debates in the Academy, through Aristotle's mediation (and the further research conducted by Apollonius of Perga and Hipparchus of Nicaea in the third and

---

[71] An alternative hypothesis was formulated by Heraclides Ponticus: 'In proposing that the Earth is at the center and moving in a circle, and that the sky is at rest, Heraclides Ponticus thought he was preserving the natural phenomena' (Heracl. fr. 67 Schütrumpf); on Heraclides' astronomical theses, their presumably Pythagorean origin, and their connection with Plato's *Timaeus*, see Gottschalk 1980: 58–87; Todd and Bowen 2009.

[72] A clear presentation may be found in Berti 2010: 42–50; in more detail see Yavetz 1998.

second centuries BC, and Ptolemy in the second century AD) was the model of the universe which was destined to remain dominant up until Copernicus' and Galileo's scientific revolution.

Metaphysics and cosmology (broadly understood) were no doubt two very important disciplines for the Academics. What is more difficult to assess is how much interest they showed in other scientific disciplines, particularly mathematics and geometry. The aforementioned comic fragment presents the Academic philosophers as engaging in the difficult task of classifying a pumpkin: this has been taken to suggest that the Academy was a sort of scientific institution, seeking to promote all forms of research on the natural world. Certainly, we must not underestimate the importance of – and the time devoted to – enquiries of this sort, but nor should we overestimate their importance (and this also applies to the more technical aspects of astronomic investigations).[73] Ultimately, what is really significant in the comic fragment is not so much the object of enquiry (the pumpkin, and hence biology), but the method adopted (dialectic, which we shall discuss in the next section).

As regards mathematics, an entrenched historiographical myth has it that the Academy crucially contributed to the development of the mathematical sciences: Plato gathered around him the leading mathematicians of his day, and constantly challenged them with increasingly complex problems. As has recently been noted, however, this picture of Plato as the 'architect of the mathematical sciences'[74] is actually the product of a later representation, based on Book 7 of the *Republic*.[75] No doubt, leading mathematicians frequented the Academy,[76] but this is not enough to make it the centre for mathematical and geometric research par excellence.[77] Ultimately, it is evident that the Academics paid much attention to numbers, but many of their theses concern metaphysics more than the mathematical sciences as such. Besides, already in the

---

[73] See now Bodnár 2020, arguing that at least Speusippus was interested in naturalistic investigations.

[74] Philod. *Acad. ind.* Y.2–12.

[75] See Zhmud 1998, whose conclusions also scale down the importance of astronomical investigations.

[76] See Procl. *In Eucl.* 66.8–68.4 for a list of the mathematicians reportedly surrounding Plato in the Academy.

[77] Zhmud 2006: 82–116.

Republic Plato had made it quite clear that mathematics serves a propaedeutic function with respect to dialectic (i.e. philosophy).[78] In other words, the Academy is not the place where science in the strict sense of the term emancipated itself from philosophy.

Epistemology and Dialectic

The fact that the Academics were not engaged in pure mathematical research does not mean that they were not interested in the potential of such research. We have already seen how they used numbers in their metaphysical doctrines; what is even more interesting is their epistemological and methodological engagement with the mathematics and geometry. In the fourth century BC significant progress was made in disciplines such as mathematics and astronomy, which became paradigmatic models of exact knowledge, based on a rigorous method and capable of attaining precise and incontrovertible results. By engaging in such disciplines, an attempt was made to establish the foundations of a theory of knowledge (*episteme*, whence the modern term 'epistemology'). This was the case with the Academics, as it had been for Plato – and justifiably so, since the problems which the philosophers discussed were of the sort mathematicians tackled.

One urgent question for mathematicians of the time such as Menaechmus – who according to our sources regularly visited Plato and the Academy – concerned knowledge of the first principles or elements at the basis of the whole system. If knowledge had an 'analytical' character, meaning that it consisted in breaking down a given object into its constituents, then there was a risk of infinite regress,

---

[78] Particularly revealing, in this respect, is the *Epinomis* (probably the work of Philip of Opus): although the science of numbers and astronomy would seem to mark the height of wisdom ([Plat.] *Epin.* 976d–978b), the mathematical sciences are nonetheless presented as a preparation (990c2–6; cf. 991b10–11) to theology and dialectic. Also significant, in this respect, is the testimony by Plut. *Vit. Marc.* 14.9–12: Plato was indignant at the fact that Eudoxus and Archytas sought to derive practical guidelines from their investigations: 'he inveighed against them as corrupters and destroyers of the pure excellence of geometry which thus turned her back upon the incorporeal things of abstract thought and descended to the things of sense'; see also Plut. *QC* 8.2 (this anecdote would appear to reflect not so much Plato's position as that of the Academics: Bowen 1983: 21–4).

which undermines the very possibility of knowledge, and if the first elements could not be known, then neither could what sprung from them.[79] One possible solution was to posit a different kind of knowledge of the first principles: a direct and intuitive kind of knowledge, rather than one based on analysis and definition. Such problems and solutions were well known to the readers of Plato and Aristotle, and they crop again in relation to the other Academics, starting from Speusippus. As already noted – and as we shall now verify – the sources would seem to suggest that Speusippus exploited the potential of mathematics and the mathematicians' insights to solve certain difficulties related to Plato's epistemology.

In the later dialogues, the philosophical method par excellence is *diairesis*, whereby one seeks to grasp the nature of a given object by charting its relations to all other objects. The same perspective, a kind of epistemological holism, is recorded in relation to Speusippus. However, as already highlighted in the *Parmenides* (136b–c), there was clearly a risk of embarking on an endless research, since the things that surround us are potentially endless.[80] If in order to know an object we must know its relations to all other objects, then – as noted by Neoplatonist commentators – we risk slipping into scepticism, understood as the impossibility of ever bringing our research to an end.[81] The choice of a mathematising metaphysics would appear to suggest a way out of this impasse, insofar as the intuition of the principles, conceived as numbers, entailed a different and possible mode of knowledge (by contrast to Forms, which according to Plato himself could only be known by the disembodied soul). The principles at least are fully knowable, because – as Proclus reports – according to Speusippus 'knowledge via contact, [which] is more vivid than sight is for those who

---

[79] For a discussion of Menaechmos' theses, see Fuentes Gonzáles 2005 and De Haas 2011: 216–29.

[80] See Arist. *An. Post.* 2.13.97a6–11 = Speus. fr. 38: 'There is no need for one who is defining and dividing to know everything there is. Yet some say that it is impossible to know a thing's differences from something without knowing that thing; but that without the differences one cannot know that thing – for it is the same as that from which it does not differ and different from that from which it does differ. Now, first, this is false' (all Neoplatonic commentaries on this passage confirm that the reference here is to Speusippus). On this passage, see now Falcon 2000.

[81] See Speus. frs. 39–43.

28

see', and from this first knowledge it would be possible to infer all the properties of these entities by means of demonstration.[82] This should not be taken to suggest that Speusippus completely yielded to Menaechmus, since he criticised him by defending the notion of the eternal and separate existence of mathematical entities in opposition to the 'constructivist' perspective (according to which science does not deal with what is eternal, but operates by producing new objects of knowledge).[83] Still, it would be difficult to deny the influence of mathematical debates.

As regards the knowledge of sensible things based on diairetic procedures, Speusippus' earnest pursuit of classification and definition (a commitment clearly reflected by texts such as *Homoia*, 'Similitudes', and *Horoi*, 'Definitions') shows that in his view a sceptical outcome was not inevitable, even in relation to sensible reality.[84] In a way which is difficult for us to reconstruct, he may have pointed out that the knowledge of numbers furnishes principles (sameness, difference, etc.) which enable us to order, and hence to some extent to know, all other entities, by defining their relations of sameness, similarity, and dissimilarity.[85] Simply put, Speusippus probably noted that in this field, unlike on the level of principles, there cannot be any exact knowledge (*episteme*); this thesis is far from incompatible with Plato.[86]

Compared to Speusippus' drastic choices, Xenocrates stands out because of his greater scholasticism, intended to clarify the Academy's positions. A case in point is the distinction he draws

[82] Speus. fr. 35. Thus, for example, Tarán 1981: 21–3, 53–6, 318–19; a different reading has been suggested by Bénatouïl and El Murr 2010: 59–62.

[83] See Speus. fr. 36 with the commentary in Bowen 1983.

[84] See esp. Speus. frs. 123–45 from *Similitudes*, where we read of definitions and classifications of tunas (male and female), pumpkins, shells, cicadas, moths, and mosquitoes; see Wilson 1997

[85] See Tarán 1981: 53–5, followed by El Murr 2018: 345. It may be possible to understand in such terms the distinction between 'scientific reason' and 'scientific sensation' in Speus. fr. 34: see Dillon 2003: 77–9.

[86] As Trabattoni 2016: 153 rightly notes, Speusippus' dialectic presents some interesting affinities and analogies with Aristotle: 'Platonic dialectic, in other words, is lowered by one degree by Speusippus [i.e. it passes from the intelligible to the sensible plane], notwithstanding the fact that the two methods radically differ on the level of definition: the intensional selection of a restricted group of differences in Aristotle, the extensional collection of all differences (with no distinction between essential and accidental ones) in Speusippus'. See also Kaklamanou 2010 and Dillon 2018.

between three levels of substance (the intelligible substance out-side the heavens, the sensible substance below the heavens, and the mixed one which lies between the two, namely the heavenly bod-ies); to these three levels there correspond three different modes of knowledge (intuition, sensation, and correct opinion). Besides, we may recall the distinction between wisdom (*sophia*) and practical wisdom (*phronesis*). Finally, what is particularly significant is the adoption of a scheme based on the two categories of 'per se' and 'relatives', which in later periods came to be used both as an alter-native and as an integration to Aristotle's ten categories.[87]

Ethical Issues

Regrettably, the meagre number of surviving testimonies does not allow us to get a correct idea of the ethical theses of Speusippus, Xenocrates, and the other Academics. What we know for sure is that a sophisticated debate on pleasure pitted Eudoxus against Speusippus, with contributions also by Plato (as may be inferred from the *Philebus*)[88] and Aristotle (as may be inferred from *Nicomachean Ethics* 7 and 10.1–5). While Plato and Aristotle adopted intermediate positions, seeking to find a place for pleasure without assigning it too much importance, Eudoxus and Speusippus took radically antithetical stances: the former defended pleasure, while the latter disputed the idea that it con-stituted a good.[89] The arguments preserved in the ancient sources can be viewed in parallel, suggesting that a real debate took place.

Eudoxus argued that pleasure is a good because that towards which everyone tends is a good; now, since everyone tends towards

---

[87] See, respectively, Xenocr. frs. 83, 95, 259. It is unclear whether Xenocrates was also the target of Aristotle's polemical attack in *An. Post.* 1.3 against the champions of the thesis according to which it is possible to acquire demonstrative knowledge of the first principles by using circular demonstrations. See Isnardi Parente 1982b (on Xenocrates' theory of knowledge) and Granieri 2021 (on the two-category scheme).

[88] Dillon 2003: 67–77 represents an interesting – and probably overly optimistic – attempt to glean numerous testimonies about Speusippus from the *Philebus*.

[89] Curiously enough, the anti-hedonist Speusippus was well known to have led a dissolute life as a young man (cf. frs. 1, 2, 5, 7, 22), whereas the hedonist Eudoxus was held in esteem by all for his sobriety (Arist. *EN* 10.2.1172b15–18 = Eudox. fr. 3). It is probably a universal psychological truism that in order to despise pleasure, one first needs to have intensely experienced it, and vice versa.

pleasure, pleasure must be the most important, highest good. He further defended his thesis with the argument from opposites, by observing that since everyone flees pain, pleasure – the opposite of pain – is good. But he also resorted to the argument about the end: what is most desirable is what we desire for its own sake (and not in view of something else), and this is pleasure; besides, what is added to a good so as to make it more desirable is certainly a good, and this also applies to pleasure, which, when added to just and temperate actions, makes them more desirable. Finally, he noted that pleasure, like the gods, is one of the few things which are so evidently valuable that there is no need to praise them.[90] Speusippus countered these arguments in detail. It is not true that all living beings tend towards pleasure: it is mostly children and animals that do, which is to say beings lacking reason, whereas reasonable people tend towards moderation; nor is it true that what everyone tends towards is necessarily a good. Against the argument from opposites, he noted that what is good is a mean between two negative extremes; hence, what is good coincides neither with pleasure nor pain, but with an intermediate state marked by the absence of pain and passions. Nor is pleasure an end, since it is a process, and a process is different from an end, just as the construction of a house is different from the constructed house. Even more significantly, far from increasing other goods, pleasure is often a hindrance to their pursuit, for the experience of pleasure often makes reflection difficult. In other words, if pleasure is not praised, it is not because its value is self-evident, but rather because pleasures are often blameworthy.[91]

It is interesting to note that Speusippus' thesis somehow draws upon the mainstays of Socratic ethics, foreshadowing certain Hellenistic theories (the emphasis on nature, the quest for tranquillity). His anti-hedonism should not be taken to suggest that pleasure is an evil (quite frankly, it would have been absurd for

[90] See Arist. *EN* 10.2.1172b9–25 and 1.12.1101b27–31 (= Eudox. fr. 3–4). A clear presentation of the Academic debate on pleasure may be found in Berti 2010: 173–99; Warren 2009; Fronterotta 2018.
[91] See, respectively, Arist. *EN* 7.12.1152b16–20; 10.2.1172b35–6; 10.2.1173a5–8 (= Speus. fr. 109); 10.3.1173a29–31; 7.12,1152b16–18; 10.3.1173b21.

him to defend such a thesis). Rather, the point is that no kind of pleasure is a good, because the true good is something which must give human beings serenity, shielding them from the vagaries of fate: for Speusippus, the true good is a natural condition consisting in untroubledness (*aochlesia*)[92] and can be attained through virtuous living.[93] This distinctly Platonic emphasis on virtue is also found in Xenocrates, who in turn would appear to have identified life's end with the cessation of disturbance (*ataraxia*).[94] He can also be credited with various statements which seem to specifically foreshadow Stoicism.[95] However, much of the information we have about Xenocrates has reached us via Antiochus of Ascalon, who in opposition to Academic scepticism championed the notion of continuity between Plato, the Academy, the Peripatos, and Stoicism.[96] While not wholly unreliable, his testimony must nonetheless be approached with much caution. Apart from this, what survives from Xenocrates are aphorisms, definitions, maxims, and reflections, but it does not seem as though any real ethical theory can be attributed to him:[97] as we have seen, it is in the field of metaphysics, not ethics, that we must look for the heart of the early Academics' philosophy.[98]

[92] Clem. Alex. *Strom.* 2.22.133 = Speus. fr. 101.
[93] What seems more implausible is Cicero's claim that according to Speusippus, virtue is enough to make a man happy, even when he is undergoing torture (Cic. *Tusc. Disp.* 5.87 = Speus. fr. 105; however, it is true that already Aristotle discusses this option in *EN* 7.14.1153b19–21; cf. Berti 2010: 179).
[94] Xenocr. fr. 171.
[95] See e.g. fr. 149 on indifferents or fr. 152 on the identification on the good with first things according to nature. The identification between happiness and virtue is found in Clem. Alex. *Strom.* 2.22.183 (= Speus. fr. 232), but Xenocrates also points to the need for good health and external good to ensure a happy life, which marks a break with Stoicism.
[96] See Chapter 2, The Case of Antiochus, p. 67.
[97] However, the sources credit him with the composition of numerous treatises on this topic: see D.L. 7.11–14. The most striking maxim is: 'if each individual's soul is his daemon (*daimon*), as Xenocrates believes, that he who has a good (*eu*) soul is happy (*eudaimon*); but the wise man is he who has a good soul; hence, the wise man is happy' (Xenocr. fr. 155). Playing on the etymology of happiness (*eudaimonia*, which literally means 'to have a good daimon'), and once again echoing Plato (cf. *Tim.* 90a and *Resp.* 617e), Xenocrates reverses the traditional moral dictum that happiness depends on the course of fate (i.e. one's daimon), arguing instead that happiness depends on us and on our capacities – or, rather, on philosophy, insofar as philosophy alone can help us bring order to our soul. Xenocrates compellingly illustrates the chief ambition of Greek philosophy: to put human beings in a position to lead a happy life.
[98] Isnardi Parente 1998: 225–6.

The Practical Turn: Polemo and Crantor

The election of the new scholarch Polemo marked a sharp turn within the Academy: the metaphysical interests which had been so prominent among the Early Academics would appear to have receded into the background as ethical-practical research gained prominence.

Regrettably, the limited number of sources at our disposal makes it difficult to understand how such a turn came about. Perhaps we should not underestimate the impact which Alexander's conquests had on the Greek world (Polemo became scholarch in 314 BC, roughly ten years after the death of the Macedonian general). What became more pressing were issues pertaining to everyday life, as opposed to ones pertaining to metaphysical principles. Nor should we overlook the rapid spread of new Stoic and Epicurean schools, in comparison to which the Academics' investigations may have given the impression of being utterly useless and abstract. These are merely hypotheses, yet the fact remains that even within the Academy, ethical problems acquired a centrality and importance that they could never have had with Speusippus and Socrates. Indeed, Polemo – the successor of Xenocrates who is believed to have been the head of the school for forty years, and who was well known for leading a sober life after a misspent youth (from which Xenocrates had saved him)[99] – apparently stated 'that people should get their practice in real situations and not in dialectical arguments, like someone lapping up a handbook on harmonics but not bothering to practice, with the result that they are impressive in examining a question but inconsistent in their attitude and behavior'.[100] Certainly, the emphasis on the practical dimension of philosophy is not incompatible with Plato's teaching; but it is always striking to hear an Academic criticising dialectical reasoning.

All in all, Polemo's doctrines seem to take up some of Xenocrates' insights, radicalising them by lending them more austere overtones: while not all testimonies are equally reliable, certain doctrines certainly seem to be verging on Stoicism. Thus

[99] D.L. 4.16.
[100] D.L. 4.18.

Polemo himself apparently stated that the end of life is 'to live according to nature'[101] – a formula which was to become famous precisely with the Stoics. Xenocrates had already put forward a similar thesis, but Polemo stands out from his predecessor on account of his greater rigour. Xenocrates had indeed spoken of the need to act in accordance with nature, but at the same time he had acknowledged that the possession of external goods is also required for a happy life. Polemo instead would appear to have argued that virtue is enough for a happy life, even in the absence of external goods[102] – this too is a thesis which the Stoics were to uphold as crucial. Elsewhere, however, Cicero – one of the most important sources – also attributes to Polemo the idea that natural goods contribute to a happy life,[103] a thesis which would mitigate Polemo's rigorism, bringing him closer to Xenocrates than to the Stoics. In other words, as far as Polemo's thought is concerned, the sources follow two contrasting directions, with some seeking to reinforce the connection with his Academic predecessors and others emphasising his role as a forerunner of Stoicism. This hampers a full understanding of the role which Polemo played at a time of great innovation.[104] It is interesting to note that these

[101] Cic. *De fin.* 4.14 and 50 = Polem. frs. 129–30.
[102] Clem. Alex. Strom. 2.22 = Polem. fr. 123. As regards Xenocrates, cf. *supra*, n. 95. Philod. *Acad. ind.* XIII 38 = Polem. fr. 109 also attributes the *apatheia* thesis to Polemo, but 'this information about *apatheia* would appear to concern not so much Polemo's philosophical doctrine as his attitude or behaviour' (Isnardi Parente 1998: 229 n. 46).
[103] See Cic. *De fin.* 2.33–5 and 4.14 = Polem. frs. 127 and 129, with the comments in Dillon 2003: 162–4.
[104] The sources also report that Polemo defined the cosmos as *theos*: this can be taken to mean either that the cosmos is God or that the cosmos is a god. By focusing on the former possibility, Sedley 2002 has sought to reconstruct Polemo's physics as an original teaching that largely foreshadows Stoic physics. In his view, this is confirmed by those pages of the *Prior Academics* in which Varro presents the Early Academics' philosophy according to Antiochus of Ascalon. Following in Sedley 2002's footsteps, Dillon 2003, notes that the epistemological section the the *Prior Academics* seems to provide a reliable description of Polemo's theory of knowledge. However, as has repeatedly been observed (e.g. by Reydams-Schils 2013: 40–5), the very short doxographical citation on the divine cosmos is not enough in itself to support such a difficult hypothesis, not least given that the Ciceronian text speaks of 'ancients' in the plural (meaning Plato, Speusippus, Xenocrates, Aristotle, and Theophrastus, in addition to Polemo). The *Prior Academics* aims to present the theses of Antiochus of Ascalon, and there is no reason to doubt what the text states: we will therefore be discussing this work in relation to Antiochus' thought in the second chapter. As far as Polemo is concerned, it seems quite impossible – at any rate for the time being – to assign him 'a distinct physical theory of his own' (Isnardi Parente 1998: 228), and the same holds for his theory of knowledge.

analyses and classifications (the distinction between different goods, between goods and indifferents, the relation between virtues and goods, etc.) progressively defined an agenda of shared problems (and a shared language), which later came to serve as the basis for Hellenistic debates.

We know little about Crates, the scholarch who took Polemo's place, and nothing philosophically noteworthy. Something instead remains to be said about Crantor, a pupil of Xenocrates' and later Polemo's, and the last significant figure from the Early Academy. In antiquity he earned great renown through a consolatory work *On Pain*, 'a golden little volume', as Cicero describes it,[105] which once again confirms the prominent role of ethics at this stage in the Academy's life. Judging from the meagre picture it is possible to reconstruct, Crantor's teaching revolved around the notion of *metriopatheia*, or moderation of passions, which suggests an attempt to draw closer to the Aristotelian tradition to the detriment of Stoicism (which instead commended the elimination of all passion, or *apatheia*).[106] The same can be said about his acknowledgement of the power of fate, *tyche*, another thesis dear to the Peripatetics but unacceptable to the Stoics,[107] and about his acceptance of external goods.[108]

Proclus reports that Crantor was the first Platonic commentator. Indeed, quite a few sources inform us about his interpretation of some *Timaeus* passages.[109] However, it would be rash to identify Crantor as the author of the first systematic commentary on the whole dialogue (i.e. the sort of commentary that was to become increasingly common in the Imperial age), as some scholars have done.[110] After all, we have already seen how the other Academics' speculation, and particularly Xenocrates', was closely connected to the text of the dialogues: the fact that Crantor was interested in the *Timaeus* hardly

[105] Cic. *Ac.* 2.135.
[106] Cf. ps-Plut. *Cons. ad Ap.* 102c–d and Cic. *Tusc. Disp.* 3.71 = Crant. fr. 3a–b Mette.
[107] Cf. *SVF* 2.966.
[108] Sext. Emp. *Adv. Math.* 11.51–9 = Crant. fr. 7a Mette.
[109] Cf. Procl. *In Tim.* 1.76.1–2 = Crant. fr. 8 Mette. A systematic presentation of the passages discussed (the Atlantis myth, the eternalist interpretation of the world, the generation of the World Soul: essentially, as far as we can tell, Plat. *Tim.* 24d–25d, 28b, and 35a–37b) may be found in Krämer 1983: 161–2 and Dillon 2003: 218–24.
[110] Sedley 1997: 114 n. 1.

constitutes an innovation in and of itself; hence, it is not enough to justify the difficult thesis of a continuous commentary on the dialogue.[111] Still, we should not completely reduce Crantor to his predecessor's views: whereas Xenocrates' exegesis seems to be designed to critically reappraise Plato's philosophy, Crantor's appears to be driven by 'more explicitly and purely exegetical aims'.[112] This may have given Proclus or a philosopher before him the idea that Crantor was the first systematic commentator on Plato's dialogue.

Coming to Plato's Aid

It is not easy to appraise this first period in the long history of Platonism, and not merely because of the limited number of (often polemical) testimonies that have survived. Ultimately, the real problem is that in appraising these philosophers we inevitably tend to compare them to their two great counterparts, Plato and Aristotle. It is hardly surprising, then, that far from favourable opinions have been expressed on the work of philosophers such as Speusippus, Xenocrates, and Crantor.[113] To the extent that they are compared to Plato and Aristotle, it would be pointless to deny that there is some truth to this assessment. Yet we should not push things too far, since other clues point to the need for more nuanced judgements. In particular, these philosophers appear to have exercised considerable influence over the following centuries, although this influence is difficult to assess on account of the dearth of testimonies. Without indulging in wild speculation, it is possible to ascertain that the Academics' reflections somehow prepared and shaped the development of Hellenistic philosophy.[114]

---

[111] See e.g. Ferrari 2000: 179–80.

[112] Isnardi Parente 1998: 231, who notes that Crantor – unlike Xenocrates – dropped all references to the doctrine of principles in the exegesis of the passage on the generation of the soul; see also Krämer 1983: 162.

[113] Consider the case of Margherita Isnardi Parente, mentioned *supra*, The Doctrine of Principles and the Abandonment of the Theory of Forms, p. 20.

[114] The most systematic attempt in this respect remains that of Krämer 1971; see also the influential Sedley 2002 on theology and cosmology, and more cautiously Ademollo 2012. More recent interpretations adopt a more cautious approach, drawing a distinction between the possible direct influence of Plato and the indirect influence of the Academics: see Reydams-Schils 2013: 32–40, and – more generally – all the essays in the volume edited by Long 2013.

What is even more noteworthy – and even harder to demonstrate in any detail – is the influence they exerted on Imperial Platonism, and specifically on so-called Middle Platonism. Theses such as that put forward by Hans Joachim Krämer, who in a pioneering 1964 study presented Imperial Platonism as a resurgence of the Early Academy, probably go too far. Still, it is indisputably the case that many Early Academic theses provided crucial stimuli for later Platonists, who indeed often refer to them in respectful terms. Nor is this the only reason why we should refrain from facile criticism. Even more important is the fact that the Academics help us understand certain salient traits of the complex phenomenon of ancient Platonism. For quite some time, many scholars held a monolithic view of Platonism, presenting it as a single body of doctrines transmitted across the centuries in a more or less unaltered form. The metaphysical speculations of the Early Academics were taken as evident proof of the underlying orthodoxy at the heart of Platonism. More recent research, promoted by scholars of the calibre of Harold Cherniss and Margherita Isnardi Parente, has shown just how misleading a reconstruction of this sort can be. If we can speak of Platonism in relation to the Early Academy, it is not in terms of orthodoxy, but rather of 'aid': a primary role continued to be assigned to Plato's philosophy – his underlying project – yet not through the kind of passive attitude of someone merely repeating what he has learned. The Academics were Platonists to the extent that they partook in the Platonic project, defending it against accusations but also correcting, adapting, or modifying whatever they deemed fit. Ultimately, it is this philosophical freedom that represents the true foundational moment of Platonism and the guiding thread running through its long history, stimulating different and sometimes unexpected interpretations, such as that of the Hellenistic Academy, to which we must now turn.

37

2

PLATONISM AND SCEPTICISM? THE ACADEMY IN THE HELLENISTIC CENTURIES

Platonism and Scepticism?

On 13 June 323 BC, in the middle of a military campaign that was destined to become the stuff of legend, Alexander the Great died. This date is conventionally taken to mark the beginning of a new period in the Greek world: the Hellenistic Age (323 BC–31 BC). Undoubtedly, the lightning-fast conquest of the Greeks' long-standing enemy, the Persian Empire, which extended to the very edges of the known world, radically changed political institutions and life practices in the Greek world: what counted now were no longer individual cities (*poleis*), but kingdoms and monarchies in which the Greeks mingled with other peoples. Along with every-thing else, philosophy was deeply influenced by these transforma-tions and by the need to find answers to new questions: there is some truth to Bevan's rather exaggerated claim that Stoicism was a 'system built on the spur of the moment to come to terms with a disoriented world'.[1] As far as the Platonist tradition is concerned, however, one must wait a few more decades before witnessing any real innovation. While hardly comparable to Alexander's con-quests, this innovation raised a series of truly relevant questions in the history of Platonism, and of philosophy more generally.

Between 268 and 264 BC (the sources do not allow us to be any more precise than this), Crates died and the young members of the Academy elected Socratides, an almost unknown figure, who however turned down the appointment.[2] Arcesilaus of Pitane was appointed scholarch in his place. With him scepticism entered the Academy: throughout the Hellenistic age, the Academy became the sceptical school.

[1] Bevan 1913: 32.
[2] D.L. 4.32; Philod. *Acad. ind.* XVIII 1–7.

38

If we consider the teaching of Arcesilaus' predecessors, and even more the systematic Platonism of the Imperial centuries, we can see how the innovation introduced was a significant one indeed. This explains the surprise, or even doubts and hesitation, shown by many scholars, as well as the tendency to regard the Hellenistic Academy as a sort of interval that has little or nothing do to with Plato's philosophy and the tradition stemming from his thought. Sure, as already noted, there was no dogmatic orthodoxy in the Early Academy, and Arcesilaus himself stressed the link with his predecessors (whose pupil he was, after all).[3] However, with hindsight it is difficult to deny that Arcesilaus marked an important turning point. Ever since antiquity heated debates have raged, which range from the accusation that Arcesilaus used Plato's name without sharing his ideas to the far more serious charge of betrayal and defection. In a world already far removed from the Hellenistic one, Proclus was to speak of the sceptical stage as the dark centuries of Platonism, lending support through his authority to the notion of an incompatibility between Plato (and Platonism) and the Sceptical Academy.[4] This interpretation became the dominant one over the centuries. The experience of Greek scepticism was often reappraised (recall David Hume, or the rediscovery of Cicero in the Renaissance), yet only rarely was any serious thought given to the link with Plato.

Might this not be too rash a conclusion? As we shall see, from Arcesilaus to Philo, numerous testimonies inform us of these thinkers' desire to lay claim to the Platonic heritage. Besides, it was in this period that the first efforts were made to organise and publish the corpus of the dialogues.[5]

These data too must be considered in order to provide a correct assessment of Academic scepticism.[6]

---

[3] On Arcesilaus, Polemon, Crates, and Crantor, see D.L. 4.22 (informing us, among other things, that according to Arcesilaus his predecessors 'were gods of some sort, or remnants of the golden race') and 29; Philod. *Acad. ind.* XV 3–27 with the commentary in Long 1986: 437–44 and Tarrant 2020.

[4] Procl. *Theol. Plat.* 1.1; on these polemics, see Bonazzi 2003a: 56–95.

[5] See Carlini 1972: 29–30, whose arguments are taken up by Lucarini 2010–11. Many pseudo-Platonic dialogues would also appear to date from this period: see Görler 1994: 841–5.

[6] Among the most complete overall studies, one might mention: Long 1974: 88–106; Ioppolo 1986; Long and Sedley 1987; Görler 1994: 719–980; Lévy 1997:181–215; Chiesara 2003: 36–101. What are still missing, instead, are commented editions of the testimonies and fragments pertaining to the main Academics: in general, one may refer

The Academy in the Hellenistic Age

'Carneades! Who was he?' said Don Abbondio to himself, seated in his large chair, with a book open before him. 'Carneades! this name I have either heard or read of; he must have been a man of study, a scholar of antiquity; but who the devil *was* he?' (Alessandro Manzoni, *The Betrothed*, Ch. 8)

Every idea of Carneades triumphed. (Numen. fr. 27.44)

Don Abbondio's question is revealing in terms of the limited reception of the philosophers of the Hellenistic Academy outside specialist circles. It marks a clear contrast to their own age, when the popularity of their polemics made them leading figures on the intellectual scene of the Athenian schools, as even one of their harshest detractors, Numenius, was forced to acknowledge. Carneades himself was one of the most celebrated philosophers of the ancient world, and it was precisely in the Hellenistic Age that the Academy attained the height of its prominence. Before moving on to discussing their philosophical views, it is worth providing a short description of the most notable figures.[7]

As already mentioned, the first noteworthy thinker was Arcesilaus of Pitane, who remained in charge of the school for over twenty years, from 268–264 to 241/240 BC. Born in Pitane, in the region of Aeolis, in the early third century BC, he first studied mathematics and attended lectures in the Peripatos together with Theophrastus, before joining Polemon, Crantor, and Crates' Academy at a time in which particular attention was being devoted to moral issues. In contrast to these philosophers, Arcesilaus engaged in a polemic with the Stoic school, which was then gaining increasing prominence. His polemic with Zeno with regard to the possibility of acquiring knowledge and the motivations for human action marked one of the most brilliant stages in the history of ancient philosophy, and was destined to challenge the wits of the principal philosophers for centuries to come.

The Stoics did not remain inactive, but used these attacks to refine their doctrines, and countered Arcesilaus' criticism point by point. A particularly important role was played in this debate

---

to the collections in Mette 1984 and 1986–7; as for Arcesilaus, see also Vezzoli 2016; as for Philo, see also Brittain 2001.

[7] For the chronological reconstructions, see the succinct overview in Dorandi 1999.

by the school's third diadochus, Chrysippus of Soli, whose contribution to the systematisation of the Stoic doctrines was such as to give rise to the saying 'Without Chrysippus there would have been no Stoa'. Nor 'there would be me, if there were no Chrysippus', Carneades was to reply.[8] Carneades of Cyrene is the second leading philosopher of the Hellenistic Academy. Through his close engagement with Stoic doctrines, he displayed a subtle philosophical intelligence, enabling the Academy to acquire a central position with respect to the other Athenian schools. Born around 214/213 BC and appointed diadochus around 170 BC, Carneades is also famous for the embassy to Rome he led in 155 BC together with two other philosophers, the Stoic Diogenes of Babylon and the Peripatetic Critolaus of Phaselis: on this occasion he delivered two lectures, praising justice on the first day and criticising it on the second, before a rapt audience of young men. Cato himself made sure to have the philosopher immediately expelled.[9] Carneades stepped down from his position as scholarch in 137/136 BC because of health problems and died in 129 BC.

Under Carneades the Academy reached its apex, establishing itself as the most authoritative school both within and beyond Athens. It is said that Carneades' main opponent, the Stoic Antipater of Tarsus, was incapable of facing him directly and only composed polemical books, thereby earning the nickname of *kalamoboas*, 'screeching quill'.[10] Following Carneades' death, his authority increased to such an extent that the Academics started focusing on the interpretation of his ideas even more than on those of Socrates and Plato – a truly unprecedented development.[11] Indeed, the subtleness of Carneades' arguments made his position an elusive one: Clitomachus, who was born in Carthage

---

[8] D.L. 4.62.
[9] On this embassy, see Appendix 1, Platonists and Politics, p. 173.
[10] Plut. *De garr.* 514Cc–d.
[11] See, among others, Brochard 20024: 186 and Long – Sedley 1987, vol. I: 448. Outside Athens, there is evidence of schools connected to Carneades' Academy in Larissa, under Callicles' direction (cf. Philod. *Acad. ind.* XXXV 36), and in Alexandria, under the leadership of Zenodorus of Tyre (cf. Philod. *Acad. Ind.* XXXIII 8; XXIII 2). Carneades' success also helps explain why some ancient sources felt justified in presenting Carneades' Academy as the 'New Academy', relegating Arcesilaus' Academy to a phase of transition.

in 187/186 BC and served as scholar from 127/126 BC down to his death in 110/109 BC, wrote 400 books on Carneades, only to admit that he was not sure he had grasped the ultimate meaning of his teaching. Carneades' pupils essentially developed two main interpretations of it: the first is the one endorsed by the aforementioned Clitomachus, who championed a systematic and radical adoption of scepticism; over the course of time, a more moderate interpretation also emerged that is nonetheless quite interesting (also with respect to the thorny problem of the relationship with Plato, to which we shall return at the end of the present chapter). Initially developed by Metrodorus of Stratonicea, this interpretative approach became the official one when it was embraced by Philo of Larissa, the last diodochus of the Academy (110/109– 84/83 BC).

Those figures we have here mentioned are the most prominent, yet the sources inform us about many other Academics too. We also know of contrasts, discussions, or even schisms.[12] Ancient classifications, which speak of three Academies (Plato's Old Academy, Arcesilaus' Middle Academy, and Carneades' New Academy), or even five (adding Philo and Antiochus),[13] reveal that contemporaries were already aware of these internal tensions, which further confirm the highly dynamic quality of this institution throughout the Hellenistic period. The same liveliness also marked cultural and political life in Athens at large: mention has already been made of the embassy of 155 BC, when Carneades scored a great success for Athens by persuading the Roman Senate to abolish a fine of 150 talents for the sacking of the city of Oropus. Probably also for this reason, in addition to his intellectual merits, Carneades was awarded an honorary statue in the agora (its base is still visible today).[14] However, the relationship between the school and the city was not always a happy one: in 306 BC, Athens even passed a law – proposed by Sophocles of

---

[12] The most striking case is the break between Philo and Antiochus in the 90s. However, it is interesting to note that even in earlier years, before becoming scholarch, Clitomachus too had quit the Academy for some time in order to teach in the Palladium between 140/139 and 129/128 BC.

[13] Cf. SE *P* 1.220; Eus. *PE* 14.4.16; D.L. 1.19; Clem. Alex. *Strom.* 1.14.63–64.

[14] On this statue, see Zanker 1996: 181–2.

Sounion – forbidding the teaching of philosophy.[15] The new law, however, was abolished the following year: the importance of philosophical schools, not least in economic terms, could no longer be ignored. Later, in 124/123 BC the three schools (the Academic, the Epicurean, and the Stoic) received official acknowledgement as educational centres.

For any reader who might be interested, the sequence of the Academy's *diadochoi* in the Hellenistic Age runs as follows: Arcesilaus of Cyrene (268/264–241/240 BC); Lacides of Cyrene (241/240–226/225); Telecles and Evander of Phocaea and Egesinus of Pergamon (226/225–167/166 BC); Carneades of Cyrene (167/166–137/136 BC); Carneades the son of Polemarchus (137/136–131/130 BC); Crates of Tarsus (131/130–127/126 BC); Clitomachus of Carthage (127/126–110/109 BC); and Philo of Larissa (110/109–84/83 BC). Regrettably, the scarcity of testimonies prevent us from knowing exactly the theses and views endorsed by these authors: the two most authoritative thinkers, Arcesilaus and Carneades, did not write anything, while the other philosophers' works are all lost. Fortunately, however, there are plenty of authoritative testimonies, starting from those by Cicero and Sextus Empiricus. The former, a staunch champion of Academic theses, sought to defend them and to present them to a Roman public that was potentially hostile to the sceptics' subtleties;[16] the latter, an unwavering opponent, sought to show why the Academic theses could not be regarded as being genuinely sceptical.[17] In both cases, the outcome was a detailed and exhaustive analysis which still allows us to reconstruct many of the theses of Arcesilaus, Carneades, and Philo in a reliable way. No less important, as far as biographical information is concerned, are Diogenes Laertius' *Lives of Eminent Philosophers* (which in Book 4 informs us about Arcesilaus, Lacydes, Carneades, and Clitomachus) and the so-called *Index Academicorum* by the Epicurean Philodemus of Gadara (which is part of a more extensive work on Hellenistic schools and constitutes a crucial tool to reconstruct the history

[15] See Haake 2008.
[16] An important work on Cicero's academic philosophy is Lévy 1992; see also Appendix 1, Two Political Platonists: Marcus Tullius Cicero and Flavius Claudius Julianus, pp. 178.
[17] On Sextus and the Academy, see Spinelli 2000 and Ioppolo 2009.

of the Hellenistic Academy).[18] Other authors still, while polemical (Numenius) or at any rate not always reliable (Plutarch, Augustine), help further clarify the problems under investigation.

Discourses on Method

As just noted, Arcesilaus and Carneades did not produce any written works. Likely, this was a conscious choice meant to establish a connection with Socrates' teaching, at a time in which other philosophers too – Stoics and Cynics – were seeking to lay claim to his legacy. Further evidence of Socrates' importance is to be found in the interest shown in dialectic and in the two scholarchs' efforts to define their argumentative strategies.[19] This was indeed a crucial issue for philosophers who did not promote any doctrines of their own, but felt that their main task was to put other people's theses to the test: this had been the case with Socrates, and it was also the case with Arcesilaus and Carneades.

A shared starting point, however, did not translate into shared methods. Particularly significant, in this respect, is the case of Arcesilaus, who presented his method as a resurgence of the famous method of Socratic refutation.[20] While laying claim to a connection with Socrates, Arcesilaus was also keen to distance himself from Socrates' well-known profession of ignorance, noting that the very claim to know that one does not know risked slipping into a form of dogmatism which would hamper true research.[21] Arcesilaus' effort to distance himself from Socrates, which presented the latter's position in far too schematic terms,[22] is the first example of the perceived need for greater rigour – and greater formalism – that was destined to shape Hellenistic debates.

A second example is arguably to be found in the development of the discussion *in utramque partem*. Socrates would simply ask an interlocutor to present his own view on a subject in order to

---

[18] See Long 1986 (on Diogenes on Arcesilaus) and Hatzimichali 2020 (on Philodemus).
[19] See now Castagnoli 2019.
[20] Cic. *De fin.* 2.1–2.
[21] Cic. *Ac.* 1.45.
[22] Burnyeat 1997: 290–300.

then show that this view was incompatible with other opinions of his. By contrast, Arcesilaus would invite his interlocutor to present his thesis in order to then counter this with the opposite thesis; he would then allow the interlocutor to defend the same thesis again, only in order to refute it a second time.[23] Finally, an even more sophisticated argumentative style was adopted by Carneades, who would personally expound arguments in support of and against a given thesis (the most famous example of this being the two speeches on justice he delivered in Rome). Socrates would expose his interlocutor's state of confusion but, in principle, could not rule out that one of the theses this person endorsed was correct. With Arcesilaus and Carneades, instead, the interlocutor was inevitably forced to suspend all judgement. The only point that remains to be clarified is whether this also applied to the two Academics themselves or not (an issue we shall return to later on). No doubt, debating with one's colleagues required the adoption of more rigorous techniques than those Socrates had used to show his fellow citizens what contradictions their beliefs entailed.

The Debate on Knowledge

As has just been noted, the revival of the Socratic approach, where what mattered was the investigation of other people's theses, without any preconceived claims to knowledge, made it necessary to identify who could be regarded as a worthy object of engagement, that is, who apparently had persuasive solutions to offer. Finding interlocutors of this sort was not a problem in the world of Hellenistic schools: already Epicurus and his pupils had claimed to have a solution to the problem of knowledge, and the Stoics were equally confident of their own views. It was therefore by engaging with the doctrines of these schools, especially the Stoic one, that the Academics developed their research.

According to the Stoics, knowledge is formed from sensations, yet not just any sensations: in their view, certain sensations differ from others insofar as they are capable of faithfully representing

[23] Cic. *Ac.* 1.46; D.L. 4.28.

the perceived object – and that alone.[24] These were known as cataleptic impressions (φαντασίαι καταληπτικαί).[25] Cognition is assent to impressions of this sort.[26] The sum of such acts of cognition was believed to constitute the basis of knowledge:[27] in a striking metaphor, Zeno compared a cataleptic impression to an open hand, assent (συγκατάθεσις) to a hand with folded fingers, actual cognition (κατάληψις) to a clenched fist, and knowledge (ἐπιστήμη) to two hands, one folded over the other.[28]

This short presentation is enough to show the importance of the notion of cataleptic impressions, the ultimate foundation of all Stoic epistemology. It is hardly surprising, therefore, that precisely defining this kind of impression was a crucial task for the philosophers of the Stoa. An impression can be termed 'cataleptic' if: 1) it derives from an existing object, 2) it reproduces this object in an exact way, and 3) it is such that it cannot derive from a non-existent object.[29] In other words, in order to be cataleptic, an impression must meet two essential prerequisites: it must stem from a truly existing object, and it must reproduce this object in an exact, clear, and accurate way. However, while these two requirements could be met by the first clauses of the Stoic definition, it is the third requirement that reveals the underlying meaning of the cataleptic impression, namely the reality of the object and conformity to it: only real objects, as truly existent objects, possess the kind of clarity and accuracy that is capable of producing a true representation. Impressions are 'cataleptic' when they are capable, on the one hand, of 'grasping' their object and, on the other, of seizing the subject by dragging him towards assent.[30] In Stoic epistemology, what truly matters is being able to identify a class of sensations capable of truly representing the perceived object, as though they were truthful messengers.

---

[24] For a succinct yet exhaustive overview of Stoic epistemology, see M. Frede 1999a.
[25] Cf. e.g. D.L. 7.50, SE *M* 7.247–52.
[26] D.L. 7.397 and 151.
[27] Cic. *Ac.* 2.145; Stob. *Anth.* 2.73.16.
[28] Cic. *Ac.* 2.145.
[29] See D.L. VIII 50; SE *M* 7.248; Cic. *Ac.* 2.77.
[30] Cic. *Ac.* 1.41; SE *M* 7.257. The same etymology may also be found in the modern terms 'comprehension' and 'perception', which indeed derive from Cicero's translation (*comprehensio* < *prehendere* and *perceptio* < *capere*) of the Stoic terms cognate with *katalepton* and *katalepsis*.

The key point of the Stoic theory thus lies in the possibility of identifying cataleptic impressions: this is the *condicio sine qua non* for the attainment of knowledge. And this is precisely the main target of the Academics' criticism:[31] impressions are not such as to rule out the existence of false sensations which correspond to true ones and are identical to them from a qualitative perspective.[32] To prove this assumption, the Academics resorted to different arguments that could be divided into two basic groups: on the one hand, we have the example of identical twins, or of coins from the same coinage, that is, different objects that produce the same sensation; on the other hand, we have the case of hallucinations and illusions, that is, impressions that stem from what is non-existent, and yet are capable of inducing assent just as compellingly as cataleptic impressions. The key point in the Academics criticism, then, is not an attempt to dispute the existence of true impressions, but rather the possibility of distinguishing between true sensations (cataleptic impressions) and untrue sensations (non-cataleptic impressions). To draw upon a metaphor used before, out of many messages we are incapable of making out the reliable ones.[33]

This discussion may schematically be presented as follows:[34]

1) some sensations are true, others are false;
2) false sensations cannot be known;
3) every true sensation is such as to admit of a corresponding sensation that is false yet qualitatively identical to it;
4) but if two sensations do not differ from a qualitative standpoint, it is inconceivable that one sensation can be known, but not the other;
5) therefore, nothing can be known.

---

[31] However, they were not the only target, as the notion of comprehension (*katalepsis*) was no less problematic: insofar as assent precedes comprehension, there is the risk of assenting to what is not yet known, and hence of assenting to what is false (Cic. *Ac.* 1.45). Arcesilaus noted a further ambiguity in the Stoic notion of comprehension which, despite always being the same, sometimes appeared to coincide with knowledge, and at other times with opinion, depending on whether the person assenting was a wise man or an ordinary man (SE *M* 7.150–3). Sextus also informs us of a further criticism: assent is given to judgements, not impressions, which in themselves do not convey anything at all with respect to the object perceived (SE *M* 7.154–5).
[32] Cic. *Ac.* 2.78.
[33] SE *M* 7.163.
[34] Cic. *Ac.* 2.40–2; 77.

The outcome is *akatalepsia*, the refutation of the Stoic claim that something cataleptic exists: if it is impossible to identify cataleptic impressions, then it is also impossible to attain knowledge, given that this stems from assent to a cataleptic impression. In other words, what is being disputed is not the existence of impressions accurately corresponding to their objects, but rather the possibility of knowing such impressions with absolute certainty.[35]

On the other hand, the Stoics had also claimed that one of the defining traits of the wise man is that he only gives assent to cataleptic impressions, for otherwise he would slip into opinion, or *doxa*:[36]

6) if the wise man were to assent to an untrue sensation, he would slip into opinion;
7) but the wise man never slips into opinion;
8) therefore, the wise man will never give his assent to anything, but will suspend assent (*epoche*).

Epoche, the suspension of judgement, is the second key term in Academic vocabulary. It derives from the impossibility of circumscribing true sensations and from the need to avoid error: it is the outcome to which Stoics are necessarily bound, if they wish to remain coherent with their starting assumptions. This is the conclusion envisaged by Arcesilaus, who leaves at least one way out for the Stoic, by inviting him to become a sceptic, that is, to suspend judgement and to continue his research (*skepsis* in Greek). As we shall see, Carneades further radicalised this conflict by stating that it is impossible not to have any opinions.[37]

Undoubtedly, the Academic arguments offer some interesting insights and display considerable subtlety. At first sight, their focus

---

[35] Here the Academics exploited a suggestion implicitly made by Epicurean epistemology: Epicurus had argued that, if a single sensation were to prove false, even just once, we ought to never trust any sensation whatsoever (Cic. *Ac.* 2.79).

[36] Cic. *Ac.* 2.66–8. As far as the Stoic theory is concerned, see e.g. *SVF* 3.548: 'according to the Stoics, the wise man never falls into a false supposition, and does not assent to what is ungraspable (*akatalepton*); therefore, he has no opinions and there is nothing he ignores. For ignorance amounts to an unstable and weak assent; but the wise man is not weak in his judgement: indeed, he is certain and confident, which is why he does not content himself with opinion'.

[37] Cic. *Ac.* 2.67; cf. 59 and 78.

on particular, pathological cases might seem forced. Actually, though, the points the Academics make are not wholly unjustified, and the underlying problem they address is clear. In the confrontation between the Academy and the Stoa, the dispute ultimately revolves around the ordinary realism of sense-perception, which is typical of a philosophy such as the Stoic one, which never abandoned the ordinary mode of thinking, in contrast to the Platonic Academy, according to which in evaluating knowledge we should never overestimate the spontaneous faith we have in our sensations.[38] What may seem like abnormal impressions or pathological states actually reveals a recurrent feature of our way of engaging with the world, namely the impossibility of distinguishing impressions from the objects that produce them. In contrast to light, which reveals both itself and the objects on which it shines, we have no way of comparing an impression with external reality,[39] which is why the only consistent option we are left with is the sceptic's suspension of judgement.

The problem which remains to be clarified, then, is whether Arcesilaus' and Carneades' arguments are to be understood in merely dialectical terms or whether they can be regarded as personal stances. This issue has engendered a heated discussion among scholars and no consensus has yet been reached.[40] No doubt, the dialectical aspect is predominant, insofar as the Academics developed their theses about *akatalepsia* and *epoche* precisely by exploiting the theses of their Stoic opponents. However, based on what has just been noted with regard to the overall evaluation of sense-perception and its limits, it cannot be ruled out that both Arcesilaus and Carneades eventually adopted the sceptical conclusion as their own personal stance: the only stance befitting the desire for knowledge typical of the true wise man. The Academic wise man is someone who, without taking any easy but misleading

---

[38] See Lévy 1997: 189.

[39] SE *M* 7.163.

[40] This is particularly the case with Arcesilaus: while the supporters of the dialectical hypothesis (who are especially numerous in the English-speaking world) can draw on Couissin 1929a and 1929b, in recent years the alternative suggestion formulated by Ioppolo 1986 has gained considerable traction: see Castagnoli 2019: 212–17 and Lévy 1992: 45–6 on Carneades.

shortcuts, untiringly continues his research. For, as von Arnim rightly noted, 'the essential mark of wisdom is not possession of knowledge but freedom from error'.[41]

Knowledge, Opinion, and Action

Having resolved the problem of knowledge in negative terms (insofar as it is impossible to identify true sensations, it is equally impossible to attain knowledge), what remains to be clarified is the issue of opinion: as we have just seen, suspension of assent (*epoche*) was used precisely in order to avoid slipping into opinion. However, Carneades had also argued that it is impossible not to have any opinions. What are we to make of this claim?

Carneades' position becomes clear if it is viewed as a response to the accusation of *apraxia*, that is, of making life impossible, which the Stoics and other opponents had levelled against the Academics.[42] The sceptics claim that nothing is knowable: so how are human beings supposed to live? If nothing can be known, we will have no criteria by which to relate to the reality around us and to decide what to do. The suspension of assent rules out any kind of decision-making, and condemns the sceptic to a sort of intellectual and practical paralysis: the theses of *akatalepsia* and *epoche* make life impossible, petrifying human beings like the Gorgon.[43] Besides, why does the sceptic pass through doors instead of running into walls?[44] Why does he not fall into wells and down cliffs? The sceptics refute themselves, insofar as their own theses do not prevent them from acting in a practical fashion in everyday life. If *akatalepsia* and *epoche* do not lead to inaction, this means they are being put aside.

---

[41] Arnim 1895, col. 1166.
[42] Plut. *Adv. Col.* 1108d and 1109c–d; D.L. 9.104; Cic. *Ac.* 2.31 and 99.
[43] Plut. *Adv. Col.* 1122a. Given that this criticism is not meant to show that scepticism is self-contradictory, but only that it entails paradoxical consequences in terms of individuals' life conduct, the sceptics could even have responded by accepting their opponents' conclusions: it is hardly the sceptics' fault if everything is as uncertain as whether the number of stars in the sky is odd or even. While legitimate, this line of defence received little interest, and was rejected as a position only fit for desperate people (Cic. *Ac.* 2.32; the identification of these thinkers is still an object of lively debate among modern scholars).
[44] Plut. *Adv. Col.* 1122e.

Continuing along a trajectory originally traced by Arcesilaus, who had envisaged the possibility of following what is reasonable (*eulogon*),[45] Carneades vigorously responded to this criticism by introducing new concepts that contributed to further defining the potential of Academic scepticism. Although we can never be sure about the veracity of a sensation (as *akatalepsia* entails), nothing prevents us from following those sensations which are found to be persuasive (*pithana*), which do not contradict one another, and which have been carefully evaluated.[46] The wise man must not give his assent to anything, but rather must follow what is found to be convincing and persuasive (*pithanon*, probable). Carneades' 'probabilism' (a term we should use very cautiously in order to avoid anachronistic interpretations: the Greek term alludes to what seems 'convincing' or 'persuasive')[47] makes it possible to find a criterion even in a context marked by the unknowability of everything. Therefore, it is not an act of assent, but of approval:[48]

In fact as we hold that he who restrains himself from assent about all things nevertheless does move and does act, the view is that there remain presentations of a sort that arouse us to action, and also answers that we can give in the affirmative or the negative reply in reply to questions, merely following a corresponding presentation, provided that we answer without actual assent; but that nevertheless not all presentations of this character were actually approved, but those that nothing hindered.[49]

Suspending judgement on a sensation does not mean adopting an attitude of complete indifference towards it, because there is a kind of reaction to sensations that avoids the two extremes of dogmatic assent and complete indifference: it means following

---

[45] Cf. SE *M* 7.158 and Plut. *Adv. Col.* 1121b–1122d.

[46] SE *M* 7.166–89. Like many other terms, the concept of 'probable impression' is part of the Stoic philosophical lexicon, where it is used to describe the kind of impressions which produce a quiet movement in the soul and which can be either true or false: cf. ibid. 7.242 (= *SVF* 2.65).

[47] See for instance Long and Sedley 1987: 459. 'Probable' is how Cicero chose to translate the Greek *pithanon* (not without doubts and second thoughts; see Glucker 1995): from this perspective, 'probabilism' describes what persuades (*peithein* in Greek) and convinces. Therefore, the differences compared to contemporary language are evident, insofar as in today's parlance the probable stands in contrast to what is certain and necessary or, more precisely, is defined as the relative frequency of the occurrence of an event with respect to a given class of alternatives.

[48] On this distinction more generally, and on its applicability, see Bett 1990.

[49] Cic. *Ac.* 2.104.

(*sequi, adprobari*) what is convincing or persuasive (*pithanon, probabile*), by evaluating sensations based on their degree of persuasiveness (*pithanothes, probabilitas*), yet without compromising one's stance with dogmatic assertions about their veracity. Besides, already the Stoics had noted[50] that we can receive impressions without holding them to be true, acknowledging that it is possible to distinguish between the acceptance of a sensation as true and the mere fact of having a sensation, caused by external factors beyond our control.[51] By applying this distinction, Carneades could thus defend the thesis that it is possible to perform an action without regarding the sensation causing it as true, while also showing that this is a voluntary action: a man fleeing a presumed ambush does not need to believe that it is necessarily an ambush, or that it is right for him to flee – his action is caused by the suspicion that there might be an ambush, and he acts without taking account of his doubts as to whether he should flee or not.[52] As regards the charge of *apraxia*, the sceptic will not make life impossible, but will rather act like everyone else, without compromising his stance with dogmatic claims about things that are obscure. And given that according to the Stoics opining simply means accepting judgements whose veracity has not been confirmed, Carneades is not only able to describe the way in which men behave, but also forces the Stoics to admit that the wise man too must opine if he wishes to live.[53] Indeed, as already noted by

---

[50] Cic. *Ac.* 1.40–41.

[51] Cic. *Ac.* 2.145; SE *M* 8.397.

[52] SE *M* 7.186. From a historical standpoint, these arguments of Carneades' also have the merit of improving upon Arcesilaus' position, which had been criticised by Chrysippus precisely in that he did away with assent (since all that is needed for action is the impulse deriving from a sensation: cf. Plut. *Adv. Col.* 1122a–f): for the Stoics, Arcesilaus' position was incapable of accounting for the difference between voluntary and rational human actions and instinctual animal actions (whereas the criterion of the *eulogon* – i.e. that which can be reasonably justified, cf. SE *M* 7.158 – ought to be based on some kind of theory of knowledge, which Arcesilaus was incapable of providing): in addition to Striker 1980, see Bett 1989. A different reconstruction of this aspect of Arcesilaus' thought is provided by Ioppolo 1986: 167–76 and Trabattoni 2005, with some interesting remarks on the relation to Plato.

[53] Simply put: if knowledge is impossible and action requires assent, in order not to remain inactive, the Stoic wise man must give assent to impressions even when he is not sure that they are true – in other words, the wise man must opine.

Arcesilaus, it is precisely by abandoning any claim to knowledge that it is possible to live in such a way as to achieve success and happiness.[54]

Other Polemics against the Stoics: Freedom, Fate, the Gods, and Ethics

The debate about knowledge, its conditions of possibility, and its limits constitutes one of the most interesting aspects of Hellenistic philosophy. However, it was not the only widely debated topic: there was hardly any question or doctrine on which Academics and Stoics did not lock horns, often displaying considerable acumen and originality. Without claiming to cover all these topics, in what follows I will outline the most interesting issues.

As one would expect, from Arcesilaus onwards a favourite target for Academic attacks was one of the most famous and controversial Stoic doctrines, namely the thesis that everything is determined by fate.[55] The problem, for Zeno, was to reconcile this determinism with human responsibility (if everything is predetermined, meaning that it stems from a preordained chain of causes, it makes little sense to speak of freedom, or indeed of responsibility). His solution was easily criticised by Academics: to argue, as Zeno had done, that at least assent depends on us is inconsistent, because 'if all things take place by fate, all things take place with an antecedent cause; and if impulse is caused, those things which follow impulse are also caused; therefore assent is also caused'; therefore, not even assent is within our power and it makes no sense to speak of praise or blame. But a conclusion of this sort seems very difficult to support indeed, so it is more reasonable to assume that 'not everything that takes place takes place by fate'.[56] The debate was then carried further by Chrysippus and Carneades, attaining very subtle heights, distinguishing between logical and causal necessity. With regard to the problem of determinism too, then, we find an underlying divergence between Stoics and Academics,

---

[54] SE *M* 7.158.
[55] The reference study is now Bobzien 1998; see also Hankinson 1999. The ancient source of reference is Cicero's treatise *On Fate*: see the recent commentary in Maso 2014.
[56] Cic. *De fato* 40.

which points to two different ways of conceiving man and reality. Through the charge of *apraxia*, the Stoics intimated that the Academics made responsible action impossible. By introducing the notions of *eulogon* and *pithanon*, the Academics explained that it is possible to act consciously even in the absence of certain knowledge; and by developing the notion of fate, they further showed that, if anything, it was the Stoic theory of fate which presented human action as something automatic and irrational.

Carneades' dialectical skill and ability to disprove other people's claims did not spare theological conceptions.[57] The Stoics had sought to demonstrate the existence of God through a teleological argument, based on the acknowledgement of an underlying order and finality in the universe, and through a proof 'by degrees' by arguing that insofar as some beings are better than others, there must necessarily be some beings who are the best of all, namely gods. Against the first argument, Carneades drew upon the theories of the Peripatetic Strato of Lampsacus, according to whom the world 'may have come into being by itself, through a natural process, without any divine intervention, and without [serving] any natural end'.[58] Against the proof 'by degrees', Carneades instead noted that it is impossible to establish what is better and what is worse, and, most importantly, that to suppose that there exist some beings who are the best of all is not to prove their existence.

No less revealing of the Stoic efforts to provide a rational foundation for traditional beliefs about the gods is their defence of the providential character of god and their attempt to reconcile the belief in the existence of a single god with popular polytheism, based on the assumption that the traditional gods are but attributes of the one god. Like Epicurus, Carneades argued against providentialism by remarking that it is incompatible with the existence of evil and injustice (unless we are willing to admit that God does not concern Himself with human affairs or is too weak to oppose evil). As far as the second point is concerned, Carneades instead

---

[57] See Long 1990, Mansfeld 1999 and Sedley 2020. The most important ancient source is Cicero's treatise *On the Nature of the Gods*: see Pease 1955–8.

[58] Chiesara 2003: 82; it is noteworthy that a similar thesis is upheld by atheists in Book 10 of Plato's *Laws*.

resorted to the so-called 'sorites' argument,[59] to show that if we accept traditional mythology, we risk 'endlessly watering down the notion of God',[60] usually reaching a paradoxical outcome: 'if gods exist, are the nymphs also goddesses? If the nymphs are, the Pans and the Satyrs also are gods; but they are not gods; therefore the nymphs also are not. Yet they possess temples vowed and dedicated to them by the nation; are the other gods also therefore who have had temples dedicated to them not gods either?'[61] It is always dangerous to criticise traditional beliefs, as Socrates' case shows; yet it seems as though Carneades never incurred similar risks, for it was clear that he did not intend to deny the existence of the gods, but only to show that the Stoics were incapable of adequately justifying their theses.[62]

Finally, something remains to be said about ethics, and more specifically the famous 'Carneadean division' by which the Academic philosopher had sought to classify the theses upheld by the various schools with regard to the highest good (i.e. the good we must attain in order to lead a happy life).[63] In this case too, the polemical target was Stoicism, with its distinction between intention and actual realisation. To explain this difference, Antipater, a pupil of Chrysippus', distinguished between 'end' (*telos*) and 'purpose' (*skopos*): just as an archer must do everything he can to hit his target, even though the fact of hitting it does not ultimately depend on him, so the wise man must do his best to attain natural goods, without worrying about their actual attainment (for what matters is to conform oneself to God's will, and everything that occurs is the will of God). To this thesis Carneades objected that an archer will do everything he can not merely to aim at the target, but to actually hit it: for doing one's best to attain a given good without worrying about its actual attainment would mean locating one's happiness in an indifferent object.

---

[59] Couissin 1941. *Sorites* means 'heap' in Greek: the argument known by this name was used to illustrate the difficulty in exactly determining distinguishing features. So, to keep to the example of a heap, having established that a given heap comprises thirty elements, we might ask ourselves whether, once we remove one element, we are still dealing with a heap or not, and so on, until the heap ceases to be a heap.

[60] Lévy 1997: 205.

[61] Cic. *De nat. deor.* 3.43.

[62] Cic. *De nat. deor.* 3.44.

[63] See Algra 1997; Annas 2007; Bénatouïl 2007.

Philo of Larissa and the Moderate Turn

To witness a significant turn away from the rigorous scepticism of Arcesilaus and Carneades, we must wait until the last scholarch of the Academy, Philo of Larissa. But even in his case, we cannot grasp the significance of the innovations he introduced without taking Carneades' arguments into account. As already noted, the subtlety and acumen of these arguments was such that it is difficult to discern what views he personally endorsed, independently of his anti-Stoic polemics. In particular, one problem was whether it was legitimate, and in some cases necessary, to hold opinions – that is, whether the (sceptical or dogmatic) wise man could follow opinions. As already noted, the legitimacy of opinions was based on the existence of persuasive impressions (*pithanai phantasiai*), which Carneades had introduced in order to respond to the accusation of making living impossible. There was nothing to prevent the sceptic from following those sensations that, once vetted, proved to be convincing, without thereby having to subscribe to any dogmatic position. But what was the philosophical value of these probable or convincing sensations? How was the *pithanon* to be understood?[64]

At least two paths remain open to clarify the exact significance of Carneades' position. Both of these paths were actually followed by Academic philosophers. According to Clitomachus, who here agrees with most modern scholars, Carneades' arguments must be understood in an exclusively dialectical sense: nothing that Carneades states in an argument should be deemed to reflect his own philosophical beliefs. The true sceptic follows convincing sensations without assenting to anything: he only acts in accordance with them, without thereby considering them to be true. Without having found the truth (for the principle of *akatalepsia* holds), he continues to suspend assent (*epoche*), as accepting a proposition might divert him from his research. In ordinary life he instead merely follows what is found to be convincing: the *pithanon* thus

---

[64] Cic. *Ac.* 2.78, 148.

emerges as a form of passive acceptance limited to direct sensations useful in practical, everyday life (and not in the ethical realm).[65] Alternatively, another interpretation is possible, which was first put forward by Metrodorus and was then further developed by Philo of Larissa (who in the initial stages of his scholarchate had instead adopted Clitomachus' interpretation): while primarily designed to refute the dogmatists' doctrines, these distinctions also reflect Carneades' ideas to some extent. By following what seems convincing (the *pithanon*), the wise man can hold opinions, as long as it is clear that these are provisional and are advanced with the awareness that they might even be false. In other words, the principle of *akatalepsia* holds (i.e. the impossibility of identifying absolutely true sensations on which to establish certain knowledge), but *epoche* is no longer necessary, since there is nothing to prevent the sceptic from giving his assent to non-cataleptic impressions, insofar as he is aware that he is endorsing opinions and not truths:

Nothing can be perceived, but the wise man will assent to something not perceived, that is, will hold an opinion, but with the qualification that he will understand that it is an opinion and will know that there is nothing that can be comprehended and perceived (*Adsensurum autem non percepto, id est, opinaturum sapientem existimem, sed ita ut intellegat se opinari sciatque nihil esse quod comprehendi et percipi possit*).[66]

It is evident that Metrodorus' and Philo's position introduced a more moderate version of scepticism within the Academy. In their classification, the ancients speak of a Fourth Academy: the sceptic can personally support certain philosophical views, because he remains aware of the fact that he is opining and that nothing can be known with certainty. In granting assent, he is aware that he is assenting to an opinion deriving from an impression whose veracity is not guaranteed, an impression which occurs within a context marked by the unknowability of everything (i.e. the thesis of *akatalepsia*).

---

[65] Cf. Cic. *Ac*. 104–5: passively following what is probable does not require assent even when it comes to yes or no answers, since such answers correspond to 'it is probable that things are in this way rather than in any other way', and in turn this statement corresponds to 'things seem to me like this'; on Clitomachus, see now Ioppolo 2007.

[66] Cic. *Ac*. 2.148; cf. ibid. 78: 'the wise man might perceive nothing and yet form an opinion (*licebat enim nihil percipere et tamen opinari*)'.

In other words, what we have is a provisional assent, which is given because certain sensations are regarded as being provisionally reliable, yet always open to revision. Compared to Clitomachus' radical interpretation, we thus witness a broadening of the field of application of the *pithanon*, which is no longer used merely to determine the plausibility of sensations in ordinary life, but also serves to verify the reliability of philosophical theses.

Philo's interpretation ultimately prevailed and established itself as the official doctrine of the Academy not only in antiquity but even in modern times, through the influence of his pupil Cicero.[67] Without wishing to downplay Clitomachus' version, Philo's main merit lies in the fact that he envisaged scepticism as the outcome of a rational and conscious activity, rather than as the passive acceptance of mere appearances.[68] And given that awareness of the provisional nature of every doctrine also applied to the fundamental thesis of *akatalepsia*, the supporters of this moderate version of scepticism could not even be accused of negative dogmatism (i.e. of knowing at least one thing, namely that nothing is knowable).[69]

Was this Philo's ultimate stance? Between 89 and 86 BC, at the time of the Mithridatic Wars, the scholarch went to Rome, where he composed what Cicero calls the *Roman Books*, in response to Antiochus of Ascalon's criticism. I shall be referring to the historiographical thesis of the unity of the Academy later on; as regards Philo's epistemological theses, whether they presented any substantial innovations remains a matter of heated scholarly debate, particularly following the publication of Charles Brittain's influential monograph, which has defended the thesis of a third phase in Philo's philosophical reflection.[70] According to this interpretation, Philo continued to maintain the anti-Stoic stance by arguing

---

[67] Crucial observations, in this regard, are provided by the closing pages of M. Frede 1984: 273–8.

[68] See Cic. *Ac.* 2.7. For a general assessment of Philo's modernity, see the observations in Brochard 2002: 433.

[69] This is also a measure of these philosophers' distance from Stoicism, insofar as opinion is no longer regarded as a weak and obscure form of assent (cf. e.g. SE *M* 7.151 = *SVF* 2.90), but redefined as a sort of assent which is conscious of its limits. In general, see Burnyeat 1997: 305–8.

[70] Brittain 2001; a similar stance, however, had already been expressed by Barnes 1989: 68–78; Görler 1994: 920–2; Striker 1997: 263–4.

that it is impossible to know anything if one keeps to the Stoic criterion of truth (cataleptic impressions: with regard to this point, all Academics shared the same critical perspective). At the same time, Philo would also have supported a new way of understanding cognition, no longer bound to the requirement of infallibility: there exist apprehensive impressions (which is to say evident ones) that ensure true yet fallible knowledge (precisely because these impressions are not infallible). In other words, the principle of *akatalepsia* remains true if one accepts the Stoic thesis, whereas without the Stoic bias the possibility of *katalepsis* can be admitted (thereby abandoning both *akatalepsia* and *epoche*). Certainly, in the absence of clear testimonies, these are subtle distinctions; thus it is hardly surprising that other, no less authoritative scholars have rejected this hypothesis, arguing that Philo's Roman discussions only further developed the old Athenian polemics between Philo and Antiochus.[71] In antiquity, the Pyrrhonist Aenesidemus had directly opposed this whole debate, accusing all Academics of having become like Stoics fighting other Stoics – an accusation that was no doubt overblown and motivated by the need to carve out a new theoretical space for resurgent Pyrrhonism.[72]

Scepticism and Platonism

One problem tackled by ancient philosophers and modern scholars alike concerns the overall significance of the experience of the Hellenistic Academy. This experience is not easy to assess: according to a metaphor that is highly revealing of the disorientation produced by the Academic theses, Arcesilaus was like a cuttlefish squirting out black ink to prevent others from grasping his thought. Carneades was no less enigmatic: although he was able to prevail over all his opponents, his pupil Clitomachus – the author

---

[71] See e.g. Glucker 2004 and Lévy 2005.

[72] On Aenesidemus see Bett 2000. From surviving testimonies it is unclear whether, before relaunching a new form of Pyrrhonism (which had little to do with Pyrrho), he had studied in the Academy (see, most recently, Mansfeld 1995) or in Alexandria, in milieus steeped in empirical medical thought (an original take on this can be found in Decleva Caizzi 1992). Be that as it may, given that the rebirth of Pyrrhonism does not directly concern Academic scepticism, I have chosen not to discuss its innovative aspects here.

of 400 books – was forced to admit that he struggled to grasp the meaning of his teaching. As we have seen, the main difficulty was to establish whether these philosophers' statements had only dialectical significance or whether they also expressed their personal beliefs (the most reasonable hypothesis is the one that preserves both options). Another notable reason for this disorientation is these authors' institutional position: after all, the Academy was Plato's school. But what kind of relationship can there be between Plato and scepticism? This is the problem I introduced at the beginning of this chapter and to which we must finally return.

For many, both ancient thinkers and modern scholars, the only possible answer is: none at all. As we shall soon see, the most drastic position in antiquity was that of Antiochus, yet similar beliefs were also expressed by many other, non-Platonic philosophers outside the Academy. Thus the Stoic Aristo of Chios mockingly described Arcesilaus as follows: 'Plato in front, Pyrrho behind, Diodorus in the middle.'[73] Plato was the head, as though Arcesilaus sought to muddy the waters by invoking an impossible loyalty to his school, whereas the real sources of the Academic's teaching were to be sought elsewhere. An opposite, yet ultimately convergent, tradition was to attract Augustine's interest: the legend of an esoteric teaching within the Academy, based on the most rigorous kind of dogmatism, which Arcesilaus allegedly only revealed to his most faithful disciples (but of all the hypotheses suggested, this is the most unlikely).[74] Again, the underlying assumption would appear to be the impossibility of reconciling Platonism and scepticism.

Similar ideas have long influenced the reception of the Hellenistic Academy. The radical rejection of Antiochus was widely shared in the ancient world, and particularly by most later Platonists, who regarded the sceptical Academy as the dark ages in the history of Platonism. The currently most widespread interpretations

---

[73] D.L. 4.33. A similar interpretation was also suggested by Timo of Phlius, a pupil of Pyrrho's, who jokingly associates Arcesilaus with Pyrrho, the Eristic debater Menedemus of Eretria, and the dialectician Diodorus Cronus: see Tim. Phl. frs. 31–32, with the commentary in Long 1978.

[74] This thesis has been upheld by Credaro 1889–93 and Gigon 1944; however, Lévy 1978 has shown the untenability of this hypothesis.

are not all that different: many scholars of Platonism are unwilling to give the Academy much room, while many scholars of the Academy have searched for the roots of scepticism outside the Platonic tradition, finding them – based on the Aristo verse just mentioned – either in Pyrrhonism or in the dialectical tradition. In particular, scholarly literature has long been dominated by the hypothesis of Arcesilaus' dependence on Pyrrho.[75] However, while possible from a chronological standpoint, this dependence is unlikely from a philosophical perspective, as Pyrrho's position is profoundly different from that of the Academics: Pyrrho's scepticism (assuming this term is applicable to his thought)[76] is based on the claim that the reality around us is indeterminate (and thus unknowable), whereas Academic scepticism – as we have seen – has more to do with the limits of knowledge, which is to say with the impossibility of grasping reality in its objectiveness: unlike Pyrrho, who talked about reality, the Academics never discussed the ontological status of what surrounds us.[77] Clearly, these are two different positions, which were only to converge to some extent with the phenomenalistic redefinition of Pyrrho's thought by Aenesidemus (first century BC) and Sextus Empiricus (second to third centuries AD) – but in this case we can at most posit an Academic influence on neo-Pyrrhonism, not the reverse.[78]

As regards the Megaric or dialectical tradition, it certainly played an important role, insofar as it helped Academics refine their polemical strategies in view of their debates with the Stoics.[79] A sharper argumentative focus is actually typical of all schools and clearly stems from their constant confrontations: as the sophists had already shown (consider Plato's *Euthydemus*) and as Aristotle

---

[75] See, recently, Görler 1994: 812–15. For an overall discussion of all these problems, see Lévy 1992: 9–57.

[76] Precisely because it is based on a clear-cut ontological thesis (albeit a peculiar one: the indeterminate character of reality), Pyrrho's position hardly meets the typical requirement set by scepticism, namely not to commit oneself to any strong claims.

[77] For an overview, see Decleva Caizzi 1986.

[78] 'It seems that Pyrrhonism is not so much a revival of Pyrrho's philosophy, but a revival of classical Academic skepticism under the name of Pyrrho, to distinguish it from the dogmatism which Aenesidemus and Sextus associated with the later skeptical Academy': M. Frede 1984: 273. On the affinities and differences between the Academy and neo-Pyrrhonism more generally, see Striker 1981.

[79] See Sedley 1977 on Diodorus; however, there is no need to hypothesise a direct discipleship from Arcesilaus.

knew well (consider his *Sophistical Refutations*), mastering argumentative techniques was crucial in order to prevail in a discussion, and discussions were the bread and butter of Hellenistic philosophers. Yet while no doubt important, not even the dialectical tradition constitutes the main influence on Academic scepticism.[80]

To understand its nature and overall significance, therefore, it is necessary to more carefully examine how Academics presented their philosophy. The thinker we know most about is Arcesilaus, whom the sources repeatedly credit with an interest in epistemology and an attempt to tone down his innovations (most notably, *akatalepsia* and *epoche*) by invoking many past authorities and a well-established philosophical tradition. In addition to Plato and Socrates, Arcesilaus continued to express great esteem and admiration for his predecessors within the Academy, whom he described as gods or remnants of the Age of Gold,[81] as though to stress his desire for continuity with the Platonist tradition.[82] In addition, he also drew upon the pre-Socratic tradition.[83] What are we to make of this connection between Plato and the previous tradition? In this case too, one possible explanation comes from a comparison with Stoicism: the emphasis on the allegedly sceptical character of the whole Greek philosophical tradition no doubt played a useful role in anti-Stoic polemics, insofar as it helped present Stoic theses as eccentric with respect to the awareness of human limits which had always characterised the best expressions of the Greek tradition. In other words, according to Arcesilaus' presentation, originality (understood in a negative sense,

---

[80] Another interpretation connects Academic scepticism to the dialectical analyses of the Academy and of Aristotle (and Theophrastus): see Weische 1961; Krämer 1971. This is a very interesting hypothesis, which is at least partly confirmed by the fact that neither Arcesilaus nor the other Academics ever sought to make a break with the ancient Academy. However, as Lévy 1992: 20–2 and 31–2, has shown, in itself it is incapable of accounting for everything. The problem does not lie simply in the analysis of the formal procedures of dialectical discussions: the problem is the relationship with Plato.

[81] D.L. 4.22; see *supra*, n. 3.

[82] Besides, we should not forget that the expression 'New Academy', which ancient sources use to describe the Hellenistic Academy, comes from erudite categorisation efforts or hostile sources, not from the representatives of the Academic tradition themselves: see Lévy 1992: 12.

[83] More precisely, Plutarch speaks of Plato, Socrates, Heraclitus, and Parmenides, whereas Cicero speaks of Democritus, Anaxagoras, Empedocles, Parmenides, Xenophanes, and 'almost all ancient philosophers' (*Adv. Col.* 1122a); see also Cic. *Ac.* 1.44, and *Ac.* 2.14 and 72.

of course) is to be found among the Stoics (and Epicureans), not the Academic sceptics: innovation, and indeed a reversal of the most genuine Greek thought, is brought about by those seeking to turn men into gods, not by those who through their reflection remind us of the distance separating us from the gods.[84] From a general perspective, this is the meaning which Arcesilaus – and with him other Academics – attributed to philosophy.

Clarifying this point can help us understand the meaning of the reference to Plato, who stands as the cornerstone of this tradition. Plato taught philosophy as the pursuit of knowledge, not the possession of truth. More specifically, in this context of discussions and divergent perspectives, different scholars have suggested that Arcesilaus was most influenced by the so-called 'Socratic' or 'aporetic' dialogues. This is a reasonable hypothesis, which becomes even more interesting when we consider the fact that in the early Hellenistic Age a great battle was waged around the figure of Socrates, as different schools sought to claim his mantle and to present themselves as his true heirs.[85] By presenting the dialectical method under Socrates' aegis, Arcesilaus defended a 'Platonic' image of the Athenian philosopher (i.e. the image we can infer from the dialogues) in contrast to the Stoic and Cynic attempts to turn Socrates into a model of the infallible and perfect wise man (in the footsteps of Xenophon's presentation). However, it was not simply a matter of selecting a few passages from the dialogues that could justify such views. The problem more generally concerned the meaning of Plato's philosophy.[86]

Over time, as the Academy gained more and more ground, the problem increasingly shifted from Socrates to Plato, coming to a head with the polemic between Philo and Antiochus. The latter's attempt to deny the legitimacy of any connection between Plato and the Academy elicited a prompt response from Philo, who in the so-called *Roman Books* took an open stand in favour of the unity of the whole Academic tradition, starting from the scepticism championed in the Hellenistic period. In his view, in other words, there was no break between Plato and the Hellenistic

---

[84] On this thesis, see Lévy 1993.
[85] See Long 1988.
[86] This is rightly noted by Lévy 1992: 18–19.

Academics, because not even Plato had ever claimed to have attained incontrovertible knowledge. On the contrary, as we read in a famous Cicero passage, complete scepticism would appear to mark the culmination of the philosophy of Plato,

in whose books nothing is stated positively and there is much arguing both *pro* and *contra*, all things are enquired and no certain statement made (*cuius in libris nihil adfirmatur et in utramque partem multa disseruntur, de omnibus quaeritur, nihil certi dicitur*).[87]

This rather radical statement clearly reveals Plato's importance: contrary to what many scholars suggest, it seems as though a crucial stimulus for the development of Academic scepticism was provided precisely by the Platonic dialogues, and particularly by a requirement on which the Socrates of the dialogues repeatedly insists in his discussions, which is to say the need to never bring philosophical research to an end. Despite Antiochus' reservations, Philo's interpretation clearly explains what the significance of Plato's philosophy might have been within the Hellenistic Academy, from Arcesilaus to Philo.

This is an important point which must be further elucidated. Scholars have often identified an anti-empiricist polemic as the defining trait of Academic scepticism, as the key point in their confrontation with the Stoics. However, it is evident that if this interpretation were correct, any emphasis on the connection with Plato would be reductive: the polemic against empiricism is evident in Plato, but it would be reductive to limit his philosophy to anti-empiricism. What about his idealism? Anti-empiricist interpretations of the Academy have always run up against this issue, which is why doubt has often been cast on the sincerity of the Academics' appeal to Plato. The situation changes, though, once we realise that Plato's teaching is primarily a matter of method. One ubiquitous aspect of the dialogues is precisely the reflection on philosophy, on its methods and limits; and it is this legacy that the Academics claimed as their own, by reframing it within an overall interpretation of the Greek tradition – with Plato in the front but also behind, to quote the above-mentioned Aristo.

---

[87] Cic. *Ac.* 146; cf. *Ac.* 2.74.

It thus seems as though the Academics' philosophy took shape by fully developing 'the seeds of scepticism' (Brochard) already clearly present in the dialogues, and this development did not depend so much on external influences (such as Pyrrho's teaching) as on the need to defend an underlying requirement of Plato's philosophy within a context marked by radical theses, namely: the defence of the human and hence fallible character of knowledge by opposition to the Stoic claim to furnish human beings with certain knowledge, of the sort that only gods can possess. It is in this 'tradition of humility' against newcomers' arrogance that the Academics' faithfulness to Plato is to be found, not in their adherence to any alleged doctrinal orthodoxy.[88]

Naturally, this does not solve all problems. Cicero reports that when he first learned about these theses, Antiochus, 'one of the gentlest of people began to lose his temper (*stomachari coepit*)':[89] a reaction that, while perhaps over the top, is at least partly understandable, as it is difficult to believe that Arcesilaus' and Carneades' radical scepticism correctly describes the philosophy of the dialogues, even though it may have been inspired by Socrates' and Plato's dialectical method. Nevertheless, it remains true that Arcesilaus and Carneades have suggested an interpretation of Plato, albeit a rather strained one in some respects. A slightly different assessment ought to be drawn in Philo's case: even though, here too, the lack of any reference to the intelligible dimension strikes the reader as odd, his fallibilism presents much stronger affinities with Plato's thought – for while it is true that Plato never reached the conclusion that is necessary to suspend judgement about everything, it is equally true that he never attained incontrovertible results. Instead, he always chose to present his theses as provisional, as what seemed to him to be the best provisional outcome, which he was nonetheless always willing to take as his starting point for further enquiries. While the claim that Plato invites us

---

[88] Lévy 1993; the expression 'tradition d'humilité' may be found in Lévy 1992: 623. One aspect of Lévy's interpretation that is more difficult to share, not least in the absence of explicit testimonies on the matter, is the thesis that, insofar as they attacked sensations, the Academics' discussions also implied an openness to the transcendent and intelligible dimension.

[89] Cic. *Ac.* 2.11.

to suspend judgement is certainly a strong one, the thesis that the dialogues' philosophy is primarily a philosophy of finiteness seems far more reasonable: it is a thesis that has been upheld by many scholars, including contemporary ones, and it helps us appreciate the importance of Academic arguments in view of a more rounded understanding of the phenomenon of scepticism.

The Case of Antiochus

In the previous pages I have repeatedly mentioned an internal opponent of Academic scepticism, Antiochus of Ascalon (c. 130 –68/67 BC), a controversial figure who continues to divide critics even today.[90] As we shall see in the following chapter, after Philo and Antiochus the history of Platonism would appear to have undergone a radical change: after the aporetic centuries of the Hellenistic Academy, a metaphysical and systematising idea of Plato's philosophy became dominant, in which any room for cautiousness and doubt was drastically reduced (albeit without disappearing entirely). In this context, Antiochus would appear to occupy a strategic position, insofar as he was the first – after a long period – to dispute the idea of a connection between scepticism and Platonism, while at the same time endorsing a new, doctrinal version of the tradition stemming from Plato. However, it is not easy to establish just how influential his contribution was: was it limited to his polemic against scepticism or can many of the doctrines of Imperial Platonism be traced back to his teaching? In other words, can we speak of Antiochus as the 'father of (Imperial) Platonism'? Or is he but the last representative of the great Hellenistic season, an Academic who switched to Stoicism?[91]

---

[90] Collections of fragments and testimonies: Mette 1986–7 and Sedley 2012: 334–46.

[91] An alternative to the Platonicising or Stoicising interpretation (which I will more extensively present in the following notes) is the 'syncretistic' interpretation put forward by Barnes 1989: quite simply, Antiochus' aim would have been to highlight as many possible points of convergence between Platonism, Aristotelianism, and Stoicism, in order to create a holy alliance against the two *bêtes noires* of philosophy, namely scepticism and Epicureanism. This interpretation is not entirely implausible. However, as I shall endeavour to show, the surviving testimonies point to a greater awareness and profoundness in Antiochus' thought.

What is certain is that Antiochus was one of the most prominent figures of his day. A pupil (from c. 110 BC) and then companion of Philo's,[92] around the 90s he clearly distanced himself from all forms of scepticism, promoting a return to the most authentic Academic-Platonist tradition (or, rather, what he regarded as the most authentic Academic-Platonist tradition) and gaining increasing public recognition. Antiochus was among the most famous philosophers of his time, and the most sought-after by the powerful Romans who visited Athens to learn philosophy: while Cicero repeatedly recalled his lectures,[93] Lucius Lucullus even recruited him as an adviser during his journeys to the East;[94] and it was on a journey with Lucullus, this time in Mesopotamia, that Antiochus met his death.

Philosophically speaking, much of Antiochus' fame was due to his anti-sceptical polemic, which did not merely concern arguments, but also entailed important consequences in terms of philosophical identity. In other words, his anti-sceptical polemic was also an attempt to establish a different Platonist identity, alternative and opposed to the one upheld within the Hellenistic Academy. According to Antiochus, the true Academic tradition was the one stretching from Plato to Polemo,[95] whereas the Hellenistic Academy was excluded as a subversion of the most genuine elements of Plato's thought.[96] Antiochus' reconstruction, however, was not based on mere exclusion: equally significant was what it included. Alongside 'official' Academics we find two Peripatetics, namely Aristotle and Theophrastus: despite certain errors, they too were seen as heirs to Plato's teaching.[97] Even more striking is the reconstruction of the history of this tradition in the Hellenistic period: Plato's heritage had been betrayed by Arcesilaus and his companions, but had found some followers among the Stoics.[98] The Stoics, who had been the Academics' opponents for the past two centuries, came to be regarded as the torch-bearers of Plato's philosophy! Evidently, the polemic

---

[92] Cic. *Ac.* 2.63, 69.
[93] Cic. *Brut.* 315; *De fin.* 5.1; *De nat. deor.* 1.6; *Ac.* 2.113.
[94] Cic. *Ac.* 2.4; Plut. *Vit. Lucull.* 42.3; Ael. *VH* 12.25; Philod. *Acad. ind.* XXXIV 39–42.
[95] Cic. *Ac.* 1.13 and 34; *Ac.* 2.70.
[96] Cic. *Ac.* 2.15.
[97] Cic. *De fin.* 5.7 and 14; *De or.* 3.67.
[98] Cic. *Ac.* 2.15; *Ac.* 1.7, 37, 43; *De leg.* 1.54; *De nat. deor.* 1.16.

against scepticism was also a polemic against any sceptical attempt to lay claim to Plato's teaching.

So far, Antiochus' position is clear, and amounts to a philosophical and ideological polemic against the sceptical Academy of Arcesilaus, Carneades, and Philo. We soon run into problems, however, because once we have introduced the idea of a proximity to Stoicism, we need to clarify its meaning. What was the relationship between Stoicism and the Platonist tradition? The very moment he acknowledged this proximity, Antiochus also made sure to acknowledge the differences between Stoicism and Platonism, arguing that the Stoics had made some 'corrections' to the Early Academics' philosophy.[99] For many modern scholars, who are in agreement with most ancient authors in this, the very fact of speaking of a correction implies a yielding to Stoicism, seen as the perfecting of the Academic-Platonic tradition; in other words, Antiochus would merely be an Academic who switched to Stoicism – a *germanissimus Stoicus*, as Cicero calls him.[100] The Hellenistic debate was a debate between scepticism and Stoicism, and in his battle against the sceptics Antiochus would ultimately have come to agree with the Stoics.

This is a reductive interpretation. Upon closer scrutiny, Antiochus' position is more nuanced and seems to disclose new possibilities that go beyond the Hellenistic debates, inaugurating a new phase in the history of Platonism.[101] It was not a matter for him of switching to Stoicism, but rather of stressing the affinities between the two traditions for the purpose of subordinating Stoicism to the Academic-Platonic tradition. What Antiochus implemented, in other words, was a more subtle (and – as some have noted – somewhat perfidious)[102] strategy, based on two

---

[99] Cic. *Ac.* 1.37 and 43.
[100] Cic. *Ac.* 2.132; cf. also 69 and 137; SE *P* 1.235; August. *Contra Ac.* 3.41 and *De civ. Dei* 19.3; among modern scholars, see esp. Görler 1994 and Brittain 2012. Besides, before studying under Philo, Antiochus had followed the lessons by two Stoic philosophers, Dardanus and Mnesarchus: see Cic. *Ac.* 2.69; August. *Contra Ac.* 3.41; and Numen. fr. 28. Antiochus was also on good terms with another Stoic, Sosus, a pupil of Panaetius' who also hailed from Ascalon.
[101] In defence of this thesis, see the pioneering study by Theiler 1930: 38–56; more recently, see Donini 1982: 73–81, Dillon 2011, and Bonazzi 2012a.
[102] Donini 1982: 81.

steps: first of all, he downplayed the alleged opposition between the two intellectual traditions, by showing that the Stoics were actually repeating the Academic theses by couching them in new terms;[103] this then enabled him to appropriate Stoic theses, integrating them into the ancients' doctrinal system. While apparently neutral, this strategy actually entailed the distortion of many Stoic doctrines and the subordination of Stoicism to Platonism, as may be inferred in particular in the fields of epistemology and ethics, the two disciplines in which Antiochus was most interested.[104]

At first sight, the case of knowledge is more complicated, owing to an underlying opposition between Stoic empiricism and Platonic innatism. Indeed, the Stoic theory of knowledge, which assigns so much importance to sensible experience, can hardly be seen to agree with any form of Platonic epistemology: anti-empiricism would appear to be one of the hallmarks of the Platonic tradition.[105] Nevertheless, Antiochus was able to trace an intermediate course, by downplaying the problem of the senses and identifying a common criterion between the two schools.[106] The problem of the apparent opposition between the two schools as regards the value of sensations was circumscribed, by showing, on the one hand, that the Platonists too assigned some importance to the senses (like the Stoics – and in contrast to the sceptics – they did not radically reject the senses) and, on the other hand, that in any case sensations are not the sole criterion for the Stoics. Even the most orthodox Stoics were willing to acknowledge that sensations alone are not enough to ensure true knowledge (*episteme*). What matters is rather the possession of so-called common notions (*ennoiai*): within herself each human being possesses a series of notions which she has developed over the course of her life and which, once articulated into definitions, will enable her to grasp the essence of a given object. This is what true knowledge consists of. By stressing this point, Antiochus could highlight the affinities

---

[103] Cic. *De fin.* 4.72; 5.90; *De nat. deor.* 1.16; *De leg.* 1.54.
[104] Cic. *Ac.* 2.29.
[105] For a detailed analysis of this problem, I shall refer to Bonazzi 2015a, Ch. 1. It is also noteworthy – although this problem exceeds the scope of the present study – that Stoic epistemology could hardly be reduced to mere empiricism: see M. Frede 1994.
[106] The most important testimony is Cic. *Ac.* 1.30–33.

with a theory of knowledge of Platonic inspiration. Ultimately, Antiochus' theory would appear to have been this: Stoic theory does not present substantial differences compared to that of the ancient Platonists, once common notions have been replaced with Forms, for the latter seem to fulfil the same function (the names are what change, not the things to which they refer). By exploiting the functional similarity between notions and Forms, Antiochus could thus argue for a structural affinity between the two philosophies. Yet in doing so – and this is the second step – Antiochus was not pursuing the mere goal of harmonisation and syncretism, as though it were a matter of highlighting the virtual equivalence between the two systems; on the contrary, by showing the dependence of the Stoic doctrine on Academic doctrine, he could appropriate Stoic doctrines and terms while subordinating Stoicism to Platonism. It is interesting to note that this theory enjoyed considerable popularity within Imperial Platonism.[107]

Much the same can be said about ethics, on which we are better informed thanks to Book 5 of Cicero's *De finibus*.[108] Drawing upon Polemo and Aristotle,[109] Antiochus claimed for the Academic tradition the formula which identifies 'living according to nature' as the goal of human life,[110] a formula traditionally associated with Stoicism. Once a degree of underlying continuity had been ensured, it was a matter of toning down the alleged peculiarities of which the Stoics were so proud, by showing – once again – that these philosophers were merely repeating old doctrines with new terms. This was the case with the basic thesis of the self-sufficiency of virtue, one of the cornerstones of Stoic doctrine: Antiochus acknowledged the centrality of virtue for happiness (only the virtuous is happy), yet also stressed the need to

---

[107] See Chapter 3, Epistemology and Logic, pp 97–100.
[108] See Bonazzi 2009 and Tsouni 2019 (underling the importance of the relation with Peripatetic philosophy).
[109] Cic. *De fin.* 5.14.
[110] Cic. *De fin.* 5.24. The emphasis on this formula marks a rather strong break with the theories upheld by later Platonists (see Chapter 3, The Ethical Doctrines and the Problem of Fate, pp. 100–103); however, it might be connected to what some of the Early Academics argued. We should always leave room for doubt, however, given that – considering his underlying thesis – Antiochus is hardly a source we can unconditionally trust: see Chapter 1, Ethical Issues, pp. 30–32.

attain goods according to nature (e.g. good health), if one wishes to lead a most happy life. This thesis, typical of the Peripatetic tradition,[111] was completely unacceptable for the Stoics, yet it was attributed to them based on the fact that they too acknowledged that what is according to nature is 'preferable' to what is not (e.g. good health is preferable to sickness).[112] According to Antiochus' (arbitrary) reconstruction, all verbal distinctions aside, the Stoics too accepted the thesis that happiness lies in living according to nature, 'enjoying the primary gift of nature with the accompaniment of virtue'.[113]

Likewise, another major point of disagreement between the two schools was addressed, namely the problem of passions (*pathe*), of which the Stoic wise man – unlike the Academic-Peripatetic one – is free.[114] It was an arduous task to reconcile the Stoic thesis of *apatheia* with the Academic and Peripatetic belief that it is possible to govern the passions, yet never to fully eradicate them (the so-called thesis of *metriopatheia*). However, Antiochus set himself to this task with considerable skill by exploiting the Stoic notion of *eupatheiai*, the positive feelings proper to the Stoic wise man. By refusing to acknowledge the deep meaning of this concept and by labelling it as a mere neologism, Antiochus noted that Stoicism too accepted the existence of positive emotions; and by identifying these with the condition of inner equilibrium consequent upon the governing of the passions (i.e. consequent upon *metriopatheia*), he concluded that the two doctrines ultimately coincided. Yet in this case too it is evident that reconciliation amounts to the subordination of Stoicism to Platonism and Aristotelianism: in Antiochus' presentation, Stoicism comes across as a new, terminologically updated version of a more ancient and more authoritative doctrine.[115]

Reconstructing Antiochus' physical doctrines proves trickier, as all we can go by is the succinct and not always satisfactory account

---

[111] It might also be an Early Academic tradition but see the previous notes.
[112] Cic. *De fin.* 5.71.
[113] Cic. *De fin.* 2.34 and 5.27.
[114] See Cic. *Ac.* 2.135 and *Ac.* 1.38–39.
[115] For a more in-depth discussion, see Bonazzi 2009: 44–50.

that Cicero provides in the *Academica*.[116] Essentially, it seems that what can safely be inferred is an interpretation of the *Timaeus* profoundly influenced by Stoic terms and doctrines: there are only two principles, an efficient force which operates and a passive matter that is ordered by it; this encounter gives rise to the four fundamental elements (water, air, earth, and fire), from which bodies are formed. This is the origin of the universe, which is eternal (an important difference compared to Stoic doctrine), one, and providentially governed by a world soul. In itself, this combination of Platonic and Stoic elements is not particularly problematic, whereas some difficulties emerge from the concession that Antiochus apparently makes to Stoic materialism, by envisaging a close interpenetration between the two principles, which would leave no room for the existence of a separate and incorporeal entity.[117] Given the impossibility of resolving this difficulty, we are forced to acknowledge that Cicero's testimony in this case is less clear than we would like it to be.[118]

The doubts increase when we attempt to make sense of the meaning of an apparent absence: that of the Forms, which played such an important role in the Platonic and Early Academic theory of knowledge. Actually, upon closer inspection, a few traces would seem to emerge where emphasis is placed on the notion of *forma* and the first principle is described as 'mind'.[119] A description of the first divine principle in such terms raises the problem of its possible objects of thought: clearly, Forms are the ideal candidate to fulfil this function. In this regard, it is interesting to note that some testimonies, from Varro and Seneca, explicitly bear witness to the theory according to which Forms are the thoughts of God (i.e. the first principle) – a theory destined to play a prominent role in the metaphysics of the early Imperial Age.[120] Therefore, it

---

[116] Cic. *Ac.* 1.24–29. A very useful analysis is provided by Inwood 2012; more controversially, Sedley 2002 has attempted to trace these chapters back to Polemo; see also Algra 2017.

[117] Cic. *Ac.* 1.24: 'each of the two principles was present in the combination of both (*in utroque tamen utroque*)'.

[118] Donini 1982, p. 79. An alternative reconstruction of Antiochus' physics, which disputes his alleged materialism, may now be found in Lévy 2008. No less thorny problems concern the presumed determinism of Cic. *Ac.* 1.29.

[119] Cic. *Ac.* 1.26 and 29.

[120] Varro *Antiq. rer. div.* fr. 306 (= August. *De civ. Dei* 7.28); Sen. *Ep.* 65.7–9. This theory, or at least an embryonic form of it, is already featured in Plato (*Crat.* 407b), and

would not be surprising if Antiochus had adopted it, possibly by exploiting the Stoic theory of *logoi spermatikoi* (the testimonies from Varro and Seneca too present a version of Platonism that is deeply steeped in Stoic elements). However, we must once again acknowledge that the sources are less clear than we would like them to be.[121]

Be that as it may, even leaving the problems related to physics open, the analysis of epistemological and ethical discussions seems to confirm that Antiochus unquestionably belonged in the Platonist camp. Antiochus repeatedly engaged with Stoicism, borrowing quite a few elements from that philosophy; this has been seen to confirm many ancient and modern scholars' prejudices about his alleged adherence, or yielding, to Stoicism. However, this is not at all the case: Antiochus rather sought to bring Stoicism back within Platonism; with the excuse of searching for a way to reconcile the two, he actually pursued the aim of subordinating the former to the latter, leading to substantial misunderstandings of Stoic philosophy. Within the field of epistemology, the identification between *ennoiai* and Forms also seems to entail an innatist bent which the Stoics would never have accepted: unlike Forms (understood – beyond all metaphors – as innate concepts), *ennoiai* are formed and develop on the basis of sensible experience. Even more evident are the violations in the field of ethics: the thesis which places the Peripatetics' goods according to nature and the Stoics' preferable things on the same level betrays the meaning of the Stoic theory which, by considering things according to nature to be indifferent, exclusively focused on virtue as the aim of a happy life. As far as *eupatheiai* are concerned, it is evident that the idea according to which the wise man too experiences emotions (if only positive ones) entails a dualistic psychology (with an

different scholars have sought to trace it back to Xenocrates (this hypothesis is one of the main ones in Krämer 1964; see also Dillon 2003: 107–8). These antecedents may have played some role, but it is probably rash to argue that the thesis was fully developed within the Early Academy (where, as we have seen, Forms were widely criticised). What is beyond dispute is that the thesis in question enjoyed considerable popularity in the early Imperial Ages: see Chapter 3, The Doctrine of Principles, p. 92.

[121] The attribution to Antiochus of the theory that the ideas as God's thoughts lies at the basis of Theiler 1930's Platonicising interpretation of Antiochus; for a more recent (and cautious) discussion of the problem, see Bonazzi 2015b.

irrational part opposed to a rational one): a psychology perfectly in line with the Platonist and Aristotelian tradition, yet absolutely incompatible with Stoic monism. In other words, Antiochus cannot be deemed a Stoic, if not at the price of profound misunderstandings: the camp he belongs to is the Platonist one, and it is noteworthy that all the doctrines we have discussed (the revival of Forms, psychological dualism, *metriopatheia*) were destined to enjoy extensive circulation in the following centuries. It would probably be too much to categorically state – as some scholars have done – that Antiochus was the father of Middle Platonism. However, it is an indisputable fact that he contributed to renewing Platonism (not least through the revival of early Academic doctrines). Deeply rooted in the world of Hellenistic debates, Antiochus was the first philosopher to dare to tread new paths, which over the following centuries were to lead to a radical renewal of the tradition stemming from Plato.

3

TOWARDS THE SYSTEM: PLATONISM IN
THE EARLY IMPERIAL AGE

The End of the Academy and the Decentralisation
of Philosophy

According to a historiographical legend that still crops up from
time to time, the Academy continued to operate up until AD
529, when Justinian issued a law prohibiting any non-Christian
form of teaching. The date is certainly intriguing, as that same
year St Benedict founded his monastery at Montecassino: a new
world was replacing the old one. This thesis found support in the
great German philology of the nineteenth century: Karl Gottlob
Zumpt collected all available information on Platonists into a list
of Academic scholarchs stretching from Plato to the Academy's
alleged closing by Justinian. Once accepted by eminent figures –
most strikingly, Karl Prächter chose to republish Zumpt's 'Tabelle'
as an appendix to his monumental history of ancient philosophy –
this reconstruction gained universal scholarly acceptance.[1] While
no doubt fascinating, Zumpt's hypothesis is wrong: Platonist philosophers continued to live and teach in Athens, albeit without
any official connection to the Academy – because the latter had
ceased to operate between 89 and 86 BC.[2]

The early first century BC was a very turbulent period for
Athens, which led to the dictatorship of two Peripatetic philosophers, Aristion and Athenion, and to an alliance with Mithridates.
Roman reaction was not slow in coming; Silla's troops laid siege
to the city, whereas the pro-Roman *optimates* were hastily fleeing
away. Among these was the last scholar of the Academy, Philo
of Larissa, who moved to Rome, where he enjoyed a successful
career as a teacher until his death in 84/3 BC. Meanwhile, Silla,

---

[1] See Zumpt 1843; Ueberweg-Prächter 1926, vol. 12: 663–6.
[2] This has unequivocally been proven by Lynch 1972 and Glucker 1978.

who had set up camp in the outskirts of the city, ordered the devastation of the Academy's gardens in order to build war machines for the siege.[3] His army eventually broke through and ransacked the city. In this period of turmoil, with the flight of Philo and the destruction of the Academy's gardens, the school founded by Plato closed down, turning into a kind of 'tourist' destination for nostalgic visitors: thinkers ranging from Cicero to Proclus were to return there to evoke something that no longer existed.

Charged with symbolic value, this episode actually fits within a context of profound changes, which from the late second century BC onwards radically altered the way of practising philosophy in the Greek and Roman world.[4] It was in this new context that Platonism took centre stage. It is not easy to establish the exact reasons behind such changes, yet some factors cannot be overlooked, starting from the crisis of Athens as the philosophical centre par excellence. Far from being an isolated event, the closing down of the Academy (and of the Aristotelian Lyceum, which met the same fate during Silla's siege) confirms a long-term phenomenon, namely the gradual spread of philosophical schools throughout the known world. In choosing to move to Rome, Philo had hardly made a revolutionary choice; he had simply followed in the footsteps of illustrious predecessors such as the Stoic Panaetius and perhaps the Epicurean Philodemus (who was also active in Naples). Besides, another philosopher would appear to have been active in Rome in the same years, the Peripatetic Andronicus, the presumed author of new edition of Aristotle's writings.[5] The situation on the Eastern front was no different, considering that the other leading Stoic of this period, Posidonius, had opened a school in Rhodes, a city which was also home to prominent Aristotelians. Thinkers from all schools were also operating,

---

[3] See Plut. *Vit. Sullae* 12. Brittain 2001: 68 has raised some cautious doubts about the destruction of the Academy; however, it remains the case that the Academy ceased its activities in this period, after Philo's flight to Rome – see Bonazzi 2020a.

[4] Fundamental works on this issue are P. Hadot 1987; Donini 1987; M. Frede 1999b; Sedley 2003.

[5] A list of the most important philosophers active in Rome in these centuries may be found in M. Frede 1997, 218; it includes, along with the aforementioned philosophers, Asclepiades, Staseas, Athenodorus, Diodotus, Xenarchus, Arius Didimus, Nicholas of Damascus, Thrasyllus, Attalus, Sotion, Cornutus, Cheremon, Musonius, Favorinus, Epictetus, Euphrates, and possibly Numenius, Plotinus, Amelius, and Porphyry.

writing, and debating in Alexandria, a city that had shown surprisingly little interest in philosophy during the Hellenistic centuries; most prominent of all, as we shall see, were the Platonist philosophers.[6] The Early Imperial Age is the age of the pervasive spread of philosophy.

This progressive decentralisation is important not just because it bears witness to the growing success of philosophy, but also because of the consequences it entailed. The first and most crucial was the introduction of new ways of practising philosophy. Whereas the entire Hellenistic period had been dominated by debates between different schools, what now proved central was the exegesis of what were regarded as authoritative and truth-bearing texts. This new interest in texts sprung precisely from the crisis of the Athenian schools, which during the Hellenistic centuries had served as guardians of orthodoxy. The proliferation of new centres, increasingly unconnected to one another, necessarily entailed the rethinking of the meaning of one's own philosophical choices, and an answer was now sought – and found – precisely in the founding fathers' texts. In brief, the Early Imperial Age became the age of the return of the ancients (Plato and Aristotle, naturally, but also Pythagoras and Pyrrho), based on the belief that the truth had been revealed in the past and that it was simply a matter of bringing it back to life.[7]

One of the priorities was thus the systematisation of the founding teachers' writings, which fuelled the editorial work carried out on Aristotle by Andronicus, and on Plato by Thrasyllus and Dercyllides. Increasingly, the main task for a philosopher was to interpret and explain the doctrines of the founder of his school, for the purpose of clarifying their value and self-consistency. This was the age of handbooks, paraphrases, compendia, anthologies, and especially commentaries, which for centuries to come were to constitute the privileged genre for philosophical research. Philosophy, in other words, became the domain of professors: Seneca, who struggled to grasp both the reasons for the changes underway and their significance, complained that philosophy had

---

[6] On Alexandria, in addition to the classic study of Fraser 1972, see now Hatzimichali 2011.
[7] On this topic, see especially Gigon 1958; Donini 1993; Boys-Stones 2001.

turned into philology.[8] Actually, this new way of operating, far from amounting to a mere show of erudition, something quite useless for solving everyday life problems (as Seneca suggested), was to contribute to a radical renewal of philosophy – as we shall see in the following pages.[9]

In Search of an Identity: A Map of (Middle) Platonism

In the case of Platonism, even more so than in that of other schools, this new situation translated into a genuine identity crisis. Both within the Academy and outside it, divergent and frequently incompatible images and interpretations of Plato proliferated. The problem was no longer limited to the clash between Philo, an heir to Hellenistic scepticism, and Antiochus, the champion of a return to the positive doctrines of the first Academy. No less relevant were the attempts to appropriate Platonic doctrines advanced by Stoics (Panaetius and Posidonius) and Peripatetics (Aristocles, Aspasius, and possibly also Adrastus) – who sought to present Plato as an imperfect predecessor of their own theories – as well as by authors close to Pythagoreanism (a controversial category, as we shall see), who instead wished to stress Plato's dependence on Pythagoras. Finally, we have those seeking to develop a radically sceptical, Pyrrhonian interpretation of Platonic philosophy.[10] The debate, by now, increasingly revolved around Plato.

Given this situation, it is hardly surprising that a considerable portion of the Platonists' written production – and one that is unfortunately lost – was devoted precisely to the attempt to defend the significance of their belonging to Plato's tradition, at a time when the end of the Academy had stripped them of their

---

[8] Sen. *Ep.* 108; to understand the meaning of Seneca's criticism, see Inwood 2007 and Boys-Stones 2013.

[9] An impressive collection of the most important surviving testimonies from these authors is provided by the multi-volume publishing project begun by Heinrich Dörrie and carried on by Matthias Baltes: Baltes and Dörrie 1987–2020. Not less important is now Boys-Stones 2018a and the new edition of the Überweg-Prächter, *Grundriss der Geschichte der Philosophie* (Riedweg, Horn, and Wyrwa 2018, with an extensive bibliography). The two classic studies – Dillon 1996 and Donini 1982: 100–59 – remain the ideal introduction to Early Imperial Platonism.

[10] A succinct overview may be found in Donini 1987 and 1993.

most important point of reference. In concrete terms, this wealth of polemical literature was developed in two different directions: on the one hand, it was a matter of addressing the issue of the compatibility (or incompatibility) of Academic scepticism with Plato's thought, at a time in which Platonism was orienting itself towards increasingly dogmatic and systematising approaches. On the other hand, it was a matter of taking a stance vis-à-vis the criticism featured in Aristotle's school treatises, which in this very period started circulating again, attracting considerable interest.

In the former case, there was a tendency to exclude the Hellenistic period, by labelling it either as a betrayal (Antiochus) or as a period of darkness in contrast to the most genuine Platonist tradition (Proclus).[11] As far as we know, only Plutarch (c. AD 45–125) and the anonymous author of a commentary on the *Theaetetus* discovered in Egypt in 1905 (and which can be dated to the period in question) sought to also include the Hellenistic Academy so as to defend the unitary nature of the tradition stemming from Plato, by offering an openly dialectical and implicitly dualistic interpretation of Arcesilaus and his followers; that is to say, by showing that any attempt to establish philosophy on a materialistic or empirical basis (as the Stoics and Epicureans had done) was destined to meet with failure, the Hellenistic Academics – actually Platonists *in terra infidelium* – were to prove the intrinsic necessity of Platonic dualism.[12]

Closely connected to the issue of the Hellenistic Academy is a broader reflection on Hellenistic philosophy in general. While Epicureanism was unanimously condemned (as may be inferred, for instance, from Plutarch's many polemical treatises),[13] the relationship with Stoicism was more complicated. As the case of

---

[11] On the anti-sceptical polemic, see Bonazzi 2003a: 15–96 and Petrucci 2021; see also Chapter 2, The Case of Antiochus, pp. 66–69.

[12] See Sedley and Bastianini 1995 (which is also the reference edition for the commentator's text); Opsomer 1998; Bonazzi 2012c and 2015b. A historically more sensitive defence of Academic scepticism was put forward by the famous orator Favorinus of Arles, with whom Plutarch was in contact: see Ioppolo 1993. Many of Plutarch's philosophical works have been preserved; among the philosophically most noteworthy, see *Delphic Dialogues*, *On the Daimonion of Socrates*, *On the Face in the Moon*, his treatises of Platonic exegesis (*On the Generation of the Soul in the Timaeus* and *Platonic Questions*), and his treatises against the Epicureans (especially *Against Colotes*) and the Stoics.

[13] On Plutarch's anti-Epicurean polemic, see Boulogne 2003 and Kechagia 2011.

Antiochus clearly illustrates, the polemic against scepticism could lead to a reassessment of Stoicism, the system which had most opposed any aporetic turn. Besides, it was widely known that the founder of Stoicism, Zeno, had been a pupil of the great Academics of his day.[14] Leaving aside the materialism and empiricism of this school (a controversial issue, then as much as today), the similarities with Platonism were quite remarkable. What was one to make of all this? With the predictable exception of Plutarch,[15] whose defence of the Academic tradition always went hand in hand with the anti-Stoic polemic, most Platonists' stance was less clear-cut: while not openly acknowledging the convergence with the rival school, they adopted more nuanced strategies, in an effort to adapt their opponents' doctrines to the new context of Platonist metaphysics. Although scholars have not always realised it, this implicit engagement with Stoicism runs throughout the history of Imperial Platonism, significantly influencing its development.[16]

No less complex was the relationship with Aristotle, the other great name of that age, who burst back onto the scene after centuries of partial oblivion.[17] For Platonists, the renewed circulation of treatises such as the *Categories*, the *De caelo* and *Metaphysics*, which were full of Platonicising ideas and openly anti-Platonic claims, clearly raised some problems, which were even thornier than those posed by an engagement with Stoicism.[18] Conventionally, a distinction is drawn between Platonists who were for and those who were against a reconciliation with Aristotle, but this is partly misleading: as with the Stoics, it is better to distinguish between those who were firmly opposed to

---

[14] Polemo and possibly Xenocrates: see D. L. 7.2.

[15] Babut 1969 remains a fundamental work on Plutarch. Of course, it may well be that Plutarch's opinion of Stoicism was still less negative than his opinion of Epicureanism: see Opsomer 2014b and 2017.

[16] One interesting study is Reydams-Schils 1999, which sets out from the reception of the *Timaeus*. See now the essays collected in Long 2013 and Engberg-Pedersen 2017.

[17] Moraux 1973–2001 remains the reference study for Aristotelianism in this period; more recently see also Sharples 2010. On its relationship with Platonism, see Karamanolis 2006; see also Rashed and Auffret 2014.

[18] However, it is not easy to assess how interested Early Imperial Platonists were in a thorough reading of the Aristotelian texts, as Chiaradonna 2017 rightly argued (besides, the relevance of the exoteric works should also be taken into consideration). In more general terms, on the publication and actual circulation of Aristotle's works, see Barnes 1997.

any kind of reconciliation (most notably, Atticus) and those – the majority – who instead sought to draw upon Aristotelian ideas and doctrines to develop a Platonic system. It must be noted, as the controversy surrounding Aristotle perfectly exemplifies, that by the age in question such discussions unfolded with reference to other Platonists: the target was not Aristotle or Stoicism (who, as opponents, are criticised), but rather Platonist colleagues planning to employ Aristotelian, Stoic or Academic doctrines to clarify Plato's thought. These self-referential polemics are perhaps the most enlightening example of how difficult it is to give a coherent interpretation of Plato's thought.

Overall, the interaction of all these factors produced a series of orientations and tendencies within the large family of Platonism. As already noted, one first, general distinction is between the unitarist minority, seeking to find a place even for the Hellenistic Academy within the Platonist tradition (Plutarch and the anonymous commentator on the *Theaetetus*) and a separatist majority, openly hostile to any compromise with scepticism. However, this hardly explains anything at all, since the problem was to establish what Platonism positively consisted in: even for Plutarch and the anonymous commentator on the *Theaetetus*, Platonism was unquestionably a metaphysical system comprising specific doctrines. We must look elsewhere to find more significant differences.

At the risk of oversimplifying things, I will present what may be regarded as the most influential options. On the one side, we find a tradition – in such cases it is best to avoid speaking of organised currents – which was more interested in engaging with Stoicism. It enjoyed a certain degree of popularity in Athens: leading representatives of this new tendency were Antiochus in the first century BC; Atticus, Lucius, Nicostratus, and Severus in the second century AD; and Longinus in the third century AD.[19] On the other side, we find an ever more marked opposition to the

[19] Editions of fragments: Des Places 1977; Gioè 2002 (with an extensive commentary); Brisson and Patillon 2001 (with an extensive commentary); Lakmann 2017. On Atticus, see Baltes 1983, Trabattoni 1987, and especially Michalewski 2017 and 2020 (presenting new evidence from Syriac sources); on Longinus, see the rich monograph by Männlein-Robert 2001 and M. Frede 1990.

sceptical tradition being expressed by Pythagoreanising currents, which are well attested in Alexandria and soon spread elsewhere. Alexandria would appear to have been an especially important centre between the first century BC and the first century AD: it was in this city that Eudorus and Thrasyllus operated, and it is here that many pseudo-Pythagorean treatises were apparently written that played a fundamental role in the development of Platonic metaphysics.[20] In Alexandria we also find Philo, who drew upon his philosophical expertise to produce an original interpretation of Jewish thought.[21] The popularity of this Pythagoreanising tendency, however, was not at all limited to this city, but progressively extended to many other areas: from Italy, which is where Moderatus of Gades (the late first century AD) would appear to have been active, to the Anatolian coast with Nicomachus of Gerasa (the second century AD) and especially Numenius of Apamea (the second century AD),[22] one of the most original and interesting philosophers from this period.

Important as it may be, the distinction between Stoicising Platonists and Pythagorising Platonists is far from exhaustive: as already noted, the main problem lay in the relationship with Aristotle. The representatives of both traditions were clearly aware of this issue, which soon acquired a central place in the debates of those years. Indeed, it was this problem that the majority of the above-mentioned treatises (most of which are now lost) sought to address. Among surviving testimonies, the most notable attempts to integrate Aristotle into Platonism are provided by Lucius Calvenus Taurus and Alcinous, the otherwise unknown author of a handbook for the teaching of Platonic doctrines (*Didaskalikos*),[23]

---

[20] Eudorus' fragments have been brought together by Mazzarelli 1985; see now Bonazzi 2013a with further bibliography; on Thrasyllus, see Tarrant 1993. As far as pseudo-Pythagorean literature is concerned, a collection of such texts may be found in Thesleff 1965 (cf. *infra*, n. 38); for an overview, see Centrone 2014; the dating of these treatises to the 1st cent. AD, see – among others – Burkert 1972b; Baltes 1972: 20–36; Huffman 2005: 594–620.

[21] On Philo of Alexandria and Platonism, see Runia 1986.

[22] Edited by Des Places 1973; among the most significant studies on Numenius and the Pythagoreans, see Baltes 1972; M. Frede 1987; O'Meara 1989, Michalewski 2012; Boys-Stones 2018a. On these 'pythagorean' philosophers, see *infra* p. 103–110:

[23] The relevance of Taurus has now been made clear by Petrucci 2018a, who underlines the role played by the Peripatetic and doxographic tradition; as for Alcinous see Whittaker 1990 and Dillon 1993.

to which we can also add *De Platone et eius dogmate* by Apuleius of Madaura (c. AD 125–70), the most important Latin Platonist of the Early Imperial period.[24]

For quite some time, scholars have labelled this wealth of orientations and interpretations as an expression of 'eclecticism', as though to stigmatise the unsystematic and incoherent nature of these philosophers' thought. The term generally used to describe Early Imperial Platonism clearly reflects scholars' limited appreciation of these philosophers: from Prächter onwards, we tend to speak of 'Middle Platonism', as though the only value of this period lay in the fact that it paved the ground for Neoplatonism. It goes without saying that the philosophers in question would have staunchly rejected this classification, as they professed to be nothing but Platonists – which is to say, exegetes, commentators, and interpreters of a philosophy which they believed to encapsulate the truth.[25] What I will try to show is that this range of orientations and interpretations, far from reflecting the confusion of an age of transition, constitutes one of the liveliest moments in the long history of Platonism – one of the moments in which the elusive richness of Plato's philosophy was most keenly perceived.

Editions and Classifications

Despite the many differences, some common topics and more or less shared lines of enquiry are to be found which make it possible to consider the phenomenon of Middle Platonism as a whole. To begin with, all Platonists share two underlying assumptions:

---

[24] On Apuleius' Platonism (and especially the two treatises *De Platone et eius dogmate* and *De deo Socratis*), see Moreschini 1978; Trapp 2007b: 470–4, and especially Fletcher 2014 (on the *Metamorphoses* see also infra, pp. 114–115). The recent edition of a strange Latin summary of Platonic dialogues, tentatively attributed to Apuleius (see Stover 2016; *contra* Bonazzi 2017c) further contributes to our knowledge of Roman Platonism. Later, the most important Latin author is the author of an important commentary on the *Timaeus*, Calcidius, who lived in the fourth century but de facto reflects the philosophical climate of Middle Platonism, see Waszink 1962, Bakhouche 2011, and especially Reydams-Schils 2020. As regards the reception of Platonism in Rome more generally, Gersh 1986 is still a good source.

[25] On these terminological problems, see Glucker 1978 and Bonazzi 2003b. An interesting reflection on the limits and advantages of adopting the category of Middle Platonism is provided by Donini 1990; more recently, see Catana 2013, Hatzimichali 2011 (on the problem of eclecticism) and Ferrari 2018.

1) Plato is the first philosopher to have revealed the truth; and
2) the duty of the Platonist (which is to say, of the only true philosopher) is to reconstruct the doctrinal system to be found in the
dialogues, and especially in the *Timaeus*. The second assumption is the more surprising. Indeed, it is obvious that Platonists
might wish to affirm Plato's superiority, just as it is obvious that
Aristotelians might wish to affirm the superiority of Aristotle and
Pyrrhonians that of Pyrrho; what is far less obvious is the claim
that Plato's dialogues, when correctly interpreted, can be seen
to contain a perfect and exhaustive system.[26] Few people would
endorse such a claim today. Yet this idea was universally shared
by ancient Platonists: as an anonymous author quoted by Stobaeus
states, Plato has many voices (*polyphonos*), but not many doctrines (*polydoxos*).[27]

In this respect, Platonists were – at least to some extent – influenced by the similar claims made by the Stoics and the Aristotelians,
who in turn had repeatedly stressed the coherence of their own systems as a marker of the superiority of their philosophy.[28] In entering into competition with these schools, Platonists were forced to
show that their philosophy too could systematically account for
reality in all of its complexity. The importance assigned to commentaries can easily be explained as a consequence of this need
for a systematic philosophy.[29] Platonists' engagement with other
schools also brings out a specific feature of their exegesis: given
the ambiguity and reticence invariably to be found in Plato's dialogues, these thinkers became convinced that it was necessary to
go beyond the letter of his texts in order to grasp their true content.
What Platonists needed, in other words, was a creative interpretation based on the principle *ex eo quod scriptum sit ad id quod non
sit scriptum pervenire* ('to pass from what is written to what is
not written').[30] This kind of interpretation, which at times yielded

[26] See e.g. Albin. *Eisag.* 149.13–14; Attic. fr. 1.
[27] Stob. *Anth.* 2.7.4a and 2.7.3f.
[28] Donini 1987: 5027–35.
[29] On Middle Platonist exegesis and commentaries, see Ferrari 2001 and Petrucci 2018b
and 2018c.
[30] Cic. *De inv.* 2.152; see P: Hadot 1957; Donini 1987: 5081; more cautiously, see now
Petrucci 2018a: 54–64.

truly original results, distinguished Platonist exegesis from the other great exegetical tradition, the Aristotelian, which kept much closer to the letter of each text. It goes without saying that the adoption of such a criterion was far from neutral: the range of solutions proposed by the various Platonists can also be explained on the basis of such methods of interpretation.

The same requirements also contributed to the emergence of a series of propaedeutic problems that became increasingly important in a context dominated by teaching.[31] Thus, according to Albinus' *Prologue* (first half of the second century), there are three problems that it is necessary to set out in order to study Plato: 1) What is a dialogue? 2) How are Plato's dialogues divided? 3) From which dialogues should one start reading Plato? Clearly, these problems depended on the growing importance of written texts and led to very different answers. In particular, as far as the second point is concerned, we find two kinds of classification of the dialogues: one by characters (i.e. on the basis of content) and the other by tetralogies (a classification that can probably be traced back to an earlier period, but which was taken up by Thrasyllus; the classification by trilogies developed by Aristophanes of Byzantium had enjoyed a certain degree of popularity in the Hellenistic Age).[32] Even greater divergences can be found in relation to the third point: it is difficult to find two authors who agree on the reading sequence of the dialogues.[33]

However, this should not be taken to suggest a picture of complete fragmentation: Platonists might disagree as to the solutions required, but – as already noted – all sought to address similar needs. It is quite clear that the various kinds of classification, particularly ones 'by characters' (which distinguished between *hyphegetikoi* and *zetetikoi* dialogues, those adapted for instruction and the others for inquiry) shared the aim of forestalling any attempt to provide a sceptical interpretation of Plato: while certain dialogues might have an aporetic ending, this was seen as part of an overall communication and educational strategy ('maieutics')

[31] See Mansfeld 1994.
[32] See D.L. 3.49–50 and 56–62.
[33] The main testimonies are: Albin. *Eisag.* 149.2–150.12; Taur. T 11 Petrucci; D.L. 3.62; Aul. Gell. 1.9.8–11; Procl. *In Alc.* 11.3–17; Anon. *Proleg. in Plat. phil.* 24.1–26.25.

which in no way weakened the doctrinal framework of the Platonic system. Likewise, divergences with regard to the reading order all presupposed the same desire to establish a path capable of leading to an understanding of the divine first principles; as we shall see, Imperial Age Platonism increasingly took the form of a theology.

Therefore, notwithstanding divergences with regard to numerous specific points, common ground emerged within which all Platonist schools of the Imperial Age were to operate. In this respect, the divergences between Neoplatonism and Middle Platonism are less relevant than the elements of continuity between the two.

Eudorus and the Beginnings of Platonism in Alexandria

The first notable figure we have information about is Eudorus of Alexandria, who was most probably active in the second half of the first century BC. As Cicero recounts, Antiochus of Ascalon had also spent some time in Alexandria, which was later to become home to some of his pupils. The presence of certain points of convergence between Eudorus and Antiochus (for instance, their shared interest in Stoicism and in the Early Academy) has led some scholars to postulate the existence of a school headed by Antiochus in Alexandria, of which Eudorus too would have been a member: this connection might be the birthplace of doctrinal Platonism. However, caution is advised, given the limited information available: the existence of a school headed by Antiochus does not seem to be confirmed by any source;[34] as far as doctrines are concerned, while certain parallels are certainly evident, the points of divergence between the two philosophers are just as significant.[35]

The most interesting testimony is no doubt a passage from Simplicius' commentary on the *Physics*, which presents the doctrine of ancient Pythagoreanism by resorting to three quotes from Eudorus:

[34] *Contra*, see Fleischer 2016.
[35] On Eudorus, see Bonazzi 2013a, which I will refer to for a more detailed analysis of what follows; against the hypothesis of a school headed by Antiochus in Alexandria, see Hatzimichali 2011: 52–5.

Eudorus and the Beginnings of Platonism

The Pythagoreans put as secondary and elementary principles not only of physical things but simply of everything which is after the one (called by them principle of all things) the opposites; below these, which are not properly principles, they ranked also the two series. Eudorus writes on them: 'It must be said that the Pythagoreans postulated on the highest level the One as principle of all things, and then on a secondary level two principles of completed things, the One and the nature opposed to this. And there are ranked below these all things that are thought of as opposites, the good under the One, the bad under the nature opposed to it. For this reason these two are not regarded as absolute first principles by these philosophers; for if each is principle of a different set, they are not universal principles of all things, as the One is'. And again he says: 'And for this reason, in another way they said that the principle of all things is the One, in so far as matter and all beings are derived from it. This is also the God above'. And then Eudorus, being more exact, says that they set the one as principle, and states that from the one come the elements, which they call by many names: 'Then I say that the followers of Pythagoras leave the One as the principle of all things, but in another way they introduce two ultimate elements. They call these two elements by many names: the first is called ordered, definite, known, male, odd, right, light; its opposite is unordered, indefinite, unknown, female, left, even, darkness. So as principle there is the One, and as elements there are the One and the indefinite Dyad, both one being in turn principle. And it is clear that the One that is principle of all things is distinct from the One opposed to the Dyad, which they also call Monad.'[36]

This is a fundamental text in all respects. First of all, because it is one of the first attestations to the new historical and exegetical way of practising philosophy: it is no longer a matter of investigating or debating problems; rather, the aim of philosophy is to retrieve the ancient master's truth. This translates into an increasing importance of exegesis; philosophy takes the form of a commentary on authoritative texts. The latter are primarily to be identified with Plato and Aristotle: surprising as it may appear, even Simplicius' testimony bears witness to this new tendency. For the purportedly Pythagorean doctrine has nothing to do with the original Pythagoreanism, but stems from a combined interpretation of Plato's *Timaeus* and Aristotle's *Metaphysics*. The distinction between two orders of principles, between the true principle (*arche*) – that is, the transcendent principle, God (the Demiruge) – and the constitutive elements of reality (*stoicheia*) can be inferred through a 'creative' interpretation of the *Timaeus*,

[36] Simpl. *In Phys.* 181.7–30 = Eud. frs. 3–5.

87

traditionally regarded as the Platonic texts which most reflects the influence of Pythagoreanism. But there is more to this: equally if not more important is Aristotle (particularly the so-called 'theology' of *Metaphysics* 12). Not only had Aristotle vigorously affirmed the distinction between a transcendent principle and an immanent element, but he had also deployed this distinction precisely against Plato, by accusing him of having failed to grasp the importance of the transcendent principle, that is, the efficient and divine cause (whereas Forms instead function as formal causes).

Against the background of these polemics, Eudorus' aim is to defend Plato against Aristotle's accusations by identifying, in the former's texts, traces of the very doctrines whose absence the latter had criticised. Within this context, Pythagoreanism plays a crucial role, insofar as it justifies Eudorus' operation: if it is true that Plato is a follower of Pythagoreanism, and that the distinction between principle and elements is a 'Pythagorean' one, it follows that Aristotle's accusation is unfounded. Significant consequences issue from this. The complex genealogy just suggested (Pythagoras-Plato-Aristotle) entails that Plato has already been 'Aristotelised' in order to save him from Aristotle's accusations. By tracing the distinction between principle and element back to a (non-existent) Pythagorean doctrine, and by assuming Plato's dependence on Pythagoreanism, Plato has indeed been saved from Aristotle's criticism – but at the cost of attributing an Aristotelian doctrine to Plato! This concretely translates into a reversing of the letter of the *Timaeus*: in this dialogue the leading role is clearly played by the Forms, whereas the Demiurge is only assigned an intermediary role; but Eudorus' 'Pythagorean' reconstruction makes the Demiurge the highest God, the transcendent principle and true efficient cause, assigning Forms the subordinate role of formal causes.

These may seem like – and probably are – fanciful reconstructions, but what matters for the historian is the fact that they would not appear to be isolated interpretations. Scholars have long shown that in this period a series of Pythagorean apocrypha were produced in Alexandria: a series of treatises passed off as the original texts used by Plato and Aristotle (whom an anonymous *Life of Pythagoras* presents as the ninth and tenth scholarch of the Pythagorean school, respectively).[37] The most famous are *On the Nature of the Cosmos and the Soul*, attributed to Timaeus of Locri, and presented as the text that served as a basis for Plato's *Timaeus*, and Archytas' *On Categories*, alleged to have influenced Aristotle's *Categories*.[38] Usually Archytas is regarded as the more notable figure, and is credited with some of the most important treatises. An extensive fragment from a treatise *On Principles* attributed once again to Archytas states quite clearly what can be reconstructed with much effort through Simplicius' testimony about Eudorus.[39] Archytas claims that there exist two orders of causality, namely a transcendent principle and immanent principles (the components of things). While the principle is expressly defined as the Demiurge (the reference obviously being to the *Timaeus*), God, and the Mover (the reference being to Aristotle's *Metaphysics*), Forms are presented as the formal causes which lend order to matter. This doctrine of three principles (God, Forms or numbers, and matter) became the dominant one throughout the Imperial Age, and all Platonists agreed that it stemmed from an interpretation of Plato's *Timaeus*.

To sum up, the importance of this testimony can hardly be overestimated, as it perfectly illustrates the distinctive features of the new kind of Platonism, especially in its Alexandrian variety:

1) From a methodological perspective, it bears eloquent witness to the fact that by this period philosophy had come to be identified with the exegesis of authoritative texts, starting from the most important text of all, the *Timaeus* (Antiochus, by contrast, lacks this exegetical tendency); besides, it is worth noting that the exegetical tradition in question had always been strong in Alexandria, and not just in the field of philosophy.

2) From a historiographical perspective, it is the first source to attest to the return of Pythagoreanism as a point of reference to grasp the genuine meaning of Plato's philosophy: clearly,

---

[37] See Phot. *Bibl.* cod. 249.438b17–19.

[38] Regarding the *Timaeus*, see the Marg 1972 edition, along with Baltes 1972, and Opsomer and Ulacco 2014; with regard to the second text, see the annotated edition by Szlezák 1972, Boys-Stones 2017, and Hatzimichali 2018.

[39] See ps.-Arch. *De princ.* 19.5–20.17 with Centrone 1992 and Bonazzi 2013b: 386–9; Ulacco 2017: 17–54.

this marked a break with Hellenistic Academics (as well as Antiochus), who had never reckoned Pythagoras among Plato's sources of inspiration; it is interesting to note that, along with Eudorus and the authors of the pseudo-Pythagorean treatises, Thrasyllus and Philo (whom the ancients described as a 'Pythagorean')[40] were also active in Alexandria.

3) Most importantly, from a doctrinal perspective, it shifted the focus back, after a long period of time, to the Platonic problem par excellence: the issue of Plato's relationship with Aristotle (and his criticism). As we have seen, in the case of Eudorus and of the pseudo-Pythagorean treatises, the retrieval of Pythagoreanism was functional to an engagement with Aristotle. This was the main problem in Platonism, which continued to be discussed throughout the following centuries.

One widespread prejudice is the idea that exegesis is a fruitless endeavour, or at any rate one incapable of yielding any original outcomes: Eudorus' case disproves this opinion and stands as an early example of the potentiality of this new way of practising philosophy.

The Doctrine of Principles

Early Imperial Platonism has rightly been described as a battlefield in which different interpretations of Plato vied for supremacy. This fact can hardly be disputed and partly explains scholars' often far from positive opinions on the subject. However, as already remarked, we should not overemphasise the degree of fragmentation of Platonism in this period, for the debate to which it gave rise presupposes a series of recurrent elements that enabled philosophers to operate within a shared field. We have already discussed the underlying assumptions about Plato's philosophy as a perfect system of truth; no less important is the Platonists' religious attitude, which is to say their belief that philosophy must find its culmination in theology. As in the case of Eudorus, this explains why the discussion on the first principle was so central. Platonists

[40] See Runia 1995.

The Doctrine of Principles

endorsed the thesis that the cause of everything is a divine first principle, which they present at times as true being (ὄντως ὄν, the feature usually attributed to the Forms), and at times as the highest deity: this is the first teaching of the dialogues, starting from the *Timaeus*. Certainly, this combination of philosophy and religion is not exclusive to Platonism, as can clearly be inferred through a comparison with Stoicism. However, it is precisely this comparison that brings out the peculiarity and novelty of Platonism, namely its emphasis on transcendence. God is no longer conceived of as being part of our world (as had been the case with the Stoics) but is rather presented as 'other' with respect to it. This transcendent turn entails a substantial recovery of the dualism between the sensible and the intelligible realms, with primacy being assigned to the intelligible dimension.

From this shared foundation numerous variations branch out which are determined by specific problems and by the difficulty of adapting this doctrine to the *Timaeus* and the other dialogues. Clearly, one first problem concerned the nature of this God. The *Timaeus* spoke of the Demiurge, yet the *Republic* – an equally authoritative text – established the Good at the summit of the ontological ladder:[41] how could these two fundamental texts be reconciled? One solution was to identify the Demiurge with the idea of the Good, based on the notion that one of the essential properties of the Demiurge is precisely goodness.[42] Gradually, however, an alternative solution gained importance: in order to defend the idea of the absolute transcendence of the first principle (coinciding with the Form of the Good), philosophers stressed the distinction between this first principle – which, while being the ultimate cause of the universe, is not involved in its creation – and a second God (the Demiurge), who operates concretely on the basis of the first model (after all, the *Timaeus* stated that the Demiurge is good, not that he is the Good). This was to be the solution suggested by Numenius of Apamea.[43] By drawing a further distinction, a hierarchy of three principles came to be established,

---

[41] Plat. *Resp.* 508e2–3.
[42] See Attic. frs. 3.16–25, 12 and 13, as well as Procl. *In Tim.* 1.359.22–27.
[43] Numen. frs. 11–20.

91

where the first is utterly transcendent and the third is identified with the soul, in a way that seems to foreshadow Plotinus' triad of the One, the Intellect, and the Soul: this is the case with Alcinous' *Didaskalikos* and Numenius of Apamea.[44]

Clearly, the difficulties were not merely textual. Another series of problems had to do with the relationship between the divine and intelligible principle on the one hand, and sensible reality on the other: the emphasis on transcendence brought a typically Platonic problem to light, namely the need to reconcile distinct levels of reality. While separation was necessary in order to make God exempt from the imperfections of the sensible realm, it was still necessary to explain in what way the order of this sensible world depended on God's providential intervention. As one would expect from Platonists, this fundamental mediating function is assigned to Forms and mathematical entities.[45] The outcome is a doctrine of three principles: God, Forms (and/or numbers), and matter. Still, it is worth recalling that this doctrine can only be traced back to the *Timaeus* at the price of stretching the text: while the Demiurge takes the role of divine principle, Forms are assigned a mediating and therefore subordinate function – quite the opposite from what we read in Plato's texts. This is a problem we already came across when dealing with Eudorus and which all later Platonists had to face. As already noted, it cannot be ruled out that Aristotle exercised a significant influence: the *Metaphysics* offered not only a view in support of the transcendence of the first principle with respect to physical reality, but also a crucial con-tribution with regard to the relationship between God and Forms: the Aristotelian model, which stressed God's intellectual charac-ter, contributed to the development of the Platonic thesis which solved the problem of the relationship between God and Forms by regarding the latter as 'thoughts of God'. This is one first pos-sibility, which Alcinous expressed most clearly: Forms are 'in

---

[44] See Alcin. *Didasc.* 164.16–27; Numen. frs. 21–22. For an exhaustive overview of the various options, see Opsomer 2005 and Boys-Stones 2018a: 147–83.

[45] For a clear and succinct introduction to the issue of Forms in Middle Platonism, see Ferrari 2005; for a more detailed analysis, see the fifth volume of Baltes and Dörrie 1987–2020 (1998); Dillon 2011; Michalewski 2014: 47–96; Boys-Stones 2018a: 125–46.

relation to God, his thought; in relation to us, the primary object of thought; in relation to matter, measure; in relation to the sensible world, its paradigm; in relation to themselves, essence'.[46] In other words, Forms are the perfect thoughts of the 'things that are in accordance with nature'[47] that God thinks when He gives order to matter; in this respect, they constitute a model for the order of the world and a point of reference for human knowledge. No doubt, this is a brilliant solution. But it does not solve all difficulties.

In particular, insofar as Forms are the thoughts of God, they risk losing their autonomy. The limit of the Aristotelian parallel is evident here because this problem does not emerge at all in relation to the God of the *Metaphysics*, who is the thought of himself. It is hardly surprising, therefore, that an original solution was put forward by Platonists hostile to Aristotle – Atticus comes to mind – or at any rate those interested in Stoicism, such as Longinus. The solution suggested by Longinus – who in many respects is the last author who can be described as a 'Middle Platonist', since he was a contemporary of Plotinus', and Porphyry's first teacher – constitutes a fine example of the Platonists' capacity to appropriate the doctrines of other schools and to adapt them to suit their own aims.[48] To solve the problem, Longinus drew upon the well-known Stoic theory of *lekta*, which entailed a distinction between the act of thinking and the propositional content of thought, which is self-subsistent. Setting out from this view, Longinus was able to reaffirm both the thesis of the Forms' dependence on God and that

---

[46] Alcin. Didasc. 163.14–17. Other significant testimonies may be found in Aët. *Plac.* 1.3.21 and 1.10.3; Hipp. *Ref.* 1.19.2; Phil. Alex. *De opif.* 16; Attic. frs. 9.34–43. Scholars have long sought to identify which Platonist was the first to develop this theory, but the outcome has been a gamut of hypotheses that cover practically all names, from Xenocrates to Antiochus (cf. *supra*, Chapter 2, nn. 120–1), from Posidonius to Seneca (Inwood 2007: 159–61), and from Philo of Larissa (Tarrant 1985: 115–26) to Philo of Alexandria (Radice 1991). At the present state of knowledge it is probably wiser to avoid taking a strong stance: what we can say is that this thesis, which may have even originated with Plato, only acquired crucial importance in the Early Imperial Age. More precisely, as rightly noted by Runia 1986: 523 n. 103 (which I also refer to for further bibliographical references), it is possible to distinguish between the no doubt ancient thesis of a divine intellect that thinks Forms and the more structured and recent thesis that makes these Forms thought by God the paradigm for the creation of the universe.

[47] Alcin. *Didasc.* 163.24; on the Xenocratean origin of this thesis, see Chapter 1, The Doctrine of Principles and the Abandonment of the Theory of Forms, p. 19.

[48] See M. Frede 1990; Männlein-Robert 2001: 536–47.

of their extramental and eternal subsistence.[49] Discussions of this problem thus clearly bring out the two underlying options that were available: 'Stoicism and Aristotelianism would appear to be the two opposite poles between which all Middle Platonic doctrines tend to fluctuate.'[50]

Ever since antiquity, then, the theory of Forms has constituted one of the most important yet also most complex focal points in Platonism. Significantly, it was in relation to this very point that Plotinus made a break with Middle Platonism: in a well-known polemic with Longinus, reported by Porphyry,[51] Plotinus suggested a new way to understand this relationship (and hence also the meaning of the *Timaeus*), namely by identifying Forms with the Intellect: a solution that – as we shall see in the next chapter – was to contribute to a radical renewal of Platonism.

Overall, Early Imperial philosophy came to be dominated by the theory of the three principles – God, Forms, and matter. As in the case of God and Forms, plenty of problems also emerged in relation to matter. The very possibility of considering matter too to be a principle became the object of heated discussions, and rightly so: the idea of a third 'principle' was suggested – as always – by the *Timaeus*, yet it must be noted, once again, that this notion became imbued with meaning that could rather be traced back to Aristotle (or the Stoics). Speaking of Platonic *chora* (the receptacle, the space that receives the ideal Forms) as 'matter' (a term which Plato never uses) was a way to simplify this doctrine; but it also risked misrepresenting it: for it was Aristotle and possibly the Stoics who posited the need for a material causal principle, whereas in the *Timaeus*, *chora* is assigned the role of 'contributing cause', and never of a principle, since it cannot be described as something that fully exists, like the intelligible principles. Thus, some leading Platonists of the Early Imperial Age (Plutarch and Numenius) sought to assign the role of negative principle – opposed to the divine, intelligent, and animated one – not to matter, which is inert in itself, but to an evil and irrational soul, on the basis of a famous

---

[49] See Longin. frs. 17–19; Longinus probably drew upon a thesis by Atticus: see frs. 28.5–7 and 34.6, with the remarks in Baltes 1983: 41–2.

[50] Donini 1982: 116.

[51] See Porph. *Vit. Plot.* 18–21.

passage from the *Laws*.[52] As a consequence, a different doctrine of principles emerged.[53]

Cosmological Issues: The Debate on the Eternity of the Universe

One problem strictly connected to the theological perspective is the cosmological problem of the creation of the world. As already noted in Chapter 1, this problem stems from the controversial passage of the *Timaeus* stating that the world 'it has come to be' (*gegone*, 28b): how is one to understand this expression? Literally, in terms of an actual beginning of the world, or allegorically, by upholding the thesis of the eternity of the world? The debate was a long-standing one: in Book I of *De caelo*, Aristotle had expounded the thesis of creation in time in order to criticise it as absurd, and the Early Academics had responded by offering an allegorical interpretation that (implicitly) accepted the Aristotelian thesis of the eternity of the cosmos, assigning it to Plato (according to this perspective, the *Timaeus* passage was to be regarded as a didactic device adopted by Plato in order to discuss in a clear way an obscure topic such as that of eternity).[54] Most Early Imperial Platonists adopted the ancient Academics' solution, adducing a wide range of explanations.[55] However, the two staunchest opponents of the allegorical interpretation, Plutarch and Atticus, have the merit of having clearly highlighted what was at stake. The problem did not merely revolve around the exegesis of an ambiguous Platonic passage or the engagement with Aristotle; rather, the thesis of the eternity of the cosmos risked undermining the

---

[52] Plat. *Leg.* 896d–e.

[53] Plut. *De an. procr.* 1015a–b; *De Is. et Os.* 369b–d, 370e–371a; Numen. fr. 52; a fundamental work on Plutarch's doctrine of principles and his original conception of matter is Ferrari 1995: 80–104; on Numenius, see Jourdan 2013. Besides, there were many other versions of the doctrine of principles: see vol. 4 of Baltes and Dörrie 1987–2020 (1996: 377–489). Among the most significant are the doctrine of two principles, God and matter, which is attested by an authoritative source, the Peripatetic Theophrastus (fr. 230), and the Academic doctrine of the One and Dyad, which continued to circulate even in the Imperial Age (cf. e.g. Plut. *De def. or.* 428e–f; *De an. procr.* 1024d–f).

[54] See *supra*, Chapter 1, The Academy and the Sciences: Cosmogony, Cosmology, and Mathematics, p. 21–24.

[55] See Baltes 1976: 38–123, and more recently Bonazzi 2017b.

idea of God as a providential craftsman, for if the world is eternal and ungenerated, there is no need for a craftsman to create it or of a providence to preserve its existence.[56] This is why Atticus labelled Aristotle (and each of his followers) as an atheist. The main task for the Middle Platonists supporting the other reading was to show how to reconcile this sempiternalist interpretation with the theological commitment.[57]

In any case, the predominance of theological and metaphysical interests did not entail complete disinterest in more properly scientific issues, as though theology and science could not coexist. On the contrary, scientific enquiry was seen as a privileged avenue for 'theology': as a means to appreciate the beauty and goodness of the universe, as noted by Galen – a physician who was well acquainted with the philosophy of his day.[58] Indeed, in this period we witness a 'genuine scientific resurgence', clearly reflected by Plutarch's dialogue *On the Face of the Moon*, which defends the thesis that the Moon is not a fiery or ethereal body, but one which has the same nature as the Earth (a view which contrasts with the Aristotelian thesis of a clear-cut distinction between the sublunary world and the supralunary world): significantly, many arguments set out from the works of great astronomers and presuppose a considerable knowledge of problems related to the laws of refraction of visual rays. However, the text in question combines pages on such topics with a lengthy myth about daemonology and eschatology. 'Myth and science, daemonology and astrophysics, indeed have the same dignity for Middle Platonism and contribute, each in its own way, to a conception of which they are essential components' – that is, a theological conception of reality.[59] Similar considerations also apply to the arithmetical and mathematical

---

[56] Plut. *De an. procr.* 1015f–1017c; Plat. *quaest.* 1007c–d; Attic. frs. 19, 23, 25.

[57] Among the other Middle Platonists supporting the sempiternalist reading, Taurus is the philosopher whom we have the most information of. For a detailed reconstruction of his views, see now Petrucci 2018a: 76–145.

[58] Galen. *De usu partium* 2.447.23. The case of the great physician of this period, Galen of Pergamon, is rather more complex: an author deeply acquainted with Plato, he repeatedly asserted his own intellectual independence; hence, strictly speaking, he cannot be regarded as a representative of Imperial Platonism (despite the many points of convergence highlighted by Donini 1980): see, most recently, Vegetti 2015.

[59] These quotes are drawn from Donini 1982: 122; on this text by Plutarch, see the exhaustive commentary in Donini 2011.

sciences, which were particularly important for philosophers more interested in the Pythagorean tradition, as we shall see.

Epistemology and Logic

Mention was previously made of the endurance of Hellenistic topics in Early Imperial Platonism. This phenomenon is particularly visible in the case of the theory of knowledge: Middle Platonists believed that a correct reconstruction of Platos's philosophy would finally make it possible to solve the problems fruitlessly tackled by Stoics, Epicureans, and sceptics. The most revealing example of this ambition comes from Chapter 4 of Alcinous' *Didaskalikos*, which is devoted to the epistemological problem par excellence: that of the criterion.[60]

The terms and concepts employed betray a marked dependence on the vocabulary of the Hellenistic schools, yet the Platonists' dualistic approach leads to utterly new outcomes. The Platonists' strategy can clearly be understood with reference to so-called 'common conceptions' (or 'natural conceptions'), one of the Stoic criteria of knowledge.[61] For the Stoics, these common conceptions are 'a fundamental body of concepts common to all men as rational creatures', which are developed according to natural mechanisms, ensuring a correct representation of the world.[62] According to Alcinous, this theory is correct yet incomplete, since it fails to explain how conceptions are formed in the human mind. To claim that they are formed through repeated sense experiences, as the Stoics and Epicureans did, meant exposing oneself to accusations by Academic sceptics, who had argued against the possibility of attaining knowledge precisely by stressing the instability of sense perceptions. Alcinous takes up this criticism, yet without accepting

---

[60] See Alcin. *Didasc.* 154.8–9. In recent years we have witnessed a remarkable increase in studies devoted to this topic; among the most significant, see Schrenk 1991b; Sedley 1996; Boys-Stones 2005; Tarrant 2005; Chiaradonna 2007; and Bonazzi 2015a: 50–64 and 2017b (to which I will also refer for bibliographical references concerning Stoic doctrine).

[61] See *SVF* 2.105 and 473.29–30; for occurrences of the term in Platonic texts, see – among others – Anon. *In Tht.* XXIII 1–12, XLVI 43–49, XLVII 37–48.7; Plut. fr. 215f; Alcin. *Didasc.* 150.20–32. On Antiochus, cf. *supra*, Chapter 2, The Case of Antiochus, pp. 69–70.

[62] Chiaradonna 2007: 210.

the sceptical consequences deriving from it.[63] The rejection of the idea that common conceptions derive from sensible experiences does not rule out another possibility: that they may be innate insofar as they depend on a previous experience of knowledge, namely the vision of Forms before birth.[64] Thus, sensory experience helps awaken the knowledge of Forms in human beings, and this knowledge can then serve as a criterion of truth. The conclusion is that sensible reality cannot be known in itself, but only insofar as it partakes of the intelligible reality. Through this metaphysical reformulation of the Stoic doctrine, Alcinous and the other Middle Platonists, just like Antiochus before them, attempted to subordinate Academic and Stoic arguments to Platonism.

However brilliant, this theory did not so much solve the problem of knowledge once and for all as shift it onto another level: the real crux of the matter was the knowledge of Forms. In practice, in order to be really effective, the identification between Platonic Forms and Stoic common conceptions ought to have been based on an exhaustive knowledge of Forms. Actually, Middle Platonists were unwilling to uphold this view. Certainly, they often spoke of contemplation of Forms; but when it was necessary to be more precise, they were willing to acknowledge that true possession of Forms only occurred prior to the embodiment of the soul,[65] thereby admitting that true knowledge is off limits for human beings in their earthly existence. But if this is the case – if full knowledge of the criterion is impossible – then once again, albeit in a different context, there is a risk of slipping into scepticism, which had based its challenge precisely on an acknowledgement of the impossibility of identifying an uncontroversial criterion for knowledge. Ultimately, this had also been the position adopted by Plutarch, when defending the unitary nature of the Academic tradition as a whole.[66] At times scholars have sought to explain the significance of Plutarch's thesis by arguing that it constituted a resurgence of Academic

[63] Alcin. *Didasc.* 178.4–11.
[64] Alcin. *Didasc.* 155.24–34 with the commentary in Schrenk 1991a.
[65] See especially Alcin. *Didasc.* 155.22–3 and 164.13–18; for a more in-depth discussion, see Bonazzi 2017a: 135–41.
[66] See Bonazzi 2012c.

scepticism, as with Philo and Carneades. But the situation is different here: we can speak of scepticism in Plutarch's case, yet not in the Academic sense. According to Plutarch, the Hellenistic Academics must be regarded as part of the Platonic tradition not because they are sceptics, but because they have shown that scepticism is the inevitable consequence of any empiricist epistemology. It is in this sense that Plutarch can compare the Epicureans to the Pyrrhonists, while reserving a place within the dualistic Platonist tradition for the Hellenistic Academics on the basis of the belief that even Arcesilaus and his colleagues are dualists, deep down, on account of their anti-empiricist polemic. Thus far, the situation is quite clear: in full agreement with Alcinous, Plutarch too maintains that no scientific knowledge of sensible reality is possible. However, as with Alcinous, a problem emerges when we move on to the intelligible reality, the only one where this true knowledge can exist: even more so than Alcinous, Plutarch avoids stating that we can have any complete and exhaustive knowledge of the intelligible principles.[67] On the contrary, the attitude that most distinguishes the true Platonist is one of cautiousness (εὐλάβεια),[68] based on an awareness of the limits of human knowledge. This has been described as a form of 'metaphysical scepticism',[69] which is certainly an appropriate definition, once the distinction compared to the Academic scepticism of the Hellenistic Age has been defined: whereas the main problem for the latter was an epistemological one, related to the difficulty that human beings have in finding a criterion allowing them to establish a relation of certainty with reality, for Plutarch (and other Platonists like him) the problem is primarily ontological, and lies in the acknowledgement that intelligible reality (whose existence is never questioned) eludes man's full understanding. This too is a constitutive problem for Platonism, which even later Platonists were to tackle, leading to some original outcomes – as we shall see in the following chapter.

---

[67] See Plut. *De Is. et Os.* 382f–383a; *De def. or.* 422c.

[68] See especially Plut. *De sera num.* 549e–f; *De Is. et Os.* 382f.

[69] Donini 1986: 216, followed by Ferrari 1995: 20–1 and Bonazzi 2015a: 94–116. Another interesting thinker is Philo of Alexandria, whose emphasis on God's transcendence (and negative theology) also leads to some form of scepticism; see Lévy 1986 and 2016.

Generally speaking, the Early Imperial Age would not appear to have been particularly interested in the study of logic, a discipline which in the Hellenistic Age had instead received considerable attention: only the Peripatetics, who were engaged in interpreting the treatises of the Aristotelian *Organon*, appear to have seriously devoted themselves to such problems. Following a consolidated strategy, Platonists instead sought to appropriate Aristotelian doctrines, by affirming that they were already to be found in the Platonic dialogues: one revealing testimony is Chapter 6 of Alcinous' *Didaskalikos*, which presents syllogism as a Platonic tenet with a definition lifted straight out of the *Prior Analytics*. Where Platonists displayed greater originality is in their engagement with the *Categories* (one of the most widely discussed texts in those years): while Plutarch and the anonymous commentator merely stated that they were already to be found in the dialogues, other philosophers – more specifically, Stoicising Platonists opposed to any reconciliation with Aristotle (Lucius, Nicostratus, Severus, and Atticus) – embarked on a harsher polemic: on the one hand, they carefully criticised alleged inconsistencies in Aristotle's text; on the other, they developed a broader reflection on the problem of substance, with the aim of showing, against Aristotle, that even (or only) intelligible realities can correctly be interpreted as 'substances'.[70] It is easy to see how, once again, the polemic with Aristotle served to address crucial questions.

The Ethical Doctrines and the Problem of Fate

No less interesting is the Platonists' treatment of ethical problems.[71] In opposition to the naturalism which had been dominant in the Hellenistic centuries, Middle Platonists argued that the measure for virtue and that for happiness cannot lie in the human world alone but must be traced back to the divine principle. The

---

[70] See Simpl. *In Cat.* 73.15–28; 76.13–17 and 206.10–15; Attic. fr. 9, with the commentary in Chiaradonna 2005.

[71] One interesting study is Annas 1999, even though it pushes the attempt to reconcile Platonism with Stoicism too hard; the collected volume Pietsch 2013 introduces all the crucial questions. What is also interesting is an analysis of pseudo-Pythagorean treatises: see Centrone 1990.

gradual separation of God from the cosmos marks the transition from a cosmic theology to a metacosmic one: it was felt that it was no longer enough merely to conform to the laws of this world but, rather, that it was necessary to assimilate oneself to God, who is other with respect to us, although we depend on Him. We thus switch from the exhortation to 'live according to nature' to the exhortation to 'assimilate oneself to God', a formula which Middle Platonists were able to trace back to certain passages in the dialogues.[72]

It is noteworthy that this new theory also entailed a more specific conception of the human soul.[73] The soul, the most important part of man, is no longer regarded as homogeneous, but rather as being divided in two parts, a rational part and an irrational one (the latter being further subdivided, consistently with the tripartite psychology of the *Republic*, *Phaedrus*, and *Timaeus*). Whereas the irrational part is connected to the body and its needs, which must not be abolished but kept under control (Platonists are sympathetic to the Aristotelian theory of *metriopatheia*),[74] the former – which is that through which we think – enables us to approach the divine principle. Assimilating oneself to God, then, means rediscovering the divine which is within us, and living in accordance to it.

But what exactly does assimilation to God consist in? Once again, basic agreement does not rule out divergences. In particular, the introduction of a divine hierarchy gave rise to different interpretations: if assimilation concerns the first God, the aim is to live a theoretical life, devoted to contemplation; if it concerns the second God, what is privileged is instead the active, practical ideal. Again, it is interesting to see how exegetical problems ultimately serve to address traditional questions such as that of the contrast between the contemplative and the active life, which continued to

---

[72] Particularly the *Theaetetus* (176b) *Republic* (613a–b), and *Timaeus* (90c–d). The most interesting instance of the use of this formula occurs in a passage from Stobaeus' *Anthologium* (2.50.6–10) that is often attributed to Eudorus; other significant testimonies may be found in D.L. 3.78; Phil. Alex. *De opif.* 144; Plut. *De sera num.* 550d and *De an. procr.* 1014b; Asp. *In Eth. Nic.* 4.8; and Clem. Alex. *Strom.* 5.14.95.1–96.2. The most comprehensive modern study is still Merki 1952; see now Reydams-Schils 2017.

[73] Deuse 1983.

[74] A revealing testimony of this tendency is Plutarch's treatise *On Moral Virtue*: see Opsomer 1994 and Ferrari 2008.

be debated even in the following centuries. However, we should not rule out that Platonists sought to defend both positions,[75] once more proving their loyalty to Plato, given that in the Platonic dialogues too, philosophy consists in reconciling the practical dimension and the theoretical. In order to assimilate oneself to God, it is indeed necessary to engender order and harmony in one's own soul, and only an orderly soul can really engage in contemplation and understand what it means to be similar to the gods.[76]

One last topic is fate and determinism. In this case too, the Platonists' stance is based on a series of Platonic passages that are understood as being normative,[77] but at the same time depends on Hellenistic debates.[78] In the dialogues it is actually difficult to identify a clear position about what later became the fundamental problem in the debates between Stoics, Academics, and Epicureans, namely the need to reconcile the belief in providence and divine intervention with that in the autonomy of human beings' moral agency. As in many other cases, the chief polemical target were the Stoics, whom Platonists accused of being unable to defend the coherence between determinism and freedom: if everything is determined by God, there is no human freedom; if man is free, the thesis that everything is determined by God falls. The solution most typical of Platonists is the idea of conditional fate, which is expressed for instance in a pseudo-Plutarchean treatise *On Fate*: for Platonists,

fate displays the features of a juridical norm, which without imposing specific forms of behaviour on human beings, ineluctably sets forth the consequences of the choices they make. Choices are freely made, then, but their consequence are predetermined; therefore, the law of fate takes the form of a hypothetical necessity, such that while men are free to choose between p and q, p inevitably entails x, whereas z inevitably follows from q. So although fate does not determine every single event, it encompasses all events.[79]

---

[75] See Alcin. *Didasc.* 181.19–35 and Apul. *De Plat.* 2.23.
[76] Plut. *De sera num.* 550d–f; *Ad princ. iner.*, 781f–782a, see Bonazzi 2012b; on Plutarch's practical philosophy see Van Hoof 2010.
[77] Cf. in particular *Resp.* 617e; *Tim.* 41d; *Leg.* 904.
[78] On the connection with Stoicism, see Sharples 2003 and Boys-Stones 2007; interesting remarks can be found in Opsomer 2014a, which provides the clearest overview. Among the most important testimonies, in addition to the pseudo-Plutarchean *De Fato*, see Alcin. *Didasc.* 179.2–3; Calc. *In Tim.* 149; Nemes. *De nat. hom.* 38.304 ff. (an exhaustive collection of sources is discussed in Eliasson 2008: 119–67).
[79] Linguiti 2015.

In adopting this perspective, Platonists believed that they had found a solution that could make up for the limits of the Stoic thesis, insofar as the defence of the presence of the divine (which was instead denied by the Epicureans, the other enemies of Stoic determinism) in any case granted human beings some leeway for responsible, free action.

Numenius and the Pythagorising Platonists

As early as the first century BC, from Eudorus onwards, we witness a major comeback of the Pythagorean tradition within Platonism. Interesting in itself, this renewal of interest also helps qualify the importance of a historiographical category which circulated widely in the past: that of neo-Pythagoreanism.[80] Undoubtedly, in the new historical and cultural climate of the Empire, the Pythagorean ideal exercised a certain appeal, and records survive of attempts to revive the ancient Pythagorean communities' lifestyle (or, at any rate, what was deemed to have been their lifestyle). The most famous attempt was the one made by Apollonius of Tyana (although we should not forget Nigidius Figulus in Rome). However, these attempts probably concern the history of ancient religions more than philosophy: they provide confirmation for the enduring cultural prestige enjoyed by Pythagoras, yet not for any actual resurgence of his philosophy.[81] From the point of view of doctrinal contents, the situation was quite different: what was passed off as a return to Pythagoras' venerable tradition ultimately coincided with the emphasising of certain ideas typical of the Platonism of those years within the context of issues that were, precisely, Platonic concerns. To put it more clearly, the doctrines of these 'Pythagoreans' were closer to those of someone like Plutarch (or perhaps Speusippus) than they were to the doctrines of Philolaus and Archytas. In other words, we should not speak so much of neo-Pythagoreanism as of Pythagorising Platonism: this is the description that best fits Moderatus of

[80] A crucial work in this respect is Centrone 2000b.
[81] See e.g. Centrone 1996: 164–72.

Gades, Nichomacus of Gerasa, and Numenius of Apamea, in addition to the already-discussed Eudorus, Thrasyllus, and the corpus of pseudo-Pythagorean literature.

That this was an 'offshoot' of Platonism,[82] rather than a tradition alternative to it, clearly emerges from all points of view. Historically, the belief that Plato's philosophy was deeply influenced by Pythagoreanism – that Pythagoreanism lay at the heart of Platonism, as Numenius claims[83] – was an opinion essentially accepted by all Platonists. Like all other Platonists, these Pythagorising ones took Plato's philosophy to be a genuinely Pythagorean doctrine: at most they stood out from other Platonists because of their greater interest in the so-called 'unwritten doctrines' of the One/Monad and Dyad compared to the dialogues. Throughout the Imperial Age, 'Pythagorean' and 'Platonist' were de facto synonyms.

As far as contents are concerned, what distinguishes these authors is their focus on mathematical and arithmological investigations. But in this case too, it is evident that such interests were also shared by many other philosophers. For all Platonists the study of mathematics constituted a necessary step towards a full understanding of Plato's philosophy. Particularly revealing, in this respect, is the work by Theon of Smyrna entitled *On Mathematics Useful for the Understanding of Plato*,[84] and no less significant is the proliferation of commentaries on the mathematical sections of the *Timaeus*.[85] In this context, the cosmological speculations of Pythagorising Platonists pushed this tendency to its utmost limits, yet did not mark a real break; besides, it must be noted that for these thinkers too, the study of mathematics (or, more often, investigations on the mystical and symbolic value of numbers) was not intended to replace dialectic in the study of intelligible entities: with the possible exception of Nicomachus of Gerasa, these authors thus proved themselves to be faithful readers of the Republic.[86]

---

[82] Donini 1982: 137.
[83] Cf. Numen. fr. 24.70.
[84] See the recent edition of Petrucci 2012.
[85] See Ferrari 2000 and Petrucci 2019.
[86] See e.g. Moderatus *ap. Porph. Vit. Pythag.* 49–50; on Nicomachus, see O'Meara 1989: 17 and Tornau 2000.

No different is the situation as far as metaphysical and cosmological doctrines are concerned. As one would expect, what distinguishes these authors is a greater stress on the role of mathematics: it is numbers and geometrical shapes, not Forms, that are taken to mediate between the first principle – described either as the 'One' or as the 'Monad' – and matter (which is often presented as the 'dyad', echoing Academic philosophy and Plato's unwritten doctrines). Yet both the terms used to define the divine first principle and the mediating role of numbers and geometrical shapes are far from unique to these authors:[87] the use of Old-Academic terminology is common to all Middle Platonists (and, conversely, these Pythagorising Platonists do not hesitate to refer to the first principle as 'intellect' or 'God'), whereas authors such as Plutarch show that the importance of mathematical entities as mediators was also acknowledged outside 'Pythagorising' circles.[88] Scholars have further noted that these authors apparently multiplied the hierarchies of principles, and have discussed whether they distinguished between the One and the Demiurge.[89] But in this case too, if we look beyond the terminology used, we find no real differences with respect to a Platonist like Alcinous. Indeed, it may well be argued that with regard to such issues the philosophers in question display an even more evident dependence on Platonism: for these 'Pythagorising' authors too, it was ultimately a matter of building a cosmology on the basis of the *Timaeus*.

One author traditionally associated with this tradition is Numenius of Apamea, arguably the most interesting philosopher of the Early Imperial Age. In his case, the adherence to Platonism is even more clear-cut: we find the usual claims as to Pythagoras'

[87] See Nicomach. *Intr. ar.* 1.4.2; *Theol. ar.* 44.7–13.
[88] See Ferrari 1995: 115–71.
[89] In a famous article of 1928, Dodds suggested that the references to the One by these authors can be explained by reference to the *Parmenides*: according to this view, it was therefore such circles that gave rise to the metaphysical interpretation of the *Parmenides* which Plotinus was to develop further, so as to completely renew the framework of Platonism; see also Tarrant 1993. One revealing testimony in this respect concerns the doctrine of the three Ones which Simplicius attributes to Moderatus (in Simpl. *In Phys.* 230.34). However, this passage actually shows the limits of Dodd's interpretation, for it is difficult to distinguish between the original core doctrines of the 'Pythagoreans' and those which Neoplatonist commentators attribute to them – see Steel 2002b. In the absence of clear testimonies, we must be careful not to project later doctrines onto earlier authors.

superiority and priority, yet not the kind of focus on mathematical sciences that might be taken to distinguish the philosophers just discussed. For Numenius, the philosophical point of reference undoubtedly remains Plato, and more specifically the *Timaeus*.[90]

Regrettably, the biographical information we have is very limited: as far as we know, he lived in the second century AD in Apamea, a lively religious melting pot in the Orontes Valley in northern Syria, which continued to serve as an important centre for Platonism even in later periods: Plotinus' pupil Amelius moved there with the aim of studying Numenius' philosophy, and later Iamblichus too was to teach there. The information about Amelius confirms the remarkable popularity of Numenius: unlike many other Middle Platonists, he continued to attract considerable interest (as well as criticism) from the Neoplatonists; even more significant is the attention which Christians devoted to him. If we are quite well informed about his philosophy (particularly the two works *On the Dissension of the Academics from Plato* and *On the Good*), this is thanks to the many quotes in Eusebius of Caesarea's *Praeparatio Evangelica*.

The pamphlet on the Academics' betrayal of Plato is a document of primary importance on the polemic about identity that the Platonists were obsessed with in this period: with great satirical verve, Numenius accuses the Academics of having betrayed Plato's genuine message, a message which actually was only a clearer version of Pythagoras' teaching.[91] What is original in this polemic is not so much the harsh attack which the author launches against Academic Sceptics (at times with comical effects, as in fr. 26, where he recounts how Lacydes was deceived by his slaves); rather, what is most original is the fact that the charge of betrayal is directed against all Academics: according to Numenius, the first seeds of the dissension destined to tear Plato to shreds like Pentheus were first sown by Xenocrates.[92] It cannot be ruled out that this attack on the whole Academic tradition was directed not so much against what by then would have been remote figures,

[90] See Baltes 1976
[91] Numen. fr. 24.70. It is worth stressing, once more, that this statement does not change what has been argued so far: Pythagoras' priority is affirmed only in order to then present Platonic theses as Pythagorean.
[92] Numen. fr. 24.71–2.

such as Arcesilaus and Carneades, but rather against those, such as Plutarch and the anonymous *Theaetetus* commentator, who had defended a unitary interpretation of its history.[93] Also significant is the attempt to connect the truths of Plato/Pythagoras to the Oriental traditions of the Persians, Egyptians, Indians, and Hebrews (particularly famous is the statement 'Who is Plato, if not an Attic-speaking Moses?' in fr. 4; Numenius also shows to be familiar with and appreciate Jesus' teaching: see fr. 10a). The idea of an ancient Oriental lore had always fascinated the Greeks and finds interesting parallels in the works of other Platonists (for example, Plutarch's treatise *On Isis and Osiris*). With Numenius we witness an acceleration of this tendency. Indeed, it has been argued that one of his aims was to establish an 'ecumenical theology', by combining into a single system the various paths followed by human beings to reunite with God.[94] The same tendency is reflected by the numerous doctrinal convergences with the *Chaldean Oracles*, another key document bearing witness to this syncretism between philosophy and religion which enjoyed considerable prominence in late antiquity – as we shall see later on.

Despite what some leading scholars have argued,[95] this 'appeal to the Oriental wisdom' must not be understood as the subordinating of Platonism to religious traditions: on the contrary, Plato remained the point of reference and criterion for evaluating these Oriental doctrines (which in any case stemmed from widely different worlds – Egypt, Persia, India, and Hebrew Palestine). In the important fr. 1 from the treatise *On the Good* – a programmatic passage that asserts the need to look back, beyond Plato, to the doctrines of the Brahmins, Chaldeans, Egyptians, and Hebrews – Numenius does not argue that Plato derived his knowledge from foreign traditions; rather, he regards religion and philosophy as the two parallel sources of wisdom, while at the same time affirming

---

[93] Donini 1987: 5074–5.

[94] Athanassiadi 2006: 71–107: 77. More generally, on the topic of Platonism and Eastern wisdom, see the exhaustive overview in the second volume of Baltes and Dörrie 1987–2020.

[95] Puech 1934 has been particularly influential; the thesis was then taken up by Turner 2001, whose (questionable) ideas about the priority of Gnosticism over Platonism I will discuss later.

that the latter, which is to say Plato, is the yardstick for the truth of the former. Eastern traditions are valid insofar as they 'agree with Plato'.[96] Thus, Numenius exploits religion to support his metaphysical ideas.[97] In other words, as in the case of many other authors from this period, Numenius' openness to a theological dimension can hardly be disputed. Yet this should not lead to the rash conclusion that what we are dealing with is some kind of 'Eastern mirage': the Eastern that is invoked is often an ideological construct that conceals problems and ideas that are typical of Platonism.[98]

Mention has already been made of Numenius' doctrines in the previous chapters: often regarded as an eclectic and unsystematic thinker, Numenius actually proved capable of developing original solutions, destined to influence the development of Platonism over the following centuries. By setting out from a radically dualistic approach that draws a contrast between matter, which is suffused with an evil soul,[99] and the intelligent divine principle, Numenius then further divided the first principle into different levels: he distinguished between a first, transcendent God and a second principle charged with the creation of the universe. In itself, this distinction is a fine example of Platonist interpretation, insofar as it makes it possible to more clearly lay out the relationship which subordinates the *Timaeus*' Demiurge to the *Republic*'s Form of the Good.[100] The many exegetical problems raised by the *Timaeus* also account for a further division proposed by Numenius, who states that the second God must actually be understood in a twofold sense: for on the one hand we have the thinking intellect (coinciding with the eidetic paradigm), and on the other the God concretely ordering the world (coinciding with the Demiurge and possibly the world soul). Like a good helmsman, 'regulating his rudder according to the Forms', by receiving 'the faculties of judgement' through contemplation, the

---

[96] Numen. fr. 1.8.
[97] See M. Frede 1987: 144; Burnyeat 2005: 144; and especially van Nuffelen 2011: 79, who provides the most enlightening discussion on the relations between Platonism (and philosophy more generally) and religious traditions in the Imperial Age. Plutarch's case in the *On Isis and Osiris* is not different; see Petrucci 2016.
[98] Besides, Numenius would appear to have been equally interested in Greek (and Roman) religious traditions; no less significant are his interpretations of Homer, which we know about from Porphyry's *On the Cave of the Nymphs*: Lamberton 1986: 54–77.
[99] See Numen. fr. 52 with the commentary in Jourdan 2013.
[100] Numen. fr. 20.

Demiurge steers the world across the sea of matter'.[101] Compared
to the traditional interpretation, which are more or less implicitly
forced to support the thesis of the Demiurge's superiority over
Forms, Numenius' solution is certainly brilliant.

A leading representative of Platonism, Numenius is also the philosopher who radicalised some of its tendencies. We have already
noted his emphasis on the transcendence of the first principle;
much the same holds true with regard to his dualism: the opposition between two souls, one good (the divine intellect) and the other
evil (and connected to matter), also applies to human beings, who
in turn are marked by this polarity and opposition between a rational soul and an irrational one.[102] Given the connection between
this irrational soul and matter and evil, it is also easy to understand
why Numenius' philosophy entailed a highly ascetic attitude and
a desire to take flight towards the realm of divine principles.[103]
Undoubtedly, all these ideas – from the tripartition of principles
to asceticism – foreshadow tendencies that shortly afterwards
were to be fully developed within Neoplatonism. Significantly,
Plotinus was accused by his contemporaries of having plagiarised
Numenius.[104] However, as others have rightly observed, it is not in
doctrinal ideas that Numenius' influence must be sought:

What is most striking is not so much the similarity or identity of certain doctrines:
the triadic structure of the divine figures and the succession of hypostases find
equally precise parallels in the Middle Platonist field. Rather, what brings these
figures closer to Plotinus and his successors than to Alcinous, or to Apuleius,
Plutarch, and Galen, is their narrowing down of the philosophical perspective to
the metaphysical and theological dimension. In the neo-Pythagoreans we no longer find any trace of the colourful and at times rather disorderly interests of the
Middle-Platonists; there is no longer any room for history, science, and novels;
it seems as though they marked the beginning of the process of compression of
philosophy into the metaphysical dimension alone.[105]

---

[101] Num. fr. 18. See also fr. 16.10–12: 'the second God, being double, is personally responsible both for producing the form of himself, and for producing the cosmos; he is on
the one hand a creator, on the other wholly absorbed in contemplation' (transl. Boys-
Stones 2018b: 180–1, slightly modified).
[102] Num. frs. 43–4.
[103] Num. fr. 2.
[104] Porph. *Vit. Plot.* 17.1–6 and 16–24; 18.1–6. Concerning the meaning of this polemic,
see Bonazzi 2015a: 117–35.
[105] Donini 1982: 146.

In this respect, authors such as Numenius would appear to represent the closest point of reference for the authors of the following centuries.

Platonism and Eastern Religions

One interesting aspect of the history of Platonism in the Early Imperial Age is its widespread popularity: the success progressively achieved by Platonist philosophers is not confined to debates between schools but concerns the cultural and intellectual life of the Imperial world as a whole. In particular, considering the theological bent of this movement, we should not be surprised to discover that it established mutually influential relationships with the varied world of religious traditions, especially the Eastern ones which in the same period spread to every corner of the Empire: from Gnosticism to Hermeticism, from Mithraism to Manichaeanism, all these religious traditions present indisputable points of contact with Platonism. De facto, this is a crucial moment in the history of Western thought, for it is in this context that the encounter with Christianity occurred (which I will briefly discuss in Appendix 2). Leaving this last issue aside, there are two cases that are particularly worthy of discussion: the Chaldaean Oracles and Gnosticism.

The Oracles are probably the most revealing testimony to the success of Platonism and its capacity to expand among religious traditions.[106] The Chaldean Oracles are a collection of oracles (many fragments of which have been preserved) that a mysterious figure, Julian (who probably lived under Marcus Aurelius, between AD 161 and 180) reportedly received not only from the gods, but also from Plato's soul (with whom Julian claimed to be in contact: his father had introduced him to the great philosopher's spirit).[107]

---

[106] The fundamental study remains Lewy 1978; for a succinct overview, see Finamore and Iles Johnston 2010; the collection edited by Seng and Tardieu 2010 instead discusses the main trends in specialist research on the topic. The reference editions are des Places 1971 and Majercik 1989.

[107] According to Michael Psellus' testimony, περὶ τῆς χρυσῆς ἀλύσεως, 216.24, quoted by Dodds 1951: 289.

This deification of Plato is certainly something new and original, yet it does not change the frame of reference of the Oracles, whose theology is but a new version of the Middle Platonist version of the doctrine: with a marked predilection for triadic forms, these Oracles present a hierarchy of three gods, respectively identified as a supreme Intellect, the Father, from whom a second intellect springs, the Son, who gives rise to a World Soul (possibly to be identified with Hecate), along with a plethora of minor deities. The references to Numenius and the usual *Timaeus* passages are evident and have sometimes been taken to suggest that the Oracles were initially formulated in Apamea, where an important temple of Zeus Bel was located.[108] While difficult to prove, this hypothesis still has the merit of highlighting the peculiarity of these oracles, which stand out not so much on account of their doctrinal content, but for the soteriological anxiety pervading them: steeped in magical elements, they introduced theurgy into Platonism for the first time, which is to say the belief that it is possible to enter directly in contact with the gods, either by bringing them to descend or by leading the human soul to ascend. Undoubtedly, the modern reader may feel inclined to smile at such matters and to view them as typical expressions of the mounting irrationalism of that epoch. However, upon closer scrutiny, we find that the recurrent problem for Platonism was at play, namely the possibility of reuniting with the first principles. This is one of the reasons why the Oracles were to enjoy such great popularity over the course of the following centuries, down to the Byzantine Age and beyond: Franz Cumont termed them the 'Neoplatonist Bible' – a fitting definition, if ever there was one.[109]

No less interesting is the case of Gnosticism. In 1945, in a cave near the Egyptian city of Nag Hammadi, a fortuitous discovery was made of 53 Gnostic treatises written in Coptic, which significantly increased our knowledge of a movement which up until then had practically only been known through the polemics

---

[108] Athanassiadi 2006: 47–64.
[109] Cumont 2006: 195 and 288, n. 87. On the importance of the Chaldaean Oracles in Neoplatonism, see *infra*, Chapter 4, The Aim of Human Life: From Ethics to Contemplation and Theurgy, pp. 166–167.

of Christians (who were rarely interested in providing an objective presentation of it).[110] More specifically, scholars identified a group of eleven treatises that, while falling within the same conceptual and spiritual coordinates as the rest, stood out because of their extensive use of doctrines and terms that could be traced back to the world of philosophical schools – Stoic and especially Platonic ones. The expression 'Sethian Gnosticism' has been coined in relation to these texts, on account of the importance played within them by Seth, the true son of Adam and true saviour. The aim of these treatises, which take the concrete form of revelations (most notably, *Zostrianos*, *Allogenes*, the *Three Steles of Seth*, and *Marsanes*), is to enlighten the believer, so as to enable him to flee from a world that is believed to be the work of an evil Demiurge: the 'Gnostic' is he who possesses true knowledge. No doubt, the emphasis on the importance on knowledge, as well as the theme of flight, are ideas that also occur in the Platonism of those years, and the same applies to many of the elements that make up the (complex or, rather, confused) cosmologies of these treatises: first of all, in a position of absolute transcendence, we find the first principle, the unknowable One or invisible Spirit (from which the threefold power of the invisible Spirit derives); we then find the intelligible realm, which is filled by a tripartite divine Intellect, the Aeon of Barbelo, which in turn encompasses three sub-aeons (Kalyptos, Protophanes, and Autogenes), which in turn preside over another realm; below these are the three lower psychic realms, which are characterised by time and movement, and which contain souls that are still transmigrating; finally, we have the 'physical' world.[111] The parallels with certain Platonist doctrines have led some scholars to suggest that the authors of these texts were inspired by Numenius.[112]

What seems more untenable is the tendency of some recent scholars to assume that these 'Sethian' Gnostics played an active role in the history of Platonism, arguing that some of the most important innovations of Plotinus and Porphyry found their first,

---

[110] A concise up-to-date overview can be found in Moore and Turner 2010.
[111] The fundamental study remains Turner 2001.
[112] See e.g. Tardieu 1996, followed by Brisson 1999.

embryonic expression precisely in these forms of 'mythological Platonism'. As far as I can tell, this is an entirely unfounded hypothesis.[113] All we know for certain from our sources is that some specific terms and theories were borrowed in religious contexts foreign to the world of Platonism, and in ways that often lead to a genuine distortion of Platonic philosophy: while Platonists may have agreed on the importance of the theme of assimilation to God, no Platonist – certainly not Numenius[114] – ever dreamt of speaking of the world as something created by an evil deity, or of dividing human beings between the elect and the non-elect. As far as the indiscriminate proliferation of metaphysical levels (so-called 'aeons') goes, we get the impression that the contrived application of Platonist terms and ideas was only a device used to ennoble a system whose structure is difficult to reconstruct, in an effort to make it less muddled. Similar considerations also hold in the case of Plotinus, whose polemic can once again be explained as an attempt to confirm the profound differences to be found between Platonism and Gnosticism despite their shared terminology.[115] Plotinus and Porphyry would always have found themselves in agreement with Numenius or Plutarch with regard to one point at least: the belief that, notwithstanding the powerful appeal of Eastern lore, with its myths and remote origins, the centre of all reflection would always be Plato and his dialogues. This is the discriminating line between the philosophy of Platonism, in all of its long and varied history, and the instrumental appropriation of traditional religious lore.[116]

---

[113] For a discussion of this proposal, see Bonazzi 2016 with a further bibliography (to which we should also add Burns 2014). Besides, without delving into the meanders of the history of religion, it is worth noting that reasonable doubts have been expressed as to the very existence of a non-Christian Sethian Gnosticism. Authors who uphold the hypothesis of its existence rely on the crucial testimony from Chapter 16 of Porphyry's *Life of Plotinus*; but in this chapter – as Tardieu 1992 has compellingly shown – Plotinus' opponents are most certainly Christians. If we wish to use Porphyry's testimony, as these scholars do, we need to clarify this problem – something they have failed to do.

[114] Cf. Numen. fr. 16.16–17.

[115] On the relations between Plotinus and the Gnostics, see the balanced overview by D'Ancona Costa 2012: 985–92.

[116] Much the same also applies, of course, to other prominent religious phenomena in the Roman world, such as Hermeticism and Mithraism: see Copenhaver 1992 and Turcan 1975.

A Philosophy for the Empire

No less revelatory of the growing success of Platonism is its impact on the literary world, an aspect that has not always received the attention it deserves. While not crucial from a doctrinal perspective, the history of this reception is highly important – for imperial philosophy even more so than for literature: it was also through the intermediation of rhetors and writers that philosophy became an integral part of *paideia*, which is to say of the system of values on which the Imperial society of Graeco-Roman municipalities was founded.[117] In this case too, Platonism played a leading role, as may be inferred from the leading figures of this period, active in different fields. Platonism was of considerable interest to Maximus of Tyre (the second half of the second century AD), one of the most widely appreciated orators of his day, whose speeches may be viewed as an effort to popularise all the most important topics discussed in the philosophical schools, from the nature of God to demonology, from *eros* to reminiscence: a popularisation effort which, as has rightly been observed, was tailored to a public eager to receive reassurance with regard to the major questions of God, providence, and the possibility of individual salvation.[118]

If we still harbour doubts as to the growing popularity of Platonism in all erudite circles of the Empire, we only need to consider two masterpieces of Imperial literature: Plutarch's *Parallel Lives* and Apuleius' *Metamorphoses* are the work of two staunch Platonists; in their own way, these texts too may be regarded as memorable expressions of Platonist philosophy. Besides, as though through in curious coincidence, these two works, when viewed together, constitute a literary transposition of the traditional tensions within Platonic philosophy, and of its fluctuation between contemplative flight and political commitment: whereas Lucius' extraordinary adventures illustrate the journey of a soul aspiring to attain the divine (they even feature his religious initiation into the cult of Isis), Plutarch, through his

---

[117] See Trapp 2007a.
[118] Trapp 2007b: 481 and Lauwers 2015; as regards Maximus more specifically, see the edition by Trapp 1997.

account of the feats of many Greek and Roman heroes, embarks on an often disenchanted enquiry into the possibility that philosophy might concretely contribute to the betterment of human society.[119] Plutarch, a firm believer in the importance of (Platonic) philosophy, captures more than any other author the friction springing from the encounter between divine philosophy and human history, as may be especially inferred from his *Life of Dio*, discussing Plato's favourite pupil, who had risked damaging his city precisely in his effort to follow Platonic precepts.[120] Even more than Plutarch's philosophical treatises, certain remarks in his *Lives* reveal just how deeply he reflected on Plato's teaching in all of its richness and variety.

---

[119] On the *Metamorphoses*, see Pottle 1978, Donini 1982: 133–5, and Fletcher 2014: 262–92; on the *Parallel Lives*, see Duff 1999 and Bonazzi 2012b, with a further bibliography.

[120] Plut. *Vit. Dionis* 47.5–8, and the remarks in Pelling 2004 and Bonazzi 2020b.

4

THE TRIUMPH OF THE SYSTEM: NEOPLATONISM

It is a widespread opinion that over the course of the third century AD a new phase emerged in the history of Platonism: these were the centuries of late antiquity and of so-called 'Neoplatonism'.[1] This classification is acceptable, but with some qualifications. The first question which must be asked concerns the very term used to describe late antique Platonism. Introduced around the late eighteenth century, this term was originally designed to convey a markedly negative evaluation: 'Neoplatonism' alluded to an exhausted tradition, which had little to do with the freshness of Plato's philosophy, as by then it had fallen prey to irrationalism and to the religious traditions stemming from the Eastern areas of the Empire, or even from beyond its borders.[2] The problem, then, is the eternal dilemma between East and West, and some eminent Orientalists of the past even looked at these Platonists' philosophy more benevolently, precisely because they harboured a more favourable opinion about Eastern civilisations. However, a reassessment of this sort matters little to anyone seeking to truly understand Neoplatonism in all its richness and complexity. After all, Neoplatonism was an essentially Greek phenomenon, and most importantly a philosophical one, in the sense that its history primarily reflects philosophical interests and motivations. Like all philosophers throughout the ages, Neoplatonists were sons of their

---

[1] Classic introductions are Wallis 1972 and Lloyd 1990; more recently, see Remes 2008, Tuominen 2009, Chiaradonna 2012, and especially the collection of studies edited by Remes and Slaveva-Griffin 2014, and the new edition of the Überweg-Prächter, *Grundriss der Geschichte der Philosophie*, edited by Riedweg, Horn, and Wyrwa 2018 (with an extensive bibliography); Sorabji 2004 too is very useful. A remarkable initiative is the translation of most of the Neoplatonist commentaries in 'The Ancient Commentators on Aristotle Project' (see www.ancientcommentators.org.uk).

[2] See Catana 2013, with an extensive bibliography. As Gersh 2019: 7 aptly remarks, the idea that Plotinus was introducing some novelties was already present in the works of Ficino and his followers (such as Francesco Giorgi, who speaks of *Platonici novitiores*).

own epoch; yet possible conditionings and external influences do not inevitably rule out genuinely philosophical themes and motifs, as we shall see again and again. Neoplatonist philosophy is an interesting philosophy both in itself and in relation to Plato's thought. As in the Middle Platonists' case, it is worth noting that the 'Neoplatonists' would disdainfully reject this label and present themselves as nothing but interpreters of Plato's truth.[3] From an exegetical standpoint as well, their reflection presents some highly interesting aspects.

Two further points may help to correctly frame our discussion of this segment of ancient Platonism's history. The first concerns the relationship between Neoplatonism and Middle Platonism: since the latter label was first introduced, we tend to think of these two philosophies as though they were different and had little or nothing in common. But this is a fallacious assessment, which risks engendering serious misunderstandings. Between the two movements there are some evident differences, as the Neoplatonists themselves were keen to emphasise in their writings. Yet these differences emerged out of a common background, which is that of philosophical schools and of the attempt to develop a systematic and consistent exegesis of the dialogues' philosophy, designed to highlight the primacy of the metaphysical and theological aspect in Plato's thought. Without going so far as to abolish the distinction between Middle Platonism and Neoplatonism (as some scholars have suggested),[4] we must certainly take this element into account.[5] And there is also a second reason why we must do so.

---

[3] Plotinus 6.3[44].1.12 and 6.2[43].1.3–5 are revealing in this respect: 'the next thing would be to say how these things look to us, trying to lead back our own thoughts to the thought of Plato'.

[4] See Catana 2013; while certainly interesting, this suggestion risks raising more problems than it solves, as already noted by Donini 1990: 82–3, when discussing a similar (yet more cautious) suggestion made by M. Frede 1987: 1041. Useful remarks can also be found in Remes and Slaveva-Griffin 2014: 1–13.

[5] No less misleading is the thesis according to which Middle Platonism is a mere 'preparation for Neoplatonism', to quote the title of the famous book by Theiler 1930: once again, the relation of continuity and discontinuity between Middle Platonism and Neoplatonism cannot be reduced to a mere relationship of subordination, whereby what comes later determines the value and meaning of what comes before it. As we shall see, certain points of continuity are indeed to be found, but there are also certain aspects of Middle Platonist philosophy that were abandoned.

Whether we realise it or not, the opposition between Middle Platonism and Neoplatonism implies an opposition between a free period and a closed one in the history of Platonism, which are evaluated differently according to each scholar's perspective. Those scholars who appreciate open research will tend to positively reappraise the apparently chaotic nature of Middle Platonism, which other scholars will instead criticise because of its alleged inconclusiveness. For the same yet opposite reasons, some scholars will criticise the rigidity of Neoplatonism, while others will praise its systematising rigour. But this is a misleading opposition, because Neoplatonism cannot be regarded as a monolithic philosophy that traversed the centuries unchanged. On the contrary, recent studies have shown the endurance of tensions and divergences against a common background – exactly as in the case of Middle Platonism, albeit for different reasons. Reconstructing this diversity and grasping the reasons for these divergences constitutes the best introduction to Neoplatonism and the clearest explanation for what makes it interesting: for in the case of these so-called Neoplatonists as well, we will find that tensions and divergences ultimately depend on the fluctuations marking Plato's writings. And if we bear in mind that Plato's fluctuations are the fluctuations of philosophy, it will be easy to understand why it is interesting and important to retrace the paths taken by the Neoplatonists.

A Map of Neoplatonism. The First Stage: Ammonius and Plotinus

Ancients and moderns agree that over the course of the third century AD, significant innovations were introduced that changed Platonism's doctrinal coordinates. Where they disagree, at least partly, is on the issue of who promoted these innovations. According to the ancients, a decisive role was played by Ammonius Saccas, an elusive figure for us: many modern scholars have studied this philosopher, but few have claimed a central place for him, choosing instead to assign such a role to Plotinus.[6]

---

[6] See esp. Hierocl. *De prov.* Ap Phot. *Bibl.* 214.172a. Among the moderns, see Schwyzer 1983, Baltes 1985, Schroeder 1987, Schibli 2002: 4–5, 28–31, and Karamanolis 2006: 191–215. The only scholar stressing Ammonius' role as a founder is DePalma Digeser

No doubt, Ammonius comes across as an important figure in third-century Platonism: his pupils in Alexandria include almost all the leading philosophers of his epoch, from Longinus to Origen and Plotinus. From a philosophical standpoint, the importance of his role would appear to be confirmed by the aim he assigned to his teaching, namely the reconciling of Plato and Aristotle; this was no doubt to prove a central problem in the following centuries. But in the absence of more explicit testimonies, these elements, however important, are not enough to justify the thesis that Ammonius inaugurated a new phase in the history of Platonism. First of all, the identity of some of his presumed pupils remains to be established; it is not clear whether the Origen who visited Plotinus' courses and accused him of having betrayed the promise not to reveal his master's teachings (*Vit. Plot.* 14.20–25) coincides with the great Christian theologian:[7] there is no certainty on this matter. Most importantly, even aside from this problem, what would the teachings that Plotinus revealed be? Actually, it is quite clear that many of Ammonius' pupils did not at all accept the most important innovations that Plotinus presented in his courses, so it is unclear why we ought to credit Ammonius with theses which we know were first developed by Plotinus, and which other pupils of Ammonius' disputed: Porphyry even informs us of a polemic between Longinus and Plotinus on the issue of intelligibles.[8] As far as Aristotle's teaching is concerned, while this was no doubt a fundamental topic for the Neoplatonists, it had already been such for the Middle Platonists; no less important is the fact that very divergent views about it were later to be held, starting once again from Plotinus, a reader of Aristotle who is as perceptive as he is polemical. The available testimonies, then, allow us to claim that Ammonius was a relevant personality, yet do not authorise us to embark on rash speculation about his alleged role as an innovator.

2012, who has gone so far as to introduce the term 'Ammonians' to describe third- and fourth-century Neoplatonists. But this thesis is certainly difficult to support in the light of our current knowledge.

[7] See the detailed analysis by Zambon 2011.

[8] On Origen and Plotinus, see O'Brien 1992 and Riedweg 2018; on Longinus and Plotinus, see Bonazzi 2015a: 126–35.

Plotinus' case is completely different,[9] as we are quite well informed about him thanks to his pupil Porphyry, who appended to his edition of Plotinus' works a rather detailed biography (albeit one that proves somewhat reticent and ambiguous at times, since it was also designed to celebrate Porphyry as Plotinus' truest disciple).[10] Born in Lycopolis, Egypt, in 205, Plotinus led a rather eventful life, despite his manifest detachment from mundane concerns: after studying under Ammonius in Alexandria for roughly ten years (232–43), he accompanied Emperor Gordian on his eastern campaign, as he was eager to become acquainted with the philosophies of the Persians and Indians. Following Gordian's defeat and death, Plotinus sought refuge first in Antioch and then in Rome (244), where he began to present his doctrines. A lively group of pupils soon gathered around him, comprising students and philosophers but also influential personalities from the Imperial court. After becoming close with Emperor Gallienus and his consort, Plotinus even sought to establish a philosophers' city in Campania which he called Platonopolis, as he wished to model it after the laws that Plato had laid out in his dialogues. Court intrigues prevented him from accomplishing this project; in the last years of his life, a sick man, he went to Campania, where he died in 270. Curiously enough, Plotinus started producing written works quite late, around the age of fifty, possibly because, along with his fellow disciples, he had sworn not to divulge Ammonius' thought in writing (but we have already noted how Plotinus' thought and writings can hardly be traced back to Ammonius in their entirety). Plotinus' pupil Porphyry then compiled these texts (sometimes in a rather strained way) into the *Enneads*, which is to say six groups of nine treatises, according to arithmological principles and their contents: the first *Ennead* dealt with ethics, the second with physics, the third with cosmology, the fourth with the soul, the fifth with Intellect, and the sixth with the One. These treatises do not

---

[9] The critical literature on Plotinus is enormous: two clear and incisive introductions are O'Meara 1993 and Chiaradonna 2009; see now Emilsson 2017 and Gerson and Wilberding 2022; another crucial resource is D'Ancona 2012, which provides a discussion of all the main issues in Plotinus' philosophy in the light of the most important studies.

[10] One exhaustive study of this biography is Brisson et al. 1982–92; see also the notes of Kalligas 2014.

make for light reading; however, they encapsulate one of the most profound reflections in ancient philosophy, one which is of crucial importance for understanding Neoplatonism, as much as for appreciating Plato's thought under a new light.

Platonism in the Third and Fourth Centuries: The Contrast between Porphyry and Iamblichus

Plotinus' most important pupil, from both a philosophical and a historical perspective, was no doubt Porphyry (234–305),[11] who was responsible for producing an edition of the *Enneads* in 301. Born in Tyre, Phoenicia, he first attended Longinus' lectures and then moved to Rome, joining Plotinus' school (263–8). It is tempting to see this move as symbolising the transition to a new form of Platonism, but the situation is rather more complex, because one of Porphyry's distinguishing features is apparently his attempt to save part of the Middle Platonist exegetical tradition by making it compatible with the new Plotinian theses.[12] Plotinus emerges as the first Platonist interested in developing a close, and often polemical, engagement with Aristotle's treatises; Porphyry is instead the first Platonist to have written systematic commentaries on Aristotle's works with the aim of showing their inherent consistency with Plato's thought.[13] This task of conciliation fit within the current inaugurated by the Middle Platonists and was developed by taking Plotinus' teaching into account: through Porphyry's mediation, Aristotelian philosophy was to find an established place within the Neoplatonic course of studies, as a subject preliminary to the study of Plato.[14] Within this work of reorganising philosophical material, we should also include a brief treatise providing an introduction to the *Categories*, and hence to logic: the *Isagoge*, which was destined to enjoy remarkable success over the course of late antiquity and the Middle Ages.

---

[11] See Karamanolis 2006: 243–330; Smith 2010.
[12] A fundamental study in this respect is Zambon 2002; new evidence is now available thanks to the recent publication of the Syriac translation of Porphyry's treatise *On Principles and Matter*, see Arzhanov 2021.
[13] The fragments of Porphyry's commentaries on Aristotle and Plato have been edited by Smith 1993.
[14] See Chiaradonna 2012: 88–92; and Karamanolis 2018.

Finally, no less significant was Porphyry's interest in Pythagoras and Pythagoreanism: he devoted numerous writings to this tradition, from a *Life of Pythagoras* (part of a four-volume *History of Philosophy*) to the treatise *On Abstinence from Killing Animals*, from a treatise on *Philosophy from Oracles* to the *Letter to Marcella*, which provides a compelling overview of Porphyry's thought.

Clearly, this reference to Pythagoreanism was hardly a new element in the history of Imperial Platonism, and the same is true of the attempt to subordinate to Plato even the truths of Eastern (Persian, Egyptian, Chaldaean, etc.) religions and traditions – let us think of Numenius or of Plutarch's *Isis and Osiris*.[15] However, what was new was the use to which Porphyry intended to put these traditions. The problem was no longer merely philosophical, and the plan to build a unitary Greek philosophical tradition, revolving around Plato, reflected a more general anti-Christian polemic: the values of Platonic philosophy were now being defended as a bastion of pagan culture. Some scholars have gone so far as to suggest that Porphyry was the mastermind behind the great persecution which Diocletian launched in 303. Intriguing as it may be, this is a widely disputed hypothesis that is difficult to prove; what is certain is that Christians were aware of the subtlety and dangerousness of his polemic, as it emerges from the treatise *Against the Christians*: at least four attempted refutations are known (Lactantius, Arnobius, Eusebius, and Methodius), in addition to an Imperial condemnation.[16]

While authoritative and well respected, Porphyry's star soon faded even in pagan milieus, where it was eclipsed by the success of a pupil of his, Iamblichus of Chalcis (c. 240–325), who eventually established his own school in Apamea (where Numenius and Amelius had already taught) in polemical opposition to his former teacher.[17] Iamblichus' break with Porphyry concerns one of the

---

[15] While sharing Numenius and Plutarch's aims (to subordinate all pagan traditions and lore to Plato's philosophy), Porphyry's project does not entirely overlap with those of these two philosophers: see Johnson 2013.

[16] On Porphyry's anti-Christian polemics, see Appendix 2, Platonists against Christianity, p. 193–194.

[17] The most detailed study remains Dalsgaard Larsen 1972, which also includes a collection of testimonies and fragments (to be integrated with Dillon 1973 and Cardullo 1995–2000); more recently, see the succinct introduction by Dillon 2010 and the new edition of *On the Soul* by Dillon and Finamore 2002.

most delicate and controversial points in Neoplatonist philosophy, namely theurgy. Porphyry's cautiousness on the matter, which reflects his position as an heir to Plotinian rationalism, stands in contrast to Iamblichus' staunch defence of theurgy, particularly in his *Response of the Master Abamon to Porphyry's Letter to Anebo* (better known today as *On the Mysteries of the Egyptians*, the title which Marsilio Ficino gave to his 1497 translation of the work). This is conceived as a refutation of the 'entire subversion of all the ceremonies of religion' (*De myst.* 5.26), and as an affirmation of the need for ritual and ceremonial practices as fundamental preliminary steps allowing one to enter into contact with divine entities. According to Porphyry, the only true path is that of philosophy; according to Iamblichus, this is no longer enough, and what is required is the true divine science of theurgy.[18] The crucial turn towards religion is undeniable, although Iamblichus denies that it translates into a form of irrationalism; indeed, as we shall see, this turn also depends on philosophical problems which are typical of Platonism (more specifically, the rejection of the thesis according to which the soul remains partly in contact with the intelligible realm).[19]

Iamblichus' heartfelt defence of theurgical practices, along with his emphasis on the *Chaldean Oracles* as the text expressing the most important truths,[20] has often stood at the basis of a non-philosophical interpretation of his thought. Yet nothing could be further from the truth, as this openness to religion does not at all entail a rejection of the more technical and scholastic aspects of philosophical reflection. On the contrary, Iamblichus is responsible for two major innovations which concern the doctrinal framework of Neoplatonist philosophy and the way in which lessons were organised in schools. The doctrinal innovation is his Pythagoreanising turn:[21] Pythagoras

---

[18] A recent edition of this fundamental text is Saffrey and Segonds 2013; see also the studies by Saffrey collected in Saffrey 2000: 39–100; another very useful work is Taormina 1999, to which we can add the more recent Tanaseanu-Döbler 2013.

[19] See Taormina 1999: 133–58.

[20] See Chapter 3, Platonism and Eastern Religions, pp. 110–113.

[21] Iamblichus is the author of the imposing work *On the Pythagorean School*, comprising ten treatises (only a few of which survive: *Protrepticus*, *Life of Pythagoras*, *On the General Science of Mathematics*, *Nicomachus' Introduction to Arithmetic*, and *The Theology of Arithmetic*). An important work on Iamblichus' Pythagoreanism is O'Meara 1989: 30–105; a helpful overview can be found in Taormina 2012: 113–21.

and Pythagoreanism had already been central for Porphyry and the Middle Platonists, but with Iamblichus they acquired a position of absolute prominence which was destined to shape philosophical research as a whole. This choice entailed significant consequences, particularly in relation to Aristotle. Iamblichus picked up Porphyry's view, reversing it: Porphyry had adopted an essentially sober stance, seeking to understand Aristotle through his writings and postponing the study of Platonism's metaphysical truths to a later stage of study; for Iamblichus, by contrast, a commentary on Aristotle cannot be developed simply by focusing on Aristotelian problems, but must unfold according to Platonic and Pythagorean intellectual principles (this is the so-called 'intellectual doctrine', νοερὰ θεωρία: see Simpl. *In Cat.* 2.13–14).[22] The best-known example of this is the *Commentary on the Categories*,[23] which shows how Iamblichus' Pythagorean sources were not the works of genuine Pythagoreans from the sixth and fifth centuries BC, but pseudo-Pythagorean treatises of the first century BC, which betrayed very strong Platonist influences: the attempt to 'Pythagorise Aristotle' thus ultimately amounted to a 'Platonising of Aristotle'.[24]

As far as school-teaching goes, it was Iamblichus who established the canon of Plato's dialogues, thereby giving definite form to a centuries-old series of suggestions and attempts. Setting out from the exegetical assumption that each dialogue had a specific *skopos*, a single central topic, Iamblichus organised the reading of Plato in such a way as to turn it into a process of ethical and intellectual purification able to lead the soul to a suitable understanding of itself and of the highest principles: a first reading cycle began with the *First Alcibiades*, as self-knowledge is a preparatory step to the investigation of external things; subsequently, with the *Gorgias* and *Phaedo*, students would approach the ethical virtues (i.e. political and purificatory ones), while the *Cratylus* and *Theaetetus* served the purpose of introducing them to the

---

[22] See Cardullo 1997.

[23] Iamblichus had also written commentaries pertaining to subjects such as *On Interpretation*, *Prior Analytics*, *On the Heavens*, and *On the Soul*; fragments survive of many of his Platonic commentaries (*Alcibiades*, *Phaedo*, *Phaedrus*, *Sophist*, *Philebus*, *Timaeus*, and *Parmenides*); see Dalsgaard Larsen 1972 and Dillon 1973.

[24] It even seems as though Iamblichus went as far as to attribute Plato's theory of Forms to Aristotle: see Elias[David], *Commentary on the Categories*, 123.2–3 Busse.

study of logical entities (names and concepts, respectively), the *Sophist* and *Statesman* to the study of the physical world, and the *Phaedrus* and *Symposium* to that of theological entities; finally, the *Philebus* would provide a first contact with that Good which lies beyond all things. This first cycle would be followed by a reading of the two most important dialogues, the *Timaeus* (on the physical world) and the *Parmenides* (on theology).[25] These were the greater mysteries, which followed the lesser mysteries, namely the study of certain Aristotelian treatises.[26] As Karl Praechter famously remarked, such innovations make Iamblichus a kind of second founder of Neoplatonism.

The little information we have makes it impossible to reconstruct fourth-century developments in detail.[27] In the past, scholars were left with the impression of an undisputed triumph of Iamblichus and his school. However, a degree of caution is advisable. Certainly, quite a few of Iamblichus' pupils ranked among the most well-respected philosophers of their day. They later came together in the Pergamon school established by Aedesius, which placed particular emphasis on theurgy. Many of the philosophers who can be traced back to this tradition even played a leading role in the Imperial court, as in the case of Sopater of Apamea under Constantine, and even more so of Maximus of Ephesus, Chrystanthius, and Priscus during Julian's short reign (361–3).[28] Yet, alongside these figures, we should not forget the names of other philosophers, operating both within and outside the Imperial court, who were reluctant to accept Iamblichus' innovations:[29] this was the case with Theodorus of Asine and Dexippus, who were closer to Porphyry, but much the same holds true for the court philosopher and orator Themistius, the author of some paraphrases of Aristotle that reveal an eloquent silence with regard

---

[25] See Anon. *Prol. In Plat. phil.* 26.39.16–40, 44 Westerink with the comments in Dalsgaard Larsen 1972, vol. I, 332–40.

[26] For a detailed description of all these reading schemes, see now I. Hadot 1990.

[27] Valuable information may nonetheless be gleaned from Eunapius' biographies: see Goulet 2001.

[28] I will discuss Julian more extensively in Appendix 1, which deals with political Platonism: see Appendix 1, Two Political Platonists: Marcus Tulles Cicero and Flavius Claudius Julianus, pp. 183–185. On Iamblichus' other pupils, see Tanaseanu-Döbler 2008.

[29] See Chiaradonna 2012: 94–6.

to any Pythagoreanising reading.[30] As is widely known, in the long run it was the Iamblichean model that prevailed, particularly in Athens, where a militant Platonic community flourished in the early fifth century.

The School of Athens

Athens today has nothing exceptional, apart from the names of the places. Just as, once the victim has been consumed, the hide remains as a trace of the beast that it was, so, philosophy having migrated from here, all that is left for a visitor to admire are the Academy, the Lyceum [...]. Athens, once home to the wise, is now only honoured by beekeepers.[31]

Synesius' judgement, while somewhat acrimonious (after all, it expresses the Alexandrian point of view), may have held true in his day, but was promptly disproved over the course of the two following centuries, which witnessed the resurgence in Athens of a staunchly (Neo)Platonist philosophical tradition. It was inaugurated in the early fifth century by Plutarch of Athens, who drew upon certain doctrinal ideas of the Syrian and Iamblichean schools (Synesius polemically alludes to him in his letter). The School of Athens was then led by Syrianus (432–7), Proclus (437–85), Marinus, Isidorus, Zenodotus, and Damascius (515–29).[32] The primary aim of this school, shared by all its representatives, was the attempt to establish a 'theological science' capable of combining a concern with mysticism and salvation (hence the interest

---

[30] His paraphrases of *On the Soul*, *Posterior Analytics*, and *Physics* have survived in Greek; those of *On the Heavens* and Book 12 of the *Metaphysics* in Arabic; on Themistius in general, see Kupreeva 2010; and on his political thought, see Appendix 1, Two Political Platonists: Marcus Tulles Cicero and Flavius Claudius Julianus, p. 184.

[31] Sines. *Ep.* 136 (written after 399). These polemics were later recalled by Damascius, who drew the following comparison between Isidore (an Alexandrian philosopher who later became the head of the Athenian School) and Hypatia (Synesius' teacher): 'Isidore and Hypathia were very different, not only as man differs from woman, but as a true philosopher differs from a mathematician' (*Hist. phil.* fr. E 164 Zintzen = 106 Athanassiadi).

[32] The most relevant figure is no doubt Proclus (412–85), who has been the object of numerous studies, including the classic Beierwaltes 1979; more recently, see Martijn 2010, Steel 2010, Chlup 2012, and d'Hoine and Martijn 2017. Among Proclus' most significant works, we should note his *Commentary on the Timaeus*, *Commentary on the Parmenides*, *Elements of Theology*, and *Platonic Theology*. As regards Syrianus, see the profile drawn in Longo 2010 and the collection of studies edited by Longo 2009.

in the *Chaldaean Oracles*, Orphism, and theurgy) with the arguments of the dialogues – especially the *Parmenides*. One crucial contribution with regard to traditional lore was provided by Syrianus, who in a (regrettably lost) work bearing the revealing title *On the Agreement Between Orpheus, Pythagoras, Plato, and the Chaldaean Oracles* reinforced the belief that Platonic philosophy was the point of conjunction of all religious traditions.[33] No less important was the role played by Syrianus (and Plutarch) with respect to the interpretation of the dialogues: exegesis was not regarded merely as a stage in the activity of teaching, but rather as part of a process of the conversion of the soul to the divine and intelligible principles. This originally Iamblichean plan was pursued by all the most authoritative representatives of the school and reached its culmination in two great works of Proclus', his *Commentary on the Parmenides* and the *Platonic Theology* (to which we may add the *Commentary on the Timaeus*).

According to Proclus, the history of Platonism, once Plotinus' light has dispelled the darkness of the Hellenistic Academy and Early Imperial Platonist babble (*Theol. Plat.* 1.1), is the history of the interpretation of the *Parmenides* (for in it lies 'Plato's only and perfect theory')[34] and of the (progressively fine-tuned) attempt to assign the correct level of reality to each of the hypotheses discussed in the dialogue. In it, Plotinus had found an allusion to an absolutely transcendent principle (the One), followed by another two hypostases. Proclus – in this respect the heir to a long season of fruitful insights and interpretive errors – was instead to account for all the *Parmenides'* hypotheses 'scientifically' by distinguishing between the first five (which set out from the hypothesis of the One in order to describe all things) and the last four (which instead deny the existence of the One).[35] In another work, the *Elements of Theology*, Proclus was to provide a thorough demonstration of this metaphysical structure, highlighting its underlying causal connections.

The *Parmenides'* importance, of course, was not to be affirmed to the detriment of the mystical truths expressed in the *Chaldaean*

[33] See Saffrey 1992.
[34] Procl. *Theol. Plat.* 1.7.32.1–12 Westerink and Saffrey.
[35] On Neoplatonist interpretations of the *Parmenides*, see Steel 2002b.

Oracles. Indeed, Proclus went so far as to argue that, out of all existing texts, he would only spare two, the *Timaeus* (on account of the truths it expresses about the physical world) and the *Chaldaean Oracles*, which he thus regarded as being on a par with the *Parmenides*, if not even clearer in their exposition of certain doctrines. No less important than Platonic dialectic and the inspired verses of the *Chaldaean Oracles* were the other pagan religious traditions, which expressed the same lofty truths in different ways (via myth, in the case of Homer and Hesiod, and via images in the Pythagoreans' case). Recombining the scattered limbs of this tradition into a 'scientific theology' so as to show their unity and coherence was these authors' aim: an aim which found a clear polemical target in Christianity, which was so despised by the Neoplatonists that it is not even mentioned in their works, if not through coded expressions known only to the initiated.

The last noteworthy philosopher, Damascius of Damascus (c. 460–540), who frequently travelled between Athens and Alexandria, emerges as the critical soul of this grand foundational project.[36] While sharing its underlying framework, Damascius embarked on a painstaking revision of all the doctrines at its basis: by highlighting their theoretical and argumentative inconsistencies, he often reached very different outcomes from Proclus (drawing closer to Iamblichus instead). This is especially true when it comes to the soul (whose impassiveness is denied)[37] and even more so to the first principle, which Damascius pushes to such levels of transcendence as to verge on absolute negation: the Platonists' quest ends in ineffable silence and 'supreme ignorance'.[38]

The pursuits of the School of Athens, a genuine ideological bastion of paganism and Neoplatonism, were not merely the concern of a self-enclosed sect, since the Emperor himself, Justinian, stepped in to close it down in 529: evidently, the School was still having an

---

[36] A succinct presentation may be found in Hoffmann 1994 and van Riel 2010; see also Napoli 2008 and Metry-Tresson 2012. Several works by Damascius have been preserved: a *Treatise on First Principles*, commentaries on Plato (*Parmenides, Phaedo, Philebus*), and a *Life of Isodorus* (also known as *Philosophos historia*).
[37] See Steel 1978: 77–119.
[38] See Linguiti 1990.

impact on the society of its day.[39] Along with another seven philosophers, Damascius then set off for Persia, to visit Khosrow I's court, in the belief that there 'as Plato's argument goes, philosophy and kingship are conjoined'.[40] This hope was soon shattered, since by 532 he and his pupils had returned within the borders of the Roman Empire, where Damascius was allowed to continue professing his religious beliefs as long as he did not divulge them. Scholars are still debating whether they stopped at Harran (ancient Carrhae, where the Roman army famously suffered a defeat in 53 BC), or whether they made their way back to Athens.[41]

Neoplatonism in Alexandria

The year 529, when the School of Athens was closed down, is the date which conventionally marks the end of ancient philosophy. In Alexandria, however, philosophers took little notice and continued to teach and comment on Aristotle and Plato for quite some time. All irony aside, the most pressing problem for modern scholars is to define the relationship between the two centres and opposing hypotheses have been authoritatively defended. In a well-known article of 1910, German historian Karl Praechter argued for a substantial difference between Athens and Alexandria, noting that the Alexandrian philosophers had chiefly focused on Aristotle, a less controversial author with respect to the ideological and religious problems of the time, devoting themselves to logical and physical issues. In 1978, Ilsetraut Hadot instead upheld the opposite thesis. Alexandrian philosophical production chiefly survives in the form of commentaries on Aristotle, which constituted the initial stage of the course of study: the fact that more challenging metaphysical theses are missing from these texts is hardly surprising and certainly cannot be invoked to defend the hypothesis of a different

---

[39] A useful overview is Di Branco 2006: 115–79. However, we should not forget that Justinian's measures were primarily directed against Christian heretics; see Wildberg 2005: 329–33 (who also suggests that the journey to Persia was made no earlier than 532).

[40] Agathias, 2.30.3.

[41] The hypothesis that Simplicius and the other Neoplatonists remained in Harran was first put forward by Tardieu 1987; it was then taken up by von Thiel 1999 and criticised by Luna 2001.

underlying orientation. Besides, the ancient sources inform us of regular exchanges between the two schools.[42] In other words, the School of Athens and that of Alexandria were closely connected and shared the same doctrinal framework. It is only the history of the transmission of their texts that prevents us from correctly reconstructing this web of relations.

As is often the case, it is likely that the truth lies somewhere in the middle:[43] in all likelihood, the Alexandrians continued to subscribe to the methods and teachings of the Athenians, with whom they remained personally in contact; but, at the same time, the different situation in Alexandria also led to the development of a different kind of Platonism, one more interested in its logical and scientific aspects (which would explain Aristotle's centrality)[44] than in theological ones (the scant emphasis on Orphic and Chaldaean texts is revealing in this respect).[45] One evident consequence of all this clearly emerges in these philosophers' relationship with Christians: whereas in Athens the rift would appear to have been unbridgeable, in Alexandria we find a greater permeability between the two worlds, marked by the influx of Christian students and even, at a later stage, by the presence of Christian teachers (besides, we should not overlook the fact that the Athenian School was a private institution, whereas the Alexandrian one depended on public funding). Along with some interesting figures (for example, Hierocles, Hermias, and Olympiodorus), the most noteworthy – or at any rate best-known – thinkers are Ammonius, son of Hermias, John Philoponus, and Simplicius of Cilicia. Ammonius (440–517 or 526) is better known for the charges levelled against him than

---

[42] To provide just a few examples: Hierocles of Alexandria was a pupil of Plutarch of Athens; Proclus initially studied in Athens, as did Damascius.

[43] See D'Ancona 2005. For a useful overview of the Justinian age, see Wildberg 2005.

[44] Indeed, numerous Aristotelian commentaries have been preserved: on the *Categories* (Ammonius, Olympiodorus, Philoponus, Elias, David), the *Analytics* (Ammonius, Philoponus), *On Interpretation* (Ammonius), *On the Soul* (Philoponus), *On Generation and Corruption* (Philoponus), *On the Heavens* (Philoponus), the *Meteorologica* (Olympiodorus, Philoponus), *Physics* (Philoponus), and *Metaphysics* (Asclepius). Also important are the commentaries on Porphyry's *Isagoge* (Ammonius, Olympiodorus, Elias, David). As far as Plato is concerned, we have Olympiodorus' commentaries on the *First Alcibiades* and *Gorgias*.

[45] See the balanced analysis by D'Ancona 2005.

for his philosophical reflections.[46] A pupil of Proclus' in Athens and the founder of the Alexandrian exegetical tradition, he was accused of betrayal because he was the only philosopher to continue his activities after the anti-pagan enquiry carried out by Nicomedes, an Imperial envoy: Ammonius was suspected of having struck an agreement with the Christian patriarch, Peter Mongus. Be that as it may, Ammonius does not discuss theurgy or the *Chaldaean Oracles*, which is to say those elements of Platonism hostile to Christianity; however, it is equally true that he continued to profess theories incompatible with Christian dogmas, such as the eternity of the universe, which led him to be attacked by his pupil Zacharias (later the Bishop of Mytilene) in a dialogue entitled *Ammonius, on the Creation of the Universe, against the Philosophers.*[47] Another pupil of Ammonius' was John Philoponus, one of the foremost Christian Platonists.[48] The author of important commentaries on Aristotle, he too took a stance against the idea of the eternity of the universe in a polemical treatise entitled *On the Eternity of the Universe against Proclus*, in which he criticised a doctrine – that of the eternity of the cosmos – that practically all previous Platonists had upheld. On account of its year of composition and publication (529), this text has been regarded by some scholars as having been composed for the sake of conformism and opportunism (Philoponus would have written it to distance himself from the other Platonists, or at any rate to curry favour with the Imperial authorities). However, this may simply have been a coincidence.[49] Finally, Simplicius (c. 490–560), who studied under Ammonius in Alexandria and then joined Damascius on his journey to Persia, may be regarded as an exemplary representative of the Alexandrian school tradition: by that time, 'philosophy had completely come to coincide with exegesis'.[50] His commentaries aim to present Platonism as

---

[46] See Blank 2010. A recent collection of essays edited by Joosse 2021 is a good introduction to Olympiodrus and the Alexandrian milieu.

[47] On Zacharias, see Champion 2014.

[48] See Verrycken 2010 and Giardina 2012.

[49] See D'Ancona Costa 2005: 12.

[50] Chiaradonna 2012, 99. On Simplicius, see Gavray 2007 and Baltussen 2008; his commentaries on the *Categories*, *On the Heavens*, and *Physics* survive, while scholars are still debating his authorship of the commentary on *On the Soul* which has been transmitted

the culmination of Greek philosophy; hence, they contain a vast number of direct quotations that make them an invaluable source (without these works, we would have little by Parmenides, for example). Simplicius, in other words, witnessed the twilight of the pagan world, yet ensured the survival of one of its loftiest legacies, which in those very centuries was beginning to spread to neighbouring areas in Syriac (Sergius, Uranius), Armenian (David the Invincible), and even Persian (Paul the Persian): this was the beginning of a long journey which many centuries later – via Latin,[51] Arabic, and Byzantine mediation – was to bring Greek philosophy back to Europe.

The Doctrine of Principles: The One and the Hierarchical Structure of Reality

The useful yet potentially misleading categories of Middle Platonism and Neoplatonism are often taken to suggest that we are dealing with two different systems of thought, united in their shared reference to Plato yet otherwise having little in common. This is an inexact, or rather incomplete, view, since Neoplatonist philosophy developed in the same school context as Middle Platonism by addressing the same problems and following similar routes. Besides, Porphyry himself is keen to mention that, during Plotinus' classes, students used to read and discuss works by the leading Platonists and Aristotelians of their day.[52] If any differences and

---

under his name in the manuscript tradition: it seems more likely that this text is the work of Priscian of Lydia, one of the last representatives of the Athenian School – see Steel 2006, 273–85. Simplicius also wrote a commentary on Epictetus' *Manual*.

[51] The main Platonic thinkers of late antiquity in the Western part of the Empire were Christians (Victorinus, Ambrose, Augustine, Boethius), which is why we will examine them briefly in Appendix 2. Obviously, though, this does not mean that there were no pagan Neoplatonists in Rome: on the contrary, even thinkers such as Macrobius (late fourth to early fifth centuries, the author of an important commentary on the *Somnium Scipionis*, the final section of Cicero's *De Republica*, and of the *Saturnaliorum libri*, a more or less fictional account of the erudite conversations of some learned Roman aristocrats in 384) and Martianus Capella (active in Africa in the fifth century, the author of the famous *De nuptiis Mercurii et Philologiae*, a sort of encyclopaedia of Classical culture) significantly contributed to the spread of Platonist philosophy over the following centuries; see Courcelle 1943 and Gersh 1986.

[52] *Vit. Plot.* 14, which expressly mentions the names of Severus, Chronius, Numenius, Gaius, and Atticus (along with the Peripatetics Aspasius, Alexander, and Adrastus).

The Doctrine of Principles

novelties are to be found, it is in the greater rigour of the answers
provided and in a greater awareness of what certain exegetical and
philosophical choices entail: Middle Platonists often seem uncertain with regard to the fluctuations, ambiguities, and difficulties
emerging from Plato's texts and the philosophical problems they
entail; by contrast, what makes Plotinus such an interesting and
significant figure is precisely the clear-cut nature of his choices
(although, as we shall see, tensions and fluctuations endure with
regard to many specific points). In this respect, his philosophy constitutes a genuine watershed in the history of Platonism.

This emerges with clarity in the case of his doctrine of principles.[53] As previously noted, arranging the material of the dialogues into a systematic theory of principles had already been
Middle Platonists' chief aim. We have also seen how, in the early
Imperial Age, philosophers constantly emphasised the existence
of a divine and unitary first principle in the development of such
doctrines. Furthermore, we should bear in mind that many later
Middle Platonists, those closest to Plotinus, always stressed the
transcendent character of this first principle. The famous Plotinian
theory that places the One at the head of the whole of reality might
therefore seem like a new variation on this theme. This is partly
true, so much so that the importance of his ideas was not immediately appreciated: to the more hostile among his contemporaries,
Plotinus was a plagiariser of Numenius – to everyone else he was
the inheritor of his teachings.[54]

Yet things stand quite differently: while setting out from the
same context as Numenius and addressing the same problems,
Plotinus developed a thesis that marked a radical break with previous theses. Certainly, the *Enneads* feature plenty of discussions of
the first principle that remind one of Middle Platonist discussions:
the first principle is identified with the Good[55] and with God,[56]
and is presented as the ultimate cause of everything;[57] it is said to

---

[53] See Linguiti 2012a, Lavaud 2008, and Remes 2008: 35–75; also very helpful are
remarks on the causality of the first principle in D'Ancona 1996.
[54] See Bonazzi 2015a: 126–35.
[55] 2.9[33].1; 5.5[32].12–13; 6.7[38].16.27.
[56] 2.9[32].6.32; 5.3[49].7.1.
[57] 5.5[32].13.35–36; 6.8[39].18.38.

133

coincide with being,[58] life,[59] act,[60] and thought;[61] and in treatise 6.8[39] Plotinus goes so far as to speak of the will and love of this first principle. However, these qualifications are part of what Plotinus describes as a 'persuasive' discourse,[62] conscious of how difficult it is to address the issue of the first principle: for all the properties we attribute to it are not actually properties of the first principle, but only our own (6.9[9].3.49–51). The philosopher displays far greater conceptual rigour when it comes to developing a complete doctrine of transcendence: the outcome is the conception of a first principle, the One, which is absolutely simple[63] and completely other compared to everything else.[64]

The One must therefore be spoken of according to a process known as the 'negative way' or 'negative theology' (also known as 'apophatic theology'): we can only speak of it by denying the predicates we would tend to attribute to it. The One, then, is an absence of determinations: it lacks any limit, shape, or parts; it is neither in one particular place nor in no place at all; it is neither in motion nor at rest; it is not in time and is devoid of being; strictly speaking, it is not even a cause, being, principle, or even one (5.5[32].6.30–37). Nor can it be said to have self-knowledge, because this too would amount to denying its unity and simplicity (insofar as having a knower and a thing that is known introduces a first form of duality):

The One is not therefore Intellect, but before Intellect. For Intellect is one of the beings, but that is not anything, but before each and everything, and is not being; for being has a kind of shape of being, but that has no shape, not even intelligible shape. For since the nature of the One is generative of all things it is not any of them. It is not therefore something or qualified or quantitative or intellect or soul; it is not in movement or at rest, not in place, not in time, but 'itself by itself of single form' [Plat. *Symp.* 211b], or rather formless, being before all form, before movement and before rest.[65]

[58] 5.5[32].13.12–13; 6.7[38].24.6; 6.8[39].16.19–21.
[59] 5.4[7].2.18–19; 6.8[39].16.32.
[60] 6.8[39].20.9.
[61] 5.4[7].2.18–19; 6.8[39].16.32.
[62] 6.8[39].13.4 and 47–50 with Szlezák 1979: 155–60.
[63] 1.6[1].7.9–10; 3.8[30].10.22.
[64] 3.8[30].9.47–49; 5.3[49].11.18; 6.7[38].32.12–13; 6.9[9].3.37.
[65] 6.9[9].3.36–45.

The Doctrine of Principles

In its state of complete separateness or aloneness […] the One is 'not something', which is 'other' than everything; and for this reason, it cannot in any way be ranked together with the things that exist through it and after it.[66]

Through this doctrine, Plotinus developed one of the most interesting theories in the history of ancient Platonism, from both an exegetical and philosophical perspective. From an exegetical standpoint (without overlooking the fact that, according to Plotinus as for all Imperial Platonists, exegesis and philosophy coincided), Plotinus' solution also represented a brilliant interpretation of Plato. Like Numenius before him, Plotinus found an important point of support in the *Republic*, which speaks precisely of the Idea of the Good as the principle which lies beyond everything: 'the Good is not being (*ousia*), but superior to it in rank and power.'[67] However, more rigorously than Numenius, Plotinus stressed the fact that the expression 'beyond' (*epekeina*) was also to be understood with reference to being: being beyond everything also implies to transcend being. Within this context, Plotinus emphasised the importance of a hitherto relatively overlooked dialogue. Middle Platonists had read the *Parmenides* – especially the second part, featuring the hypothesis on the One – as a logical and dialectical exercise. According to Plotinus, the *Parmenides* is instead the metaphysical-theological dialogue par excellence;[68] it is a dialogue dealing with true reality and leading us to the heart of Platonic philosophy: the discussion of the hypotheses on the One lays out the metaphysical structure of reality (in particular, the first hypothesis explains that if the One is, it cannot be many, but only itself). From Plotinus onwards, the most important dialogue become the *Parmenides*, which established itself as a crucial point of reference.

Through his interpretation, Plotinus found a remarkable solution to one of the problems that had always vexed Platonists, namely the need to safeguard the intelligible first principles. This is the so-called 'Third Man' problem (or problem of the self-predication of

---

[66] Linguiti 2012a: 197. This idea is already present in the works of some Middle Platonists, most notably that of Philo of Alexandria; see Whittaker 1973: 77–86 and Runia 2002: 308–12.

[67] Plat. *Resp.* 509b.

[68] The importance of the *Parmenides* for Plotinus has been highlighted in a well-known and pioneering article by Dodds 1928.

the Ideas), which we have already encountered with Speusippus:[69] not unlike the Academic, yet in a far more radical way, Plotinus emphasised the ontological difference between a cause and what is caused; by thus denying that the principle possesses that of which it is a cause, he solved the problem at its very root.

Evidently, such an interpretation of Plato entails highly significant philosophical consequences. The search for the first principle (or first cause), on which everything else depends, is a central problem in Greek philosophy. Ever since the pre-Socratics, the aim of philosophy has been to find what lies at the basis of reality, and that upon which everything depends. More precisely, the aim of this reductionism is to identify that unitary principle which orders and governs the multiplicity of reality; if the multiplicity of sensible things which we experience is defined by its composite character, it is a matter of finding the cause which holds these aggregates together; and, evidently, this cause must be simple. The Platonists' position also entailed another, crucial, point: insofar as sensible reality is defined by its composite character, the principle (or principles) we are looking for cannot be part of the sensible dimension but must be 'other' with respect to it. Usually, for the Platonists, this 'other' pointed to the intelligible world of Forms, the so-called *kosmos noetos*; but according to Plotinus, the intelligible realm lacks the kind of complete simplicity and unity we are looking for (we will be returning to this point later on) – hence the need to posit another, even higher principle that lies 'beyond' (*epekeina*). In other words, the task of philosophy is to search for that simple cause capable of ensuring the unity of the aggregates we experience; this first cause cannot be found in either a corporeal element (as many pre-Socratics, and later the Stoics and Epicureans, presumed) or an intelligible principle (previous' Platonist thesis: the intelligible too, as we shall see, entails a degree of duality). All that is left, then, is the One:

It is by the One that all beings are beings, both those which are primarily beings and those which are in any sense to be among beings. For what could anything be if it was not one? For if things are deprived of the one which is predicated of

---

[69] See e.g. D'Ancona 1992; on Speusippus, cf. Chapter 1, The Doctrine of Principles and the Abandonment of the Theory of Forms, n. 44.

them they are not those things. For an army does not exist if it is not one, nor a chorus or a flock if they are not one. [...] And again the bodies of plants and animals, each of which is one, if they escape their one by being broken up into a multiplicity, lose the substance they had and are no longer what they were.[70]

While addressing the same problem as previous philosophers, Plotinus reached unexpected conclusions in terms of the radical and compelling way in which they were developed.

The Plotinian doctrine of the One constitutes a real turning point in the history of Platonism (although, as we shall see, it should not be approached in isolation). It is therefore hardly surprising that it became the focus of the reflections and analyses of Plotinus' successors. This doctrine includes potentially contradictory ideas in the sense that the emphasis on the absolutely transcendent character of the One clashes with the thesis according to which the One is the principle at the basis of everything. As already briefly noted, in the *Enneads* we find an alternation of negative statements and positive descriptions. Later Neoplatonists also had to engage with this 'constitutive'[71] ambiguity, and given the impossibility of devising a solution, what we find is a tendency to emphasise first one aspect and then the other. While in many passages Porphyry confirms the notion of the absolute transcendence of the One, elsewhere he compares it to pure and first being; a similar thesis also occurs in an anonymous *Commentary on the Parmenides*, possibly to be attributed to Porphyry, or at any rate to someone very close to him:[72] the One is presented as pure 'being' (*einai*), anterior to any determination and hence prior to what is (*on*), which is to say to being that is determined by intelligible Forms (12.22–32). This partial reform of Plotinus' thesis provides exemplary confirmation of the typical strategy adopted by Porphyry, whose main concern would appear to have been to reconcile Plotinus with the previous Platonist tradition: without openly rejecting Plotinus' thesis, and by preserving a clear distinction between the One and the Forms, Porphyry succeeds in presenting his teacher's position in a way

---

[70] 6.9[9].1.1–12; cf. 5.4[7].1.5–15.
[71] Linguiti 2012a: 194.
[72] A crucial and pioneering study is P. Hadot 1968; the reference to the commented edition is to Linguiti 1995 (which confirms the dating of this work to Porphyry's time; recently, attempts have been made to change this picture, but with rather unpersuasive results).

that brings it quite close to the theses of someone like Numenius or Alcinous. Certainly, one may question the validity of the result achieved, but it is interesting to recall that Porphyry's reformulation (or at any rate that provided by the anonymous commentator, if he is not to be identified as Porphyry) was to enjoy considerable popularity over the following centuries, especially in the Latin world: taken up by Marius Victorinus, it constitutes the first attestation of the so-called 'Metaphysics of Exodus', the thesis made famous by Thomas Aquinas and according to which God (i.e. the first principle) is a pure being in which existence and essence coincide.[73]

As always at the opposite pole from Porphyry, Iamblichus instead radicalised the Plotinian thesis in the opposite direction, even going so far as to posit the existence of an absolutely unutterable or ineffable principle that transcends the One itself.[74] Later, Proclus was to attempt to reconcile these two positions.[75] His rejection of Iamblichus' thesis of a principle higher than the One is clear-cut,[76] yet it does not imply complete adherence to Porphyry's (and Plotinus') perspective, which is criticised as having 'contaminated' the simplicity of the One with the idea that somehow it contains – if only in a hidden or embryonic form – reality and its causes.[77] To guarantee the utter simplicity of the first principle, then, Proclus further develops a theory of his teacher Syrianus by introducing a further level of mediation between the One and the Forms, composed by so-called 'henads'.[78] This ensures the absolute transcendence and simplicity of the One, since it is not the One but henads that 'pre-contain' multiplicity; rather, all existing entities radiate from the One.[79] Proclus' proposal is no doubt an attempt to correct the ambiguities of the doctrine developed by Plotinus. However, it is quite evident that

---

[73] The expression 'Metaphysics of Exodus', coined by Étienne Gilson, refers to a famous passage from *Exodus* in which God states 'I am that I am'; on the possibility of tracing this position back to ancient Platonism, see Trabattoni 2010.

[74] In defence of this thesis, which may be inferred from Proclus' testimony (*El. Theol.* 20; *In Prm.* 7.1143.27–1144.26 Steel), see Linguiti 1988.

[75] On Proclus and Damascius, see now Greig 2021.

[76] *El. Theol.* 20; *In Prm.* 7.1143.27–1144.26 Steel.

[77] *In Prm.* 6.1105.28–1108.15 Steel; *TP* 2.5.39.22–24; 2.6.41.16–17 and 43.4–6.

[78] On Syrianus' influence, see Saffrey-Westerink 1978: xl–lii.

[79] *El. Theol.* 113–65; *TP* 3.1–6.

it merely shifts Plotinus' problems onto another level: this theory apparently guarantees the absolute and negative transcendence of the first principle, but the relationship between the henads and the One risks raising the same difficulties as that between the One and Intellect. The tendency of many Neoplatonists was to increase the number of levels of reality (to the henads we should add the Iamblichean pair limited/unlimited)[80] in an effort to approach the first principle without compromising its otherness. Nevertheless, it is clear that this unrestrained search for middle terms is incapable of solving the problems, just as one cannot square a circle by multiplying lunules.

It was thus in order to solve this and other difficulties that Damascius took up Iamblichus' thesis and developed it so as to reach even more radical outcomes, going so far as to challenge the idea that one can speak of the One as a principle: for the first principle, insofar as it is the principle of all things, is also somehow coordinated with them. In other words, between the notion of principle and that of transcendence there is an unbridgeable incompatibility;[81] hence the need to posit an entity beyond the One, one that is even higher, utterly separate and transcendent, and completely unrelated to things. We can only have an obscure foreboding of this 'something' after having given up on any attempt to rationally describe it: for any talk about it inevitably slips into contradiction; even speaking about it in negative terms is misleading, because it might create the illusion that that of which something is being denied – the subject of the negation – exists or is something: 'denial (*apophasis*) is itself a kind of discourse, and that about which the denial is made is the subject of the discourse, but the ineffable is nothing at all, and therefore no deniable can be made concerning it' (*De princ.* 1.8.21.15–16 Westerink and Combés). Even the claim that nothing can be said about the principle is

---

[80] See Iambl. *De comm. math. Scientia* 12.22–25; Damasc. *De princ.* 2.1.4–6; 25.15–17; 28.1–6.

[81] Besides, Damascius criticises the very notion of transcendence: 'For the transcendent always transcends something and so is not entirely transcendent, because it is conditioned by a relationship with that which it transcends, and generally has a fixed place in the progression of a system. If, then, it is to subsist as truly transcendent, it must not even be postulated as transcendent.' (*De princ.* 1.8.21.8–12). For a detailed comparison between Proclus and Damascius, see Napoli 2008: 371–471.

obviously self-refuting. All we are left with, then, is a form of hyper-ignorance (*hyperagnoia*), culminating in silence:

> And what will turn out to be the limit of discourse, except silence that has no power to convey it, and the agreement to continue to know nothing about that which is not permitted to enter into knowledge of, since it remains as the inaccessible? (*De princ.* 1.8.21.15–22 Westerink – Combés)

The reasons behind Damascius' thesis and the arguments on which it rests are understandable and shine for their rigour (particularly intriguing is his development of sceptical arguments).[82] Indeed, many of his theses draw interesting parallels – so much so that scholars have compared Damascius' ineffable to Heidegger's *Ereignis* and even to the black holes of contemporary astrophysics. However, one is bound to observe that Damascius' conclusions risk making all Plato's efforts come to naught, as the latter had established his philosophy in order to account for the reality which surrounds us: to talk about it correctly, not to fall into a silence filled with mystical veneration.[83]

From the One to the Many: Intellect and Soul

The doctrine of the One evidently runs into a serious difficulty: if the principle really is absolutely simple and transcendent, then it is unclear how the reality of multiple things can be generated. In other words, Plotinus introduced the One in order to explain manifold reality, but the characterisation of the One as something utterly transcendent risked separating it precisely from the reality it was meant to explain. How to solve this difficulty? The problem is to explain how reality derives from or is produced by the One without assigning the One the role of producer or creator.

Plotinus' solution lies in the so-called doctrine of 'emanation'. This is a potentially misleading term since it gives the impression that metaphysical derivation can be equated with a material process (a kind of flowing) – yet nothing could be further from the

---

[82] See Linguiti 1990: 68–73.
[83] A more favourable view of Damascius' possible relationship with Plato may be found in Trabattoni 2011.

truth for Plotinus.[84] However, Plotinus himself certainly employs metaphors connected with the sensible world to explain his thesis: the process of production starting from the One is akin to what we find in the case of a ray radiating from a light source, heat spreading from fire, cold issuing from snow, or a scent wafting from an odorous substance;[85] the One is like a spring from which water eternally gushes out.[86] All metaphors aside, it is possible to reconstruct Plotinus' thesis by dividing it into the stages of remaining in itself (*mone*), procession (*proodos*), and return (*epistrophe*):

1) The One 'remains' in itself, in its perfection.

2) Yet, from it, from this overflowing perfection, something else proceeds: the One 'overflows, as it were, and its superabundance makes something other than itself'.[87] This statement takes up – and adapts to a metaphysical context – beliefs that are typical of ancient philosophy, and particularly of Plato and Aristotle; it expresses what we might call the principle of the 'productiveness of perfection',[88] which in the Latin world came to be known under the formula *Bonum est diffusivum sui*: that which is perfect necessarily tends to generate something successive to it.[89] More specifically, this idea follows from the thesis of a 'twofold activity' (*energeia*):[90] in each thing two kinds of activity are present, one proper to the nature of the thing and the other deriving from this nature as a consequence; through this second activity, it is possible to produce an effect on something else. Let us think of fire, for instance, from whose inner activity – burning – the activity of warming the surrounding environment necessarily derives.[91]

3) This procession finds its counterpart in a movement of return towards the source and cause.[92] Again, Plotinus adapts to his

---

[84] See Dörrie 1965.
[85] 4.3[27].17.12; 5.1[10].6.27–30.
[86] 3.8[30].10.5–14.
[87] 5.2[11].1.8–9.
[88] Linguiti 2012a: 205; cf. Plat. *Tim.* 29d and Arist. *De an.* 415a26–8.
[89] Cf. Procl. *El. Theol.* 25.
[90] See Emilsson 2007: 23–68.
[91] 5.1[10].3.10–12; 5.3[49].7.21–5; 5.4[7].2.26–33.
[92] 5.1[10].7.5. This process should not be understood in chronological terms: we are dealing with two complementary aspects of a single event.

own philosophy a well-known thesis in Greek philosophy, namely the idea that the true cause is always the final one (consider, for example, the Aristotelian unmoved mover in *Met.* 12.1072a26); it is only by reuniting with its cause that that which issues from it – and which, as such, is deficient – can truly realise its own nature;[93] and it is the desire to realise one's own nature that leads to this reuniting.[94] As Pauliina Remes has aptly noted, the creation of a new order of reality can be explained in the light of three fundamental aspects of the relationship between the first cause and that which is caused: a) the act of return and conversion is in itself a change with respect to the movement issuing from the principle; b) given that this movement of return springs from a desire and sense of deficiency, the thing generated must somehow be aware of its separation and, in this respect, acknowledges itself as distinct from its source; and c) at the moment of return, the thing generated thus produces its own interpretation of the generating cause, so to speak. It is at this stage that a new order of reality is produced.

This doctrine, which was taken up by the later Neoplatonists,[95] applies to all levels and all generative processes, starting from the first and most important one, from the One to Intellect (*Nous*).[96] From the overflowing potency of the One something proceeds (5.2[11].1.8–9), an activity that is still indistinct[97] and which becomes Intellect in the moment when it gains awareness of its own origin. To quote Denis O'Brian:

> The One does not generate the Intellect. The One gives birth to something undifferentiated, which therefore is not the Intellect yet, but will become it, not by

[93] Cf. Procl. *El. Theol.* 31 and 34.
[94] Cf. e.g. 6.7[38].37.19–22; 1.8[51].2.2–5 with the commentary in Remes 2008: 52.
[95] Particularly Proclus, regarding whom Beierwaltes 1979 compellingly speaks of a philosophy of 'dynamic identity'.
[96] The process of generation of the Intellect from the One presents some additional difficulties due to the particular 'nature' of the One (which, strictly speaking, does not have any nature). As I cannot dwell on this issue here, I will refer to Chiaradonna 2009: 130–37 for a clear discussion of it.
[97] Among other things, Plotinus speaks of 'indeterminate thought' (5.4[7].2.4–7), 'indistinct vision' (5.3[49].11.12), 'intelligible matter' (2.4[12].1–5), 'otherness' (2.4[12].5.28), and 'indeterminate life' (6.7[38].17.14–15).

virtue of just any activity on the part of the First Principle, but because it constitutes itself as Intellect through a movement of return to its own origin, through the gaze that it attempts to turn towards the principle from which it has issued.[98]

To put it in Plotinus' own words:

> So when its life was looking towards that it was unlimited, but after it had looked there it was limited, though the Good has no limit. For immediately by looking to something which is one the life is limited by it, and has in itself limit and bound and form; and the form was in that which was shaped, but the shaper was shapeless.[99]

What needs to be stressed, then, is the fact that the process of generation does not entail any change in the first principle (or at any rate in the superior principle). In the specific case of the generation of the Intellect, this means that the multiplicity of the Forms that make up Intellect (and which will provide the model for physical reality) is not something present in the One, but something produced through Intellect's act of returning to its source: 'the first generated [Intellect] grasps the principle in agreement with its multiple nature and mirrors it as far as it can, fragmenting the original simplicity into the multiplicity of Forms, which constitute the structure of Being-Intellect'.[100] Plotinus is thus able to explain the formation of reality and multiplicity while preserving the fundamental heterogeneity between the principle and what depends on it.[101]

The theory of Intellect is one of the most interesting parts of Plotinus' philosophy and the one which offers the greatest proof of his ability to innovate within the scholastic context of his time.[102] The notion of an Intellect which contains and thinks the Forms was not an innovation compared to the Middle Platonist theory of

---

[98] O'Brien 1999: 55.

[99] 6.7[38].17.14–18.

[100] Linguiti 2012a: 207; cf. 5.3[49].11; 6.7[38].15.20–22. This passage is more obscure than it appears to be, as Plotinus seems to be combining two kinds of multiplicity: that which consists in the subject/object duality (Intellect which discovers and thinks itself) and the multiplicity of the Forms, which are the real thought content of Intellect; see Chiaradonna 2009: 135.

[101] Moreover, it should be noted that while this process is necessary, it implies no compulsion on the One's part, nor is it based on any decision-making or act of will on its part (5.1[10].6.26); see Donini 1982: 269.

[102] The fundamental study is Emilsson 2007; the detailed analysis of Chiaradonna 2009: 49–79 is also very useful.

Forms as God's thoughts. However, Plotinus introduces a slight alteration which produces a substantial change: for the Middle Platonists, Forms are the object of thought for God (whether he be the Demiurge or the Intellect); for Plotinus, Forms are at the same time the object and subject of the process of cognition: they are not just objects of knowledge, but also knowing subjects. To justify his proposal, and deny its obvious originality, Plotinus refers to the well-known Parmenides fragment according to which 'thinking and being are the same thing' (28A3 Diels-Kranz). Even more so, he refers to certain passages of Plato's dialogues, and in particular the pages of the *Sophist* attributing motion, life, and thought to the intelligible principles (*Soph.* 248e–249a; cf. *Tim.* 30c). Another important stimulus is provided by Aristotle (or, rather, by Alexander of Aphrodisias' interpretation of Aristotle): Plotinus found a clear description of God as thought, act, and life in Book 12 of the *Metaphysics*.[103] All in all, Plotinus' thesis is a truly original one, and it is hardly surprising that it gave rise to a bitter polemic between him and Longinus.[104] Ultimately, it was this – even more so than the doctrine of the transcendent One – which marked the real break between Plotinus and Middle Platonism.[105]

That Plotinus was well aware of the importance of his thesis is confirmed by the fact that it is the most widely discussed topic in the *Ennead*: Plotinus repeatedly returns to the topic of Intellect in an effort to clarify its nature. Intellect is 'all things together' (*homou panta*, an expression lifted from Anaxagoras), which is to say that every Form, as thought, grasps all other Forms in an intuitive and immediate way, coinciding with them and at the same time being grasped by them according to the same modes of cognition.[106] In the act of intuition (*nous* in Greek suggests precisely a direct and

---

[103] On Plotinus and Aristotelian 'theology', see Aubry 2006; we should not forget that Alexander had identified the God of *Met.* 12 with the active Intellect of *De an.* 3.4–5.

[104] Cf. Porph. *Vit. Plot.* 18 and 20, and Plot. 5.5[32].1–2, with the commentary in Bonazzi 2015: 118–26.

[105] See Donini 1982: 271–2 (who also notes that the plurality of Forms is introduced into the second principle 'via interaction with the material world' according to the Middle Platonists, but 'via contemplation of the superior principle' according to Plotinus). A crucial contribution regarding this point is Armstrong 1960.

[106] 6.6[34].6.25–26; 5.8[5].8.

intuitive kind of knowledge), subject and object, thinker and thing thought, are one and the same: thus, each Form in turn becomes a thinking intellect, a Form which thinks the whole world of Forms and coincides with it. Moreover, the relation between parts and whole in Intellect is such that the whole not only contains the parts but is also contained in each of them. In this sense, the level of Intellect represents the highest degree of unity and determinacy attainable within multiplicity. Like Leibniz's monads, individual Forms are as many views of the same city – a city which, given its purity, ought to be regarded as composed of crystal and light, that is, as completely transparent and providing an overarching view at each of its points. In the intelligible realm:

All things there are transparent, and there is nothing dark or opaque; everything and all things are clear to the inmost part of everything; for light is transparent to light. Each there has everything in itself and sees all things in every other, so that all are everywhere and each and every one is all and the glory is unbounded. [...] The sun there is all the stars, and each star is the sun and all the others. A different kind of being stand out in each, but in each all are manifest. [...] The thing itself is Intellect and its ground is Intellect; it is as if one were to suppose that in the case of this visible heaven of ours which is luminous that the light which comes from it was born to be the stars. Here, however, one part would not come from another, and each would be only a part; but there each comes only from the whole and is part and whole at once: it has the appearance of a part, but a penetrating look sees the whole in it, supposing that someone had the sort of sight which it is said that Lynceus had, who saw into the inside of the earth, a story which speaks in riddles of the eyes which they have there. They do not grow weary of contemplation there, or so filled with it as to cease contemplating: for there is no emptiness which would result in their being satisfied when they had filled it and reached their end; and things are not different from each other so as to make what belongs to one displeasing to another with different characteristics; and nothing there wears out of wearies.[107]

With respect to Intellect, the hypostasis of the Soul (*psyche*) represents a further increase of multiplicity and dispersion.[108] Intellect

---

[107] 5.8[31].4.1–31. Note that the reference to light is not a mere analogy, because Plotinus establishes a correspondence between degrees of being and degrees of luminosity. On this 'metaphysics of light', see Beierwaltes 1961.

[108] On the Plotinian theory of the soul, see Blumenthal 1971. As already noted, the generation of the Soul from Intellect occurs in an analogous way as the creation of Intellect from the One: cf. 5.1[10].3–4; 5.3[49].9; 2.4[12].3.

constituted a first form of duality in the sense that it established a duality between subject (the knower) and object (the thing known), but this duality was limited by the fact that subject and object coincided; in the case of the soul, this identity is instead lacking and we find an increase in multiplicity and dispersion: as an intelligible principle, the soul remains incorporeal, unextended, and free from spatial conditioning, but its activity unfolds in the world of bodies, which are extended and multiple. Drawing upon the hypotheses of the *Parmenides*, we might say that whereas the One is the utterly and simple One of the first hypothesis, and Intellect is the One-many of the second (ἕν-πολλά), the Soul is the One and many of the third (ἕν καὶ πολλά).[109] Here we have what tradition acknowledges as the three hypostases, namely the three levels of intelligible reality according to Plotinus (bearing in mind that the first level cannot really be compared to the other two).

Ontological differences invariably correspond to epistemological ones: at the level of the Soul, knowledge is no longer total and direct knowledge, but discursive knowledge (*dianoia*), understood as the transition from one thought content to another, achieved in time.[110] This lesser degree of unity is also manifest in the twofold function of the Soul:[111] on the one hand, the activity of thinking, which brings the Soul closer to Intellect; on the other, the function of producing and ordering the multiplicity which it generates, namely the sensible world (this division of functions would almost suggest that Plotinus distinguishes between two different hypostases: one being the higher Soul, the other the World Soul, Nature, and the *Logos*). The Soul therefore constitutes the link between the intelligible realm of the Forms and the sensible world of becoming, insofar as it represents the intelligible level responsible for the sensible world, ensuring the unity and homogeneity of everything. In other words, we should not think of the Soul as being enclosed within the cosmos (or within bodies), for the exact opposite is the case: it is the cosmos and bodies that are in

---

[109] Cf. 5.1[10].8.26; the three hypotheses are discussed in *Prm.* 137c–142a, 142c–155e, 155e–157b.

[110] 5.1[10].3–4; note that here we find the first reference to the temporal dimension in Plotinus' system – cf. 3.7[45].11.43–45.

[111] 4.8[6].7; 4.6[41].3.

the Soul, for they are enclosed by its causal power, without which they would cease to subsist.[112]

In broad strokes, such is the structure of the realm of first principles according to Plotinus. This system was never really disputed by subsequent Neoplatonists, who nonetheless – as we have already seen – sought to bring the levels of the One, Intellect, and the Soul as close to one another as possible: this was the purpose of the doctrine of henads and Iamblichus' introduction of a new pair of first principles, the limited and the unlimited. No doubt, mediation is the problem par excellence for every form of Platonism: what applies to the basic opposition between sensible and intelligible (the topic of countless discussions in the Platonic dialogues) also holds true for the various levels of being.

The Sensible World and the Problem of Evil

After the Soul, we reach the sensible world of bodies and matter, which constitutes the lowest point in the Plotinian universe. Certainly, its value and ontological consistency are extremely limited compared to the intelligible principles: the sensible realm lacks any real causal power and thus depends on higher realities. However, steering clear of banal interpretations, we must also avoid attributing to Plotinus an overly negative view of sensible reality: after all, the physical universe is still produced by the principle of the Soul, and the latter's intervention (more specifically, the intervention of the World Soul) makes the universe something harmonious that participates in a higher beauty; however imperfect, the physical universe is still an image of the divine realm.[113] Here Plotinus drew upon the teachings of the *Timaeus* and certain Stoic doctrines (while obviously rejecting the Stoics' materialistic approach); more than any other philosophical school, Stoicism had stressed the beauty and inner consistency of the world through the doctrine of 'universal sympathy', according to which everything holds together harmoniously. For Plotinus it was crucial to emphasise all this in his polemic against the Gnostics,

---

[112] 4.3[20].46–51 and 22.7–11.
[113] On Plotinian cosmology, see the commentary in Wilberding 2006 on treatise 2.1[40], *On the Cosmos*, to quote its Porphyrian title.

who, on the basis of a distorted reading of Plato, regarded the universe as the product of an evil and irrational Demiurge (particularly revealing, in this respect, is treatise 2.9).

While in terms of the general framework of his philosophy of nature Plotinus seems to draw upon Stoic ideas, when it comes to the analysis of the specific constituents of the world, namely bodies, it is rather Aristotle he engages with. From Aristotle he draws certain fundamental doctrines such as the theory of categories, the distinction between matter and form, and that between potency and act. But these borrowings are not intended to introduce into his Platonist system doctrines which are largely incompatible with it; on the contrary, Plotinus' aim is to strip Aristotelian theories of their anti-Platonic potential from within, by showing that they only work within the Platonist system.[114] This strategy becomes particularly evident in the case of the doctrine of substance: Plotinus adopts the typically Aristotelian distinction between matter and form, acknowledging the latter's priority; yet, at the same time, by exploiting some key problems with the Aristotelian doctrine discussed by Peripatetic commentators, he shows that the form in question cannot be the one inherent in bodies (this being a 'dead form' incapable of producing anything), but rather the intelligible and transcendent Form.[115] As regards matter, Plotinus' thesis is that, as being that which remains of the process of derivation of the One, it is something utterly formless, inert, unlimited, and indeterminate, and hence it cannot really receive forms.[116]

Once again, it is easy to detect a tension in Plotinus' thought: while his anti-Gnostic polemic forces him to emphasise the beauty and unity of the cosmos, his anti-Aristotelian polemic seems to lead him towards an ontological emptying of the sensible world, which almost emerges as an inert mirror (3.6[26].9 and 13, which clearly draws upon the *Timaeus*' notion of *chora*, the receptacle receiving the images of all things). Revealing evidence of such tensions

[114] This is the underlying thesis of Chiaradonna 2002: 55–146.
[115] 6.1[42] and 6.3[44].
[116] 1.8[51].7.17–23; 2.5[25].5.17–19; 4.8[6].6; 2.9[35].3; 3.6[26].13–14. Note that Plotinus thus moves beyond the Middle Platonist doctrine of the three principles; see Donini 1982: 274.

is to be found in Plotinus' doctrine of evil.[117] To quote the title of treatise 1.8[51], what are evils and where do they come from?[118] The fact that matter is identified as their source is hardly surprising given that we are dealing with a Platonist author. But when it comes to providing a more detailed explanation, the reader cannot fail to note that the *Enneads* present two doctrines that are not always easy to harmoniously combine. On the one hand, we have the aforementioned doctrine of matter as the privation of the Good: consistently with his rigidly monist interpretation, Plotinus is forced to include even matter in the process of derivation from the one without granting it any independent subsistence (which would pave the way for dualism). Matter thus emerges as the final and indeterminate residue of what is left of reality, as pure passivity, as it were; and as the lack of Good, it can be identified with evil.[119] However, elsewhere (especially in treatise I 8[51]) Plotinus speaks of matter not merely in terms of passivity and privation, but also as an obstacle, as that which resists the imposition of forms and thus of order and the Good; in this more active sense, which almost seems to suggest that matter is a principle opposed to the One and exercising a sort of negative causality, matter emerges as evil itself, as the very essence of evil.[120] Reconciling these two conceptions is not easy, as Plotinus' successors clearly realised,[121] and it was Proclus who sought to solve this tension by taking a different approach.

Proclus' solution is based on a refusal to identify matter and evil on account of the paradoxical effects that this would entail.[122]

---

[117] See O'Brien 1999.

[118] As regards this treatise, a crucial point of reference is the commentary of O'Meara 1999.

[119] We find here an application of the principle of progressive degradation whereby successive levels correspond to inferior levels of perfection. Yet this does not solve all the difficulties: 'what is difficult to understand is why the last link in this chain ought to be totally "negative". In other words, it is unclear how decreasing degrees of perfection may cause a final reversal, from the positive to the negative, such that progressively imperfect causes, which are nonetheless still "divine" and positive, will ultimately cause a perverse and evil effect [...] we are forced to acknowledge the existence of a paradox whereby the One-Good would be the cause of evil' (Linguiti 2012b: 244).

[120] I.8[51].3 and 10; 2.4[12].6; 2.5[25].5; 3.6[26].7 and 11; 4.8[6].38; 6.3[44].7.8–9.

[121] See Simpl. *In Cat.* 109.13–23.

[122] See van Riel 2001. In addition to the treatise *On the Existence of Evil* (see the commentary in Opsomer and Steel 2003), the referential texts here are *In Ti.* 1.372.25–381.21 and 384.19–385.13; *In Remp.* 1.37.37–39.1 and 96.5–100.20; 2.89.6–91.18; and *In Prm.* 3.829.16–831.16. See Steel 1998; Opsomer 2001 and 2007, and D'Hoine 2011.

Matter stems from the One and is its ultimate expression. Now, if matter coincided with evil, absurd consequences would follow: given that, according to Proclus, a cause is to the highest degree what its effects are,[123] the One, as the cause of matter and evil, would be evil to the highest degree; conversely, matter would be a good, insofar as it is akin to its cause. Nor can we posit the independent subsistence of matter-evil since this would introduce an unacceptable form of dualism. Matter and evil must therefore be separated, and matter must be assigned a more neutral value. As for evil, Proclus explains its nature by noting that it is never the proper end of any action, but rather the outcome of the failed attainment of an end, due to some weakness or deficiency. In other words, evil does not have any independent existence, but only a parasitical one: for it always depends on specific actions or events, and only concerns imperfect beings such as lower individual souls or bodies; for them, evil consists in the failure to attain their ends, in their lack of harmony with their own nature. Consider the case of an archer missing his target:[124] evil is not a proper end, but an accidental result which follows from the failure to attain the objective; likewise, an individual soul may happen to act against reason and this lack of harmony with its own nature is where evil lies, which is always a particular evil (that does not exist in itself). As has rightly been noted, Proclus' solution may prove unsatisfactory insofar as it 'weakens' the nature of evil and of the evils which have always afflicted mankind; still, one must at least appreciate his 'solid and coherent conceptual definition'.[125]

Returning to more general problems, what we note is that the Neoplatonists resumed the Plotinian plan to build a Platonist physics through a close encounter with Aristotle, yet did so by introducing a major shift of perspective. In principle, Neoplatonists

---

[123] We find here a point of divergence with respect to Plotinus: see *supra*, The Doctrine of Principles: The One and the Hierarchical Structure of Reality, p. 136.

[124] Cf. *De mal. Subst.* 4.49.9–50.14.

[125] Linguiti 2012b: 252. Closely connected to the problem of evil is that of providence: the monist Plotinian option risked leading to a form of crypto-determinism, so it was up to his successors to attempt to carve out a space for independent human action. In addition to Proclus (esp. his *Ten Questions on Providence* and *Letter to Theodorus on Providence, Fate, and What Depends on Us* – see Steel 2007), it is worth mentioning Hierocles' treatise *On Providence*; see Schibli 2002: 129–63.

The Sensible World and the Problem of Evil

agree with Plotinus, *contra* Aristotle, that the things of the physical world are something derived, and not its basic constituents.[126] With regard to this point, the convergence is strong and unambiguous. However, this does not translate into the same attitude towards Aristotle: for, unlike Plotinus, the other Neoplatonists sought to integrate Aristotle's doctrines into the Platonist system – an operation quite distant from Plotinus' perspective.[127] In other words, Neoplatonists believed that a suitable treatment of the physical world requires the study of Aristotle's treatises, but that this study is insufficient in itself to lead to a full understanding of what is truly important: Aristotle is not discarded, but his inferiority with respect to Plato is stressed.

The Neoplatonists' underlying thesis is that the physical universe cannot be explained only on the basis of physical principles (the material and formal causes), but that it necessarily depends on intelligible principles (the efficient cause, i.e. the Demiurge; the paradigmatic cause, i.e. Forms; and the final cause, i.e. the Good).[128] Unlike the Stoics and other materialists, Aristotle had acknowledged that physics is a 'second' science, subordinated to the true first philosophy,[129] namely metaphysics, which focuses on being and God: this is why the study of his treatises could become an integral part of the Neoplatonist curriculum.[130] However, unlike the Neoplatonists, Aristotle had persisted in studying this physical world without giving enough attention to the transcendent causes; he had failed to grasp that the purpose of studying nature is to enable us to attain greater awareness of such causes, and hence of the divine realm.[131] In other words, the study of the physical world must serve as an introduction to the study of the

---

[126] Remes 2008: 77.
[127] See Chiaradonna 2012: 98. For a discussion of the Neoplatonists' physical conceptions, see Martijn 2010, with the collections of studies edited by Chiaradonna, Trabattoni 2009, and Horn and Wilberding 2012.
[128] Cf. Procl. *In Ti.* 1.2.1–9.
[129] Cf. Arist. *Phys.* 192a34-b9, 194b9–15, 198a27–31, 251a6–8; *De caelo* 298b19–20; *De gen. et corr.* 318a5–6; *De motu an.* 700b8–9.
[130] Cf. e.g. Simpl. *In Phys.* 1117.3–14 and 1359.5–8.
[131] More specifically, Aristotle's error lies in his failure to realise that the efficient cause is the cause not just of the movement of things, but also of their existence, and that in the act of creation it requires an ideal model (the paradigmatic cause): cf. Procl. *In Ti.* 1.2.24–29 and 266.28–30.

intelligible one; it must help us realise that 'entities that come into existence naturally, inasmuch as they are generated from the gods, also have a kind of divine existence'.[132] Aristotle's limit lay precisely in his failure to fully accomplish this plan, which made him a merely 'daemonic' figure by comparison to the 'divine' Plato.[133] By contrast, Neoplatonist philosophers set themselves the task of exploiting the study of nature as a means to promote the soul's ascent into the intelligible realm.

Finally, something remains to be said about the cosmological problem par excellence, namely the eternity of the universe, which had been an object of heated debate ever since the first Academy. In this case too, a systematic answer was provided by Proclus' remarkable capacity for synthesis.[134] By contrast to the Middle Platonists' fluctuations, the Neoplatonists all shared the thesis that the *Timaeus* was not to be taken literally: the physical world does not have a beginning in time but exists eternally. Still, this does not mean that it is ingenerated: on the contrary, it is eternal yet also generated, because its existence depends on other causes and because it is composite.[135] In other words, the universe is eternally subject to becoming in time, as it has been generated by intelligible divine principles (which, in turn, are eternal, yet in a different way: for their eternity is of a timeless kind). It probably goes without saying that Proclus too failed to persuade everyone, since the development of a Christian form of Platonism such as that of John Philoponus was soon to reopen the question, with the formulation of new arguments in support of the opposite thesis, creation in time, the only one compatible with Christian beliefs. Simplicius' counter-response shows that what was at stake was something more than just a cosmological issue: ancient Platonists regarded the *Timaeus* not only as a cosmogony, but as a theogony as well – for in at least two passages it speaks of the sensible world as a deity.[136] Defending its eternity thus meant also defending its divine character, and exegesis also constituted

---

[132] Procl. *In Ti.* 2.217.25–27.
[133] Syr. *In Met.* 86.7; 115.25; 168.6; 192.16; cf. O'Meara 1989: 123 and esp. Saffrey 1987.
[134] See Baltes 1978.
[135] *In Ti.* 1.277.14–6.
[136] Plat. *Tim.* 34b8 and 92c7–8.

an act of piety: one last attempt to defend the pagan religious tradition which had reached its culmination with Platonic theology.[137] Significantly, Simplicius was to end both his commentary on the *Physics* and that *On the Heavens* with a prayer to the lord of the cosmos, while at the same time accusing Philoponus of impiety.[138] Like Plotinus in his anti-Gnostic polemics, after having repeatedly emphasised the imperfection of the sensible universe, these last Neoplatonists had also felt the need to praise its divine character in order to defend their brand of Platonism against the new Oriental traditions.

The Doctrine of the Soul and Debate on Human Nature

Already at the metaphysical level, the Soul (the hypostasis Soul) occupies a particular position which hardly fits the binary opposition between intelligible and sensible. While belonging to the former level, the Soul finds itself in relation with the latter: its chief function, in other words, is to mediate between otherwise disjointed orders of reality.[139] This 'amphibious'[140] position of the Soul complicates the picture, particularly when it comes to the nature of man. The discourse on the Soul is the privileged means to discuss human beings, their nature, and the place they occupy within the rich and sophisticated metaphysical system that makes up reality, as well as the aim of human existence.[141] As regards this point, as we will see, Neoplatonist thought stands out on account of its highly original and interesting theses, formulated within a lively debate and expressed from numerous distinct points of view.

What is a human being? On the one hand, we are bodies who live and operate within the system of causal relations constituted by nature. On the other hand, we possess certain functions and

---

[137] Hoffmann 2000; see Bowen 2013.

[138] Hoffmann 1987; more recently, on the importance of prayers in the Platonist tradition, see Timotin 2018.

[139] Cf. e.g. Iambl. *De an.* 7, 30, 14–27 Dillon-Finamore.

[140] Cf. Plot. 4.8[8].4.31–35; 2.3[52].9.30–31.

[141] For an initial overview, see Remes 2008: 99–133 and Eliasson 2012. One classic and still fundamental study is Steel 1978; also very useful is the annotated collection of studies by Sorabji 2004, vol. I: 245–304.

capacities (above all, thinking) which lead us beyond the physical realm. How can we account for this peculiarity? The Platonists' answer revolves around the soul[142] and the twofold function assigned to it: on the one hand, the Soul is the principle of life, that which makes bodily organisms live; on the other, it is the principle of knowledge and rational activities. This explains why, strictly speaking, we are our soul: because it is the principle of our life and of our intellectual activities. However, upon closer scrutiny, this first answer proves unsatisfactory, as this twofold function entails two options. We are our soul, but what is this soul really? The function of life is what places us within the natural system; the intellectual function is what allows us to 'transcend' the realm of nature.[143] As Plotinus notes, we are therefore twofold beings: 'so "we" is used in two senses, either including the beast or referring to that which even in our present life transcends it'.[144] In a sense, then, we are our living body, which is to say a composite being in which a soul guides a body that is subject to time and change: this is how each of us might be described. However, there is also another possibility: in a more rigorous sense, it may be argued that if what distinguishes us is our soul, and what is truly specific to our soul is its rational activity (since not just humans, but all 'living' being such as plants and animals are also alive), then what we truly are is not a composite of soul and body, but our soul alone, which is to say our rational soul, or intellect. Faced with this option, the most obvious response is to stress one more time the centrality of the composite: it is this 'us' with which we usually identify.[145] Once again displaying a radical and rigorous attitude, Plotinus instead opts for the latter possibility, developing one of the most fascinating and controversial theses of late antiquity (and beyond), namely the theory of the so-called 'undescended soul':

And, if one ought to dare to express one's own view more clearly, contradicting the opinion of others, even our soul does not altogether come down, but there is always something of it in the intelligible; but if the part which is in the world of sense-perception gets control, or rather if it is itself brought under control, and

[142] Cf. Plat. *Alc. I* 128e–130a.
[143] Remes 2008: 100.
[144] 1.1[53].10.6–7.
[145] Plot. *Enn.* 5.4[49].3.36–40.

154

thrown into confusion [by the body], it prevents us from perceiving the things which the upper part of the soul contemplates. [...] But the souls which are partial and of a part have also the transcendent element, but they are occupied with sense-perception, and by their [lower] faculty of conscious apprehension they apprehend many things which are contrary to their nature and grieve and trouble them, since what they care for is a part, and defective, and has a great many alien and hostile things around it, and a great many which it desires; and it has pleasures, and pleasure deceives it; but there is a higher part which the transitory pleasures do not please, and its life is conformable [to its own nature].[146]

According to Plotinus, the soul has a wide range of functions, which enable the 'composite' to live and interact with the surrounding world (this includes not just biological functions, but also desires and the rational discursive faculty).[147] But what we really are is something else, namely that part of our soul which is 'undescended', which has never compromised itself through dealings with matter and bodies, but which continues to live in the intelligible realm unaffected by them, enjoying the vision of the Forms. We are usually unaware of this 'part' (a term to be used with great caution: immaterial and unextended, the soul cannot have parts),[148] and thus tend to identify with the soul that relates to the body. Yet this ordinary I (or 'us', to use Plotinus' expression) is not our true I;[149] rather, what 'we' are in the proper sense is this higher soul, which is not subject to time and change, but is always active in the intelligible realm.[150] This thesis also entails important epistemological consequences. As already noted, the activity proper to the soul is the rational discursive activity (*dianoia*); yet this discursive activity is actually only an (inadequate) expression of what lies in Intellect: the soul's thinking, then, is a 'lessening of the intellect';[151] the soul is like an Intellect, which however 'sees

---

[146] Plot. *Enn.* 4.8[6].8.1–22; see also 1.1[53].10 and 12; 2.9[33], 2; 4.3[27].12. The literature on this doctrine is vast: for an initial discussion, see Chiaradonna 2009: 81–115; also very useful is the classic study Szlezák 1979; for a detailed analysis of Plotinus' concept of self, see Remes 2007.

[147] Plot. *Enn.* 4.7[2].3.15–19; 1.1[53].7.3–6; 5. 3[49].3.36–40.

[148] Plot. *Enn.* 5.1[10].1.1.

[149] Plot. *Enn.* 2.3[52].15.13–17.

[150] On this true 'us', see e.g. Plot. *Enn.* 6.4[22].14.16–21 and 1.4[46].9.28–29 and Tornau 2009. This thesis finds a compelling description in the mythological parallel between the Heracles who is perfectly happy banqueting with the gods and the Heracles who roams Hades (i.e. the sensible world) in *Od.* 11.601–4; see *Enn.* 4.3[27].32.24–27.

[151] Plot. *Enn.* 4.3[27].18.4.

something else',[152] but ultimately it is also 'the Intellect within us'.[153] Hence, we need to become aware of what we truly are and return to our intelligible origin. The task and ambition of philosophy must be to awaken us to this true I, so that we may share its cognitive activity and way of life – a cognitive activity and way of life that are fully divine:

A man has certainly become Intellect when he lets all the rest which belongs to him go and looks at this with this and himself with himself: that is, it is as Intellect he sees himself.[154]

Plotinus' thesis reveals the human soul's complexity in a way that is as incisive as it is evocative. Distinguishing between a range of different levels is a way to express an awareness of the fact that we are not necessarily aware of everything which concerns us and constitutes us. We normally live on the level of our discursive reason, yet our soul is active on other levels too: on the higher level of the undescended soul, but also on the lower level of blind passions and desires, connected to the living 'composite' of the body.[155] 'The soul, the I, and consciousness are not at all coextensive.'[156]

No less interesting are the consequences in terms of the principle of identity. Plotinus often speaks of souls and intellects in the plural, as though to suggest that each individual has a personal identity.[157] But what does each individual's personal identity consist of, if there is indeed such a thing? Certainly, this identity cannot stem from the soul's encounter with the body into which it descends,

---

[152] Plot. *Enn.* 5.3[49].3.16–17.

[153] Plot. *Enn.* 5.1[10].11.6.

[154] 5.3[49].4.29–31. Consider the famous conclusion of 5.1.[10].12.15–21: 'it is as if someone was expecting to hear a voice which he wanted to hear and withdrew from other sounds and roused his power of hearing to catch what, when it comes, is the best of all sounds which can be heard; so here also we must let perceptible sounds go (except in so far as we must listen to them) and keep the soul's power of apprehension pure and ready to hear the voices from on high'. This thesis, and hence the possibility of identifying with divine principles, also supports the thesis of the immortality of the soul, a doctrine clearly present in Plato's dialogues and hence defended by all Imperial Age Platonists.

[155] On this third level of the soul, see 4.4[28].8; 5.1[10].12; 4.8[6].8.

[156] Donini 1982: 275.

[157] See e.g. 4.3[27].5.1–14. What further emerges in this context is one of the most complex issues in Plotinus' philosophy, namely the possibility of there being Forms of individual things: see Kalligas 1997 and Ferrari 1998.

because to accept this view would be to assign too much importance to something that is inert and, properly speaking, not even real, namely matter. But can we distinguish individual souls, which somehow all depend on the hypostatic Soul? One possible solution is to emphasise the fact that all souls are potentially everything, but that not all realise all potentialities in the same way: it is in these different degrees of realisation that the possible distinctions between individual souls lie. This solution, however, is not entirely satisfactory, because it has identity depend on imperfection:[158] each soul, according to its weaknesses, distinguishes itself from the others on account of its inability to realise all potentialities. This solution is even less satisfactory in the case of the undescended soul, where the problem becomes almost impossible to solve: if 'we' ultimately coincide with the undescended part of the soul which is ever absorbed in contemplation, then very little space is left for personal identity. Indeed, in accordance with Plato's and Aristotle's epistemological theories, contemplation of the intelligible consists in the identification between subject and object; and given that the object of contemplation, Forms, is universal, it follows that the subjects contemplated, namely souls and intellects, must also identify with one another if they engage in contemplation. However, this should not be taken to suggest an error on Plotinus' part or an inability to solve the problem. Rather, we must acknowledge that his priorities are different from our own: whereas for us moderns, who have been influenced by Christianity, the notion of identity can hardly be separated from that of person, this is not the case for Plotinus, who is interested in identity as a metaphysical problem and something of normative value. The point for him is not to establish our own irreducible identity, but to understand how we can fully realise the potentialities that belong to all human souls: 'our ideal self, the undescended soul, is the normative ideal to which the ordinary self must be able to conform in order to attain its perfection'.[159] For Plotinus, unlike for us, what matters in the contrast between perfection and individuality is perfection.[160]

[158] Remes 2008: 113.
[159] Chiaradonna 2009: 133; for a more in-depth analysis, see Remes 2007 and Tornau 2009.
[160] Remes 2008: 126–7.

Plotinus' thesis is no doubt an interesting one, but it is difficult to establish whether it is compatible with Plato's philosophy. Plotinus was quite aware of the fact that the thesis of an undescended soul constituted a striking innovation for the Platonists of his day: the passage quoted earlier (4.8[6].8) confirms that Plotinus was conscious of his thesis' originality, yet at the same time he sought to defend its correctness and, even more so, its faithfulness to Plato's teaching. Significantly, however, his successors did not agree with him and almost invariably rejected his thesis, deeming it incorrect and incompatible with Plato's philosophy.[161] Neoplatonists could all agree on this point, but the alternative theses developed once again lead us back to the contrast between Iamblichus, followed by Damascius on the one hand and Proclus on the other. Porphyry instead adopted a more cautious position, glossing over the thesis of a higher soul and attempting to lead Plotinus' thesis back into the fold of more traditional Platonism.

Iamblichus' position helps us to better understand the problem under discussion: the notion that we are our soul and that our soul is what unites us with the world of Forms is, in principle, correct; yet it clashes with our everyday reality, which is that of fallen souls, that is, souls that have become embodied: according to Iamblichus, when the soul descends, it descends completely; as the soul is one, it makes no sense to argue that part of it remains in the intelligible world (less still to identify the soul with Intellect, as Plotinus' thesis risked doing).[162] In criticising Plotinus, Iamblichus thus confirms one fundamental point, which crops up again and again in the Platonists' reflection: namely, the awareness of the gulf separating us from the most authentic and divine realities. But if this is true, it follows that the soul changes

---

[161] Criticism of Plotinus' thesis can be found in: Iambl. *De an.* 6.30.12–13; 17.44.6–9; 19.44.17–19; 26.52.13–14 Dillon and Finamore; Procl. *El. Theol.* 211; *In Ti.* 3.333.38–334.27 (= fr. Iambl. *In Ti.* Fr. 87 Dillon); *Theol. plat.* 5.19.71.16; *In Prm.* 948.12–38; Dam. *In Prm.* 4.15.3–9. Only Theodorus of Asine would appear to have remained faithful to Plotinus' thesis (Procl *In Ti.* 3.333.38). Among modern studies, see Dillon 2005; D'Ancona 2006; and Remes 2008: 115–18.

[162] It is worth recalling that Iamblichus was the only Neoplatonist to associate rational souls with the fourth hypothesis of the *Parmenides*, rather than the third; in doing so, he confirmed the idea of their distance from higher levels of hypostases (including Intellect).

its nature and undergoes an essential transformation in passing from one context to the other. In other words, it is as though the soul led a double life, in the intelligible realm and in the sensible one, acquiring a different nature in each of the two contexts without ever completely identifying itself with either Intellect or sensible reality (which, once again, explains the soul's intermediate nature).[163] A different solution was suggested by Proclus, who opposed the idea that the soul could alter its substance: he thus acknowledged that the soul is not a simple nature (as Plotinus and Iamblichus had contended), but a complex one. The soul comprises a range of substances (three, like the three parts of the soul in *Republic*, Book 4), all of which descend entirely (by contrast to what Plotinus suggests) and change their activity during this descent, yet not their nature (by contrast to what Iamblichus suggests).[164] Curiously enough, Proclus' suggestion was endorsed by several Alexandrians – most notably Ammonius and Philoponus[165] – but not by the Athenians: accusing Proclus of passively conforming to Plotinus' theses, Damascius, later followed by Priscian,[166] was to take up Iamblichus' thesis again by stressing both the unity of the soul and the essential transformation it undergoes.[167] Damascius' thesis makes the most of Iamblichus' idea and offers a description of human nature that is no less fascinating than Plotinus' one. The moment it descends into the body, the soul undergoes a radical change that affects its very essence, yet this does not compromise its identity: just as a sponge remains such regardless of the amount of water it soaks up, so the soul remains the same regardless of how much divine light fills it. And the soul's essence lies precisely in this ability of fill up and empty out: the soul is a substance which changes itself. Damascius thus grasps a crucial aspect of human nature which is not unchangeable and given once and for all, but rather free to determine itself according to what it could be.[168] This dynamic conception of the

---

[163] Steel 1978: 53–60.
[164] Cf. e.g. *In Remp.* 1.207.8–11; more generally, see Perkams 2006.
[165] Cf. e.g. Philop. *In De an.* 10.4–9; 12.15–22; 205.18–206.1.
[166] Assuming, as most contemporary scholars do, that Simplicius is the author of the important *Commentary on the De anima*; see e.g. Steel 1978: 80–7.
[167] Dam. *In Prm.* 4.11.20–12.2 and 13.1–19.
[168] Steel 1978: 93–119.

soul clearly grasps its particular nature and function of mediating between the intelligible and the sensible realm.

With regard to the soul too, then, we find a rather marked divergence between Plotinus and his successors: generally speaking, all Neoplatonists endorse the underlying Plotinian thesis, namely the notion that the intelligible (and immortal) soul is what is truly important;[169] yet unlike Plotinus, they are more willing to acknowledge the soul's essential importance even in its embodied form: what they lose in rigour, one might say, they gain in humaneness.[170] As we shall now see, this will have major consequences in the ethical field.

The Aim of Human Life: From Ethics to Contemplation and Theurgy

Two well-established precepts in Platonic philosophy are rooted in the famous Socratic exhortations 'know yourself' and 'take care of yourself'. The investigation into human being – knowing who we are – is preparatory to a more practical discourse: it cannot but translate into a way of life.[171] Usually, this would fall within the field of ethics; but in the Neoplatonists' case, considering what we have said about their conceptions of the soul and the nature of human being, it is easy to see that ethics is not enough. Insofar as our aim is to rediscover our true divine nature, ethics, as the discourse concerning our practical activities, risks playing a secondary or marginal role. This risk is particularly strong in the case of Plotinus' rigorous intellectualism.[172]

Naturally, this does not imply a rejection of ethics: not only Plotinus' practical choices (asceticism and celibacy, as well as his commitment to look after the orphans entrusted to his care),[173] but also several pages of the *Enneads* suggest that he too regarded

---

[169] Eliasson 2012: 213.
[170] Remes 2008: 118.
[171] This aspect of ancient philosophy has been emphasised with very compelling arguments by P. Hadot 1981.
[172] See Chiaradonna 2009, 163–72, and more recently Stern Gillet 2014 and Tornau 2015; this thesis had already been upheld by Kristeller 1929; *contra*, see Schniewind 2003.
[173] Cf. Porph. *Vita Plot.* 9.

ethics and morality as two fundamental elements of human life. Besides, one important aspect of Plotinus' anti-Gnostic polemic was the fact that, by stressing the distinction between the elect and the non-elect, the Gnostics argued that the former were exempt from all moral rules – a claim that Plotinus found intolerable.[174] Upon closer scrutiny, however, we are forced to acknowledge that ethics has an ambiguous and merely secondary place in Plotinian thought. Certainly, in order to rediscover our true self, we must first of all free ourselves of all passions, which stem from the excessive importance assigned to everything connected with our body and earthly existence. Plotinus repeatedly recalls that the true evil for the soul, the real consequence of its fall, lies precisely in the excessive care shown for the body.[175] In this context, ethics thus plays a fundamental preparatory and purificatory role. But it is precisely only a preparatory role. The limits of ethics lie precisely in the fact that practical ethics (not to mention politics) can hardly help us to achieve our true aim (our *telos*, to use the technical term found in Hellenistic and Imperial Age philosophical debates), namely to consciously reunite with our divine part:

Our concern, though, is not to be out of sin, but to be god.[176]

This statement, drawn from treatise 1.2 *On Virtues*, is enlightening with respect to the distinctiveness of Plotinus' position. From Aristotle onwards, virtue had been the central theme in all ethical discussions; moreover, as we have already seen, the theme of assimilation to God (ὁμοίωσις τῷ θεῷ) evoked the solution proposed by earlier Platonists. A famous *Theaetetus* passage urged human beings to flee the evils of this world: 'escape means becoming as like God as possible; and a man becomes like God when he becomes just and pure, with understanding' (*Tht.* 176b). According to many Early Imperial Platonists, the aim of life was to reunite with the divine, and this could be achieved through practical engagement, insofar as, by becoming virtuous, man had the chance to approach the gods' perfect virtue.

[174] Plot. *Enn.* 2.9[33].9.25–59.
[175] Plot. *Enn.* 3.9[13].3; 5.1[10].1; IV.8[6].2 and 7.
[176] I.2[19].6.2–3, see the excellent commentary by Catapano 2006.

This view is not shared by Plotinus, however, who introduces some small variations which entail radical consequences. As we have seen, according to Plotinus the principle and the cause are heterogeneous:[177] in relation to the specific case at hand, this thesis translates into the claim that it is pointless to attribute distinctly human virtues to God (more specifically, in the divine Intellect we only find those ideal models of virtues which are not really virtues in themselves).[178] Therefore, it is not by means of virtuous behaviour that we can assimilate ourselves to God. Note that Plotinus here is not entirely rejecting the importance of ethical virtues; as already noted, they help us free ourselves from care of the body and from passions, and so in this respect they are important.[179] But what is most important lies elsewhere: we need other 'virtues' in order to fulfil our life objectives.

It is easy to grasp what these other virtues might be once we consider Plotinus' anthropology and metaphysics: if what we truly are is that 'part' of the soul which is always engaged in the contemplation of intelligible realities, and if the hallmark of intelligible reality is precisely its intellectual dimension, then it follows that the virtues enabling us to assimilate ourselves to God are the 'contemplative' virtues. The Greek word for virtue, *arete*, indicates performative excellence: contemplative virtue is therefore the capacity to accomplish our cognitive activities in an excellent way; and it is by doing so that we can attain our goal:

> One would not be wrong in calling this state of the soul likeness to God, in which its activity is intellectual, and it is free in this way from bodily affections. For the Divine too is pure, and its activity is of such a kind that that which imitates it has wisdom.[180]

Consistently with Plotinus' intellectualist perspective, Plotinus' thesis becomes paradoxical once its consequences have been fully worked out. If what matters is the undescended soul, it follows

---

[177] Cf. *supra*, The Doctrine of Principles: The One and the Hierarchical Structure of Reality, p. 136.
[178] 1.2[19].2.3–4 and 6.11–7.3. Plotinus is here drawing upon Aristotelian theses: cf. *EN* 10.8.1178b8–18.
[179] 1.2[19].2.13–26.
[180] 1.2[19].3.19–22.

that 'we' are already completely happy, regardless of all empirical forms of conditioning or practical forms of commitment:

> The man who has a life like this has all he needs in life. [...] His well-being will not be reduced even when fortune goes against him; the good life is still there even so. When his friends and relatives die he knows what death is – as those who die do also if they are virtuous. Even if the death of friends and relations causes grief, it does not grieve him but only that in him which has no intelligence, and he will not allow the distress of him to move him.[181]

Through his theses, Plotinus appropriated in a provocative and original way numerous ideas discussed in the Greek philosophical schools: for example, the idea of the self-sufficient and perfectly happy sage, 'like a god among men',[182] had stood at the basis of Hellenistic, Stoic, and Epicurean ethics. But whereas the Hellenistic philosophers had pursued this idea through the moral perfecting of the earth-bound human soul, Plotinus found a solution in a 'transcendent core of the [human] personality'.[183] And it was through this theory that he was able to defend a fully intellectualist ideal – something that not even Socrates, Plato, or Aristotle had succeeded in doing. Ethics therefore only serves a preparatory task; indeed, it is not really very important with respect to what truly matters, namely our true intellectual 'I'.[184] The attainment of our life goal consists in a purely intellectual exercise, the intelligible contemplation of primary, perfect, and divine realities: as has rightly been noted, 'Plotinus is he who ensures the final triumph of the Aristotelian ideal of *theoria*'.[185] This recovery of ourselves further serves as the basis for the attempt to reunite with the true principle of all, that absolutely transcendent One from which everything somehow derives: the mystical experience of

---

[181] 1.4[46].4.23–36; cf. 3.2[47].15.46–54.
[182] Epic. *Ep. Men.* 135.
[183] Linguiti 2012b: 237.
[184] Cf. Chiaradonna 2009: 168: 'our entire moral effort is conceived as a means to regain a condition with respect to which empirical behaviour and concrete actions de facto lose much of their value'.
[185] Donini 1982: 277. What is also closely connected to the pursuit of this ideal is the Plotinian conception of freedom, understood as self-determination: only theoretical activity, as opposed to practical activity (which depends on external circumstances), can ensure true freedom; see e.g. 6.8[39].4.7–26, 3.1[3].9.4–16, and 8.9–11. A crucial work in this respect is Eliasson 2008; see also Van Riel 2000.

unification (ἕνωσις), this flight of the alone to the Alone, 'in solitude to the solitary', driven by an erotic tension[186] which transcends man's intellectual possibilities and dissolves his personal identity,[187] marks the culmination of the process of ascent.[188]

We have repeatedly noted the key importance of the doctrine of the undescended soul in Plotinus' system in relation to man and the meaning of his existence. The later Neoplatonists' rejection of this doctrine, which entailed a greater openness to the requirements of embodied life, enabled the development of a more complex ethical system.[189] Yet even in the case of these Neoplatonists, the reassessment of ethics was only a partial one: the attempt to find an alternative solution to Plotinian intellectualism led them in a direction which had little to do with ethics.

A more in-depth engagement with ethical doctrines occurred with regard to virtues, the discussion of which led to the development of a genuine theory of virtues from Porphyry onwards.[190] Whereas Plotinus had simply drawn a contrast between preparatory (i.e. ethical) and contemplative virtues, the Neoplatonists developed the so-called doctrine of the 'degrees of virtues'. A first outline of this doctrine may be found in Porphyry's *Sentence* 32,[191]

---

[186] 6.9[9].11.51; 6.7[38].34–35.
[187] On the duration of the ecstatic experience, see Remes 2007: 253.
[188] Concerning Plotinus' 'mysticism', see the balanced remarks in Chiaradonna 2009: 172–5 and esp. Donini 1982: 280, who describes this ecstatic experience as 'the sudden flash of inspiration whereby someone – a philosopher or scientist – suddenly realises *why* things – all things – are as they are; and he [scil. Plotinus] refers this supreme experience to the level of the One, understood precisely as the ultimate reason for the existence of an intelligible order, the very order mirrored on the level of the *Nous'* intuition. If there is any truth to the parallel between the hierarchy of hypostases and the condition of a thought that goes through increasingly organised and deep stages of understanding, then there really are few possibilities to rank Plotinus among the mystics if not in the Russellian sense of the "mysticism of logic", insofar as this leads to the rational vision of a universe that has finally become completely intelligible'. See also Armstrong 1974, who stresses the importance of Plotinus' personal experiences.
[189] One interesting testimony is Simplicius' commentary on Epictetus' *Handbook*: see Hadot and Hadot 2004; and Brennan and Brittain 2002. Similar considerations can be made about politics: see Appendix 1.
[190] See now Chiaradonna 2021. On the sources for this theory and its reception (down to Psellus, Aquinas, and Bonaventure), see Saffrey and Segonds 2001.
[191] It is worth noting that the *Sentences* were apparently an attempt to explain the cornerstones of Plotinus' philosophy: once again, while divulging his teacher's thought, Porphyry sought to neutralise its most radical theses. On this crucial work of Porphyry's, see Brisson 2005.

which divides the virtues into civil (proper to the politician and fostering moderation with respect to passions), purificatory (proper to those who are approaching contemplation and who have therefore become impassible), intellectual (proper to those engaging in contemplation), and exemplary (proper to Intellect qua hypostasis). Subsequently, this list was broadened through the addition of three other types of virtue: at the base of the ladder we find natural and moral virtues, and at the summit hieratic or theurgical ones.[192] The novelty with respect to Plotinus does not lie only in the proliferation and systematisation of the types of virtue; more important still is the shift of perspective: whereas the separation between lower (i.e. ethical) and higher (i.e. contemplative) virtues is what matters the most for Plotinus, with the later Neoplatonists we witness an attempt at harmonisation, whereby what is higher encompasses what is lower without erasing it. The most important biographies of Neoplatonist philosophers, from Marinus' *Life of Proclus* to Damascius' *Life of Isidore*, sought precisely to show how these philosophical heroes possessed and exercised all these virtues, leading a truly fulfilled and happy life.[193]

No doubt, the rejection of the thesis of the undescended soul translated into greater attention towards the empirical self and hence into greater interest in ethical issues and practical action.[194] However, the doctrine of the degrees of virtue, and particularly the idea that the highest degree is embodied by theurgical virtues, shows that even for later Platonists ethics only served a vicarious function. What truly mattered were theurgical practices. And it is precisely the debate around the issue of theurgy and its value that accounts for the great rift between Plotinus and the later Neoplatonists, starting from Iamblichus.[195]

---

[192] Cf. e.g. Dam. *In Phd.* I.138–39, 144.
[193] See the above-mentioned studies of Saffrey and Segonds 2001 on Marinus and O'Meara 2006 on Damascius.
[194] Baltzly 2004; Remes 2008: 188. Note that in the above-quoted passage from I.2[19].6.2–3, Plotinus talks about 'being a god': a strong claim, quite far from the traditional exhortation to 'become similar' to God, and which other Platonists would have struggled to accept.
[195] Cf. Dam. *In Phd.* I.172: 'Some, like Plotinus, Porphyry, and many other philosophers, hold philosophy into greater account; others, like Iamblichus, Syrianus, Proclus, and all the theurgists, the sacred craft.'

Very briefly, what we mean by theurgy (literally, 'divine work') is a series of half-magical, half-theological practices designed to lead the gods to act on earthly events, and at the same time to reunite with human beings. The growing importance of such practices in Neoplatonism has generally attracted negative views from scholars: theurgy has been seen as the irrationalism of an angst-ridden age bursting into the field of philosophy with prodigies, oracles, levitations, evocations, and many other bizarre phenomena.[196] Yet this is an oversimplistic judgement: it is certainly true that in these philosophers we find a kind of yearning for salvation that we would hardly associate with philosophy nowadays; as Father Festugière noted, the history of late antique philosophy is the history of human beings in search of salvation.[197] However, we should not overlook the fact that the hieratic art's importance was also justified on the basis of strictly philosophical arguments, as may be inferred from the polemic between Porphyry and Iamblichus, a polemic which constituted a real turning point in the history of late antique Platonism.[198] As already noted, one important aspect of Porphyry's philosophical project was his defence of pagan cults and religious traditions as a bulwark against Christianity. This context also explains his interest in texts such as the *Chaldaean Oracles* and phenomena such as theurgy: this was part of a wider project, which in itself did not entail an abandoning of Plotinus' legacy, centred on philosophy. For Porphyry too, as for Plotinus before him, only intellectual contemplation ensures true access to the divine, whereas cult practices can only play a subordinate role.[199]

Iamblichus' new Platonism took shape precisely as a way of opposing this perspective. In order to clarify his ideas, Porphyry had addressed a letter to an imaginary Egyptian priest by the name of Anebo (most of this work is lost). Playing along with the fictional Egyptian context, Iamblichus reacted by drafting *The Response of the Master Abamon to Porphyry's Letter to Anebo*, in which he criticised Porphyry's 'subversion'[200] and justified theurgical cult

[196] Particularly revealing is the well-known view expressed by Dodds 1951: 283–314. An enlightening text is Eunapius' *Lives of Philosophers and Sophists*; see Goulet 2001.
[197] See Festugière 1968: 10.
[198] See now Tanaseanu-Döbler 2013.
[199] Cf. Porph. *De abst.* 2.34.3; *Ep. ad Marc.* 19.
[200] *De myst.* 5.21 and 26.

practices.[201] The underlying thesis of this work is that philosophical ascesis alone is insufficient for us to reunite with the divine; what is required are the ritual purifications of theurgy; 'it is not pure intellection that unites the theurgists with the gods: for else, what would prevent contemplative philosophers from attaining theurgic union?'; 'by means of the sacred liturgy the theurgists are established among the gods and unite with them'.[202] Without delving into a complex reconstruction of these practices, what must be stressed is the fact that there were also clear philosophical reasons for this turn: theurgy came to be perceived as necessary precisely because the possibility for the human soul to gain genuine access to divine and intelligible realities was denied – the soul was seen to lie on a different ontological level compared to the divine world. To put it more clearly, one may argue that theurgy constituted an alternative to the Plotinian doctrine of the undescended soul. Both Plotinus and his successors not only believed that the aim of human life is to reunite with divine realities, but also that this goal can somehow be achieved; since it cannot be achieved in a purely rational way (for it is untrue that part of us enjoys the presence of the divine), the only possible solution is to achieve it by a different means, namely through cult practices. Theurgy thus emerges as a philosophically grounded alternative to Plotinus' radical intellectualism.[203]

It is important to recall that Plotinus was not hostile to religious traditions in themselves or to the prospect of uniting theology and philosophy; quite the contrary. Yet the fact remains that this never translated into a subordination of philosophy. Instead, this is precisely what happens with Iamblichus, whose theses gave rise to a genuine theologisation of Platonism. As is widely known, the ancients had always conceived of philosophy as a way of life; in late Neoplatonism, this practice translated into life choices deeply marked by the religious dimension.[204]

---

[201] See the texts quoted in n. 18.

[202] *De myst.* 21.11 and 1.15.

[203] On theurgy in Proclus, see *In Tim.* 1.302.17–25; *TP* 4.2.7–9 with van den Berg 2000. Also interesting is what we read in the handbook *On the Gods and the World* by Sallust, an otherwise largely unknown figure.

[204] In addition to theurgic practices, let us think of the prayers included at key points of some Neoplatonic commentaries: exegesis was regarded as the religious action of deciphering and elucidating divine truths. On the 'pagan holiness' of the philosophers more generally, see Fowden 1982.

Platonisms: Some Final Remarks

Neoplatonism has often been judged negatively on account of its allegedly monolithic and uniform character. The aim of this chapter has been to disprove such prejudices by showing that Neoplatonism is pervaded by tensions and divergences that make it no less dynamic and problematic than Middle Platonism. Indeed, one of the outcomes I hope to have reached concerns Imperial Platonism as a whole. While divergences are to be found, so are elements of continuity, and one must take both into account. The claim that Plotinus radically renewed the philosophical scene is as self-evident as it is indisputable. However, it is no less true that many of Plotinus' most important theses, starting from that of the undescended soul, were not accepted by his successors, who thereby drew closer to some of Middle Platonist doctrines:[205] whereas a sharp division between the sensible and the intelligible level would appear to be a distinguishing feature of Plotinus' philosophical project, subsequent Neoplatonists shared their predecessors' desire to reconcile the two levels; and whereas Plotinus – consistent with his approach – aimed to develop a science of the intelligible in itself, *iuxta propria principia* (according to its own principles), Neoplatonists once again shared their predecessors' awareness that full access to intelligible realities is off-limits for human beings in their earthly condition. By this, of course, I do not wish to support the thesis of an identification of Middle Platonism with Neoplatonism, but neither does it make sense to speak of these two segments of the Platonist tradition as though they represented two radically different philosophies. Evident divergences are to be found (for example, with regard to the first principle and, more generally, in the latter's more systematic approach compared to the former), yet these divergences represent the development of one and the same project: to articulate Plato's philosophy into a complete and perfect metaphysical system.

There are also more general and important reasons why it is crucial to highlight this convergence. Over the course of the medieval,

---

[205] It is therefore hardly a coincidence that one of the foremost experts on late Platonism, Henry-Dominique Saffrey (1988: 19), spoke of Plotinus as an island in the Neoplatonist current. On Plotinus' project and its specificity, see Chiaradonna 2009: 33–8.

modern, and contemporary ages, the belief has gradually taken root that this version of Platonism represents the Platonism par excellence, which is to say the only genuine form of Platonism. This book ought to have shown that we are dealing with an error of perspective. Imperial Platonism is one possible development of Plato's thought, a development obviously based on the dialogues but also incorporating certain ideas drawn from the Stoic and Aristotelian traditions (starting from the attempt to organise Plato's doctrines into a system). No doubt, from a historical standpoint, this is the version of Platonism which became dominant, but the fact that it became dominant does not make it the only authentic version: it must be clear that, in this case too, we are dealing with an interpretation of Plato – an interpretation that, with all its strengths and limits, is certainly possible, yet is still only an interpretation, and one which stands in contrast to other possible ones.

If this conclusion is accepted, then the book will have attained the goal he had set himself: what an in-depth analysis of the thousand-year-old history of the Platonist tradition suggests is precisely that there is no single Platonism; rather, we have many 'Platonisms', several different ways of accounting for that ambiguity which represents Plato's philosophical richness. Certainly, some common tendencies are to be found – for example, an underlying anti-empiricism[206] – yet it is difficult to identify conceptual coordinates capable of uniting this tradition in a strong sense. Before choosing one or the other option, as we are indeed free to do, we must take account of all this, particularly in the light of the significance of Plato and Platonism in the history of philosophy.

---

[206] Gerson 2013 has suggested that we identify the matrix of Platonism in five oppositions: the innermost nature of Platonism would consist of a combination of anti-nominalism, anti-mechanism, anti-materialism, anti-relativism, and anti-scepticism. While certainly interesting, this suggestion is not entirely convincing. The first three points may more generally be traced back to a form of anti-empiricism, and certainly the battle against relativism also played an important role in Plato's philosophy and in Platonism. However, it is difficult to regard anti-scepticism as a common denominator in Platonism, and not merely because it would risk being incompatible with the Hellenistic Academy. Ultimately, from Speusippus to Damascius (but with the notable exception of Plotinus), almost all Platonists acknowledged – in one way or another – that full knowledge of the intelligible principles is inaccessible to human beings. And given the importance of intelligible principles on the epistemological level, it would be difficult to describe Platonism as a philosophy that solved the problem of scepticism.

This conclusion may prove disappointing for those who have definitively made up their minds as to the nature of Plato's philosophy, while it will confirm other people's impression that there is something wrong with Plato: that there must be some inconsistencies in his thought, if so many possibilities remain open. However, the best thing may be to think of all this as Plato's greatest gift to his heirs and readers – the freedom to always make a fresh start:

> Plato himself, too, shortly before his death, had a dream of himself as a swan, darting from tree to tree and causing great trouble to the fowlers, who were unable to catch him. When Simmias the Socratic heard this dream, he explained that all men would endeavour to grasp Plato's meaning (τὴν τοῦ Πλάτωνος διάνοιαν), none, however, would succeed, but each would interpret him according to his own views.[207]

How a swan may leap from tree to tree remains a bit of a mystery. But the author of this anecdote could hardly have come up with a better description of this long history.

[207] Anon. *Proleg. in Plat. phil.* 1.29–35.

THE PLATONISTS AND POLITICS

People tend to forget that it was only at the turn of the twentieth century that a 'political' interpretation of Plato became popular: an interpretation that identified practical and political engagement as the inevitable outcome of Plato's theoretical reflections, so to speak. Previously – and not just in antiquity – Plato and Platonists had often been regarded as the standard-bearers of the contemplative life. While this remains true in most cases (but not all, as we shall see), it does not justify scholars' disinterest in the relationship between Platonism and politics in the ancient world. On the contrary, we must account for this phenomenon too if we wish to gain an adequate understanding of what Platonism stood for.

Platonists and Politics

Even a superficial survey of the available sources reveals that a significant number of Academics and Platonists were engaged in political activities. Some scholars have sought to downplay this phenomenon by distinguishing between the majority of people who simply attended the Academy or Platonist schools and the few true Platonist philosophers within them: in the former group, political commitment and attending Plato's lessons or Platonic schools were not necessarily connected events. For instance, in Plato's day, the Academy was frequented by many members of the upper classes, which is to say people who, after completing their education, were destined to seize the reins of power. This was also the case with the many Roman aristocrats who attended Platonist schools in the early centuries of the Empire: certainly, it was not as Platonists that they pursued political careers.[1]

---

[1] Brunt 1993: 288.

This observation is certainly correct. Yet even accepting this distinction, and limiting ourselves to professional philosophers, the outcome does not change: for centuries a truly significant number of Platonists practised politics. This phenomenon emerges quite plainly from the very beginning and would appear to constitute an important aspect of the Academy's life: the first two scholarchs, Speusippus and Xenocrates, engaged with the new Macedonian authorities – in a favourable way in the former case and with greater reservation in the latter.[2] Indeed, philosophers were so involved in Athenian political life that in 307/306 Sophocles of Sunium famously issued a decree threatening with death any philosophers seeking to open new schools in Athens without the assembly's permission. This decree was apparently soon withdrawn, but it is still revealing of an increasingly widespread sentiment in the city: chiefly directed against the Peripatetics, it certainly also applied to the Academics, and – among other things – it was aimed at curbing an increasingly ill-tolerated degree of activism.[3]

More specifically, Platonists were directly involved in defining the legislation of *poleis* (according to the model laid out in the *Laws*) and serving as advisers to rulers (as Plato had done in Syracuse – Aristotle's role as Alexander's counsellor in Macedon being another famous example). We also know of personal attempts to seize power, according to the *Statesman*'s model of the *aner basilikos*, or to overthrow autocratic regimes: from the failed endeavour of Dion (the pupil for whom Plato had the greatest expectations, and who was killed by another Academic, Callippus, in 354) to the lesser-known case of Chaeron. This was a student of Plato's and Xenocrates' who, in Pellene in 331, attempted to introduce a series of radical reforms more or less inspired by the *Republic* (redistribution of properties, banishment or execution of noblemen, manumission of slaves, and sharing of women), but only succeeded in establishing a tyranny based on terror.[4] These different modes of political intervention caused

---

[2] For a detailed analysis of all testimonies about political commitment in the first Academy, see Isnardi Parente 1989: 63–78; Trampedach 1994; Vegetti 2003; Haake 2020.

[3] On this decree, see Haake 2007: 16–43 and Haake 2008.

[4] Dorandi 1994.

considerable perplexity already in ancient times, to the point of giving rise to two contrasting images of the Academy, which was labelled as a school for tyrants by its detractors but celebrated as a school of freedom by its champions.[5] The Hellenistic period's political developments did not change this picture: the innovations which followed Alexander's conquests broadened the stage and reduced the possibilities for direct intervention in politics, yet the new importance acquired by the Athenian schools bestowed increasing authoritativeness on philosophers.[6] Arcesilaus' apparent disengagement[7] is counterbalanced by the embassy that Carneades famously led in 155 BC, when – along with the Peripatetic Critolaus and the Stoic Diogenes – he was sent to Rome to uphold Athens' cause. The Romans, represented by the great Cato and alarmed by the negative influence that Carneades might have on young Romans, soon granted the Athenians' requests, eager to get rid themselves of the philosophers as soon as possible. The success of this mission hardly depended on shrewd diplomatic action; yet we are still dealing with one of the few cases in which a Platonist achieved success in an important political enterprise.[8] The last scholarch, Philo of Larissa, who was in all respects a more moderate philosopher than Carneades, would appear to have been on excellent terms not just with the Athenian authorities, but also with powerful Romans – so much so that he chose Rome as his destination when forced to leave Athens. The

[5] Athen. *Deipn.* 508f–509a; Plut. *Adv. Col.* 1126c–d.
[6] Two important studies on the Academy's public role in the Hellenistic Age are Haake 2007: especially 99–117; and Ferrary 2007. Useful information can also be found in Habicht 1994.
[7] D.L. 4.39: note, however, that Arcesilaus too served as an Athenian ambassador.
[8] Carneades' strategy was subtly designed to involve Rome in the charge against Athens: the *polis* risked sanctions because of its attack on the small town of Oropus. But why? If it was not right for Athens to pursue its own interests, then how could Roman imperialism be justified? Either Rome and Athens were acting justly, in which case Athens should not be punished, or Athens and Rome were acting unjustly, in which case it was difficult to understand the reasons for Rome's superiority: see Atkins 2000: 494. As Victor Brochard has compellingly noted, 'Carneades taught the Romans but one thing: that the way of acting that was usual for them, and which seemed natural to them, was deplorable' (Brochard 2002: 177). It is easy to see why Carneades was immediately expelled. From a philosophical perspective, these theses would appear to stem from a dialectical exercise which did not necessarily commit Carneades to taking any definite stance on the matter (Cic. *De rep.* 3.9); on a possible relationship with Plato, see Lévy 1992: 509–20.

other best-known Platonist of this period, Antiochus, continued the tradition of philosophers serving as advisers by accompanying one of the most influential Roman politicians, Lucullus, on his journeys to the eastern provinces.

The picture in the Imperial Age is no different, as many Platonists were directly engaged in the management of power, whether on a local scale, as in the case of Plutarch in continental Greece (between Delphi and Chaeronea), or – and this is a truly significant point – at the Imperial court.[9] A lively debate surrounds Porphyry's possible role in relation to Diocletian's anti-Christian persecution; later, many of Iamblichus' pupils held leading positions at court over the course of the fourth century (such as Maximus of Ephesus and Sopatrus). Julian's short reign is the only actual instance of a Platonist philosopher in power – a fulfilment of the famous wish expressed in the *Republic* (473c–d). In the meantime, several philosophers continued to act as advisers, including Longinus – who was implicated in Zenobia's revolt in Palmyra (and for this reason sentenced to death by Aurelian between 272 and 273) – and even Plotinus. The most unpolitical Platonist of all from a philosophical perspective accompanied Gordian on his unlucky eastern campaign, was acquainted with quite a few senators in Rome, and even attempted – in vain – to establish a city called 'Platonopolis'.

It goes without saying that with the rise of Christians to power, the pagan Platonists' importance was drastically curtailed. However, it was not entirely erased, since Justinian's decision to close the School of Athens down in 529 would appear to have been partly motivated by the need to oppose the influence of the last pagan Neoplatonists.[10] Besides, it is important to note that many leading 'Christian Platonists' – from the Cappadocian Fathers to Synesius in the East, and from Augustine to Boethius in the West – held very important political offices. This amounts to further confirmation that philosophers connected to Plato were engaged in politics.

[9] For a succinct and insightful overview, with a rich bibliography, see Chiaradonna 2013.
[10] Cf. e.g. Di Branco 2006: 115–79 (a more cautious view is expressed by Wildberg 2005: 329–33).

Two Platonic Political Doctrines from Speusippus to the Neoplatonists

When we move on to consider more strictly doctrinal contents, we soon note that most testimonies fall into two separate groups, according to whether their emphasis is on the political importance of philosophy and the need for a philosopher-ruler, or on the priority and centrality of the law (*nomos*).[11] These fluctuations reproduce the divergence between the *Republic* on the one hand, and the *Laws* and *Statesman* on the other. However, upon closer inspection, it becomes clear that it would be wrong to overstress this apparent tension: from a Platonist standpoint, the two theses are not incompatible, but rather reflect different perspectives on the same problems.

The importance of the issue of the law emerges quite explicitly already with Speusippus, in one of the few testimonies about the political reflections conducted in the first Academy. In the lost work *To Cleophon*, Speusippus reportedly observed that 'if monarchy is something noble, and only the wise man is truly a king and leader, then the law too, being a rightful discourse, is something noble'.[12] This statement presents two ideas destined to become common among many later Platonists. First of all, it constitutes an exemplary testimony about the primary importance of the *nomos* as the foundation of any lawful form of governance. Originally formulated in opposition to the Cynics, over the centuries this idea came to be repeatedly used in a variety of contexts, for explicitly polemical purposes. It found a striking expression in the image of the ruler as the 'guardian of the law':

So law is a good for all in common, and without it none of the other goods could come about. Consequently, the ruler who is placed in responsibility for the laws must have a completely pure into the absolute correctness of the laws. [...] For the preserver and guardian of laws should be as immune from corruption as is humanly possible.[13]

Secondly, this maxim clearly reveals an inclination towards the monarchy (*basileia*): a predilection for this form of government,

---

[11] Useful introductions may be found in Isnardi Parente 1979: 235–305 (Old Academy); Centrone 2000a (Middle Platonism); and Chiaradonna 2013 and O'Meara 2003 (Neoplatonism).

[12] Fr. 119.

[13] Iambl. *Ep. Ad Agrip.*, *ap.* Stob. 4.5.77.

expressed in a range of different settings, is another recurrent feature in the Platonists' reflections.

This predilection is explained and further justified by the second aforementioned thesis, namely the need for a philosopher-ruler: clearly, the belief that a (Platonist) philosopher alone can ensure fair governance for a city finds its most suitable embodiment in a monarchical regime (for it is easier to convert a single person to philosophy than the people as a whole), as Plato's journeys to Syracuse illustrate. However, the importance of the thesis of the 'philosopher in power' goes far beyond the mere endorsement of monarchical regimes (a rather predictable position, considering that from Alexander onwards the Greek world first and then the Graeco-Roman one were mainly governed by monarchs). It constituted a fundamental element for the construction of a Platonist identity and for the defence of Platonism's importance in a cultural context that was not always favourably disposed towards philosophy.

The underlying idea is the familiar one of two orders of reality: one divine and perfect, the other imperfect and human. The duty of politics is to reproduce – as far as possible – the divine and ideal order in the imperfect world we inhabit. This explains the philosopher's superiority: the only true ruler is the philosopher (alternatively, only a philosopher can correctly advise a ruler), because only a philosopher can know those truths and values which lie at the basis of everything. Hence, only a philosopher can be capable of reproducing that order which governs the life of the universe in cities and human communities:

God has established in states the light of justice and of knowledge of himself as an image which the blessed and the wise copy with the help of philosophy, modelling themselves after the most beautiful of things.[14]

As Iamblichus noted, what matters is wisdom (*phronesis*), for

It has the characteristic of directing men, and, in referring cities and households and the private life of each individual to a divine model, it portrays them in likeness to what is best, rubbing out something here, painting in something there, and in both cases bringing everything to a harmonious likeness.[15]

---

[14] Plut. *Ad princ. ind.* 781f–782a; on Plutarch's position more generally, see Bonazzi 2012b and 2020b.
[15] *Ep. Ad Asph.*, *ap.* Stob. 3.3.26; see Taormina and Piccione 2010.

Herein lies the philosopher's superiority and the need for philosophy. No doubt, as has been repeatedly observed,[16] theses such as these do not seem particularly original, given that the idea of the sovereign as God's earthly representative and an embodiment of divine *logos* is a widespread one hardly limited to Platonist schools: from Hellenistic political treatises to the works of Stoics such as Seneca and of many other Imperial Age writers, it emerges as something of a commonplace in ancient political thought.[17] Without wishing to deny this shared background, there is one element at least that might help define the specificity of the Platonists' view, namely their widely attested emphasis on the ethical dimension. A recurrent motif in Platonist thought is the belief that true politics consists in caring for people's souls: in this respect, scholars have spoken of 'a collapsing of administration into ethics'[18] and it was by stressing this point that in certain cases Platonists were able to criticise the politics of their day.

Two Political Platonists: Marcus Tullius Cicero and Flavius Claudius Julianus

Generally speaking, it cannot be denied that the Platonists meditated on politics and that their considerations are worthy of investigation. However, this is not to say that the ancient Platonists sought to defend a 'political' interpretation of Plato such as that developed by many contemporary scholars. Still, two exceptions are worth considering: we know of at least two Platonists who embodied a political ideal in the ancient world and who even sought to realise it in their lives, in the specific circumstances in which they found themselves operating. I am referring to Cicero and Julian.[19]

---

[16] O'Meara 2003: 97 and 148.
[17] See e.g. Chesnut 1978.
[18] Trapp 2004: 198; this remark concerns Plutarch, yet applies equally well to numerous other Platonists of the Imperial age.
[19] A third thinker in relation to whom we might speak of political Platonism is Plutarch of Chaeronea: see Bonazzi 2012b and Bonazzi 2020. Indeed, if there is a moment in which the political interpretation of Plato would appear to have been regarded as particularly important, it was Middle Platonism (which nonetheless also defended the contemplative life – there was no clear-cut stance on the matter).

Appendix 1: The Platonists and Politics

1. *Cicero.* The life and thought of Cicero (106–43 BC) is fatally intertwined with the history of Rome during its transition from Republic to Principate. A champion of many battles, and involved in as many resounding victories as disastrous defeats, he sacrificed his very life for the sake of his political commitment.[20] However, Cicero's reflection ultimately transcends contingencies and has established itself as a fundamental point of reference in the history of Western political thought. Readers usually tend to focus on his orations, fascinated by his greatness as a writer. Rhetoric, however, for Cicero was part of something much bigger: namely, philosophy.[21] Arguably the most ambitious, and certainly the most Platonic, feat undertaken by Cicero lies precisely in his effort to introduce philosophy into Rome in the belief that it might heal the moral sickness that was destroying the city.

No doubt, Cicero received a distinguished philosophical education, as he studied under the two most authoritative Platonist philosophers of his day: Philo of Larissa – when the latter fled to Rome – and Antiochus of Ascalon, between 79 and 77 BC.[22] Cicero was especially won over by the former's moderate scepticism (*totum ei me tradidi*, he later observed: 'I entrusted myself to him completely' – *Brutus* 306), without thereby completely rejecting the latter's teaching, particularly as far as politics is concerned.[23] Philo's scepticism did not rule out a qualified commitment to certain theses,[24] and Cicero made the most of this possibility in

---

[20] A succinct and compelling overview of Cicero's life and work is Stroh 2008; Steel 2013 is also useful. Schofield 2021 is now the reference for his political thought. Lévy 1992, and Gawlick and Görler 1994 (with an extensive bibliography), and now Atkins and Bénatouïl 2021, remain fundamental as regards Cicero's philosophical thought. More concise introductions to his political thought may be found in Atkins 2000 and Zetzel 2013.

[21] Cf. e.g. *Orator* 3.11.

[22] An intriguing reconstruction of this period is provided in the prologue to Book 5 of the *De finibus*. Cicero, moreover, attended lectures by the Stoics Diodotus and Posidonius, and by the Epicurean Phaedrus: see *De nat. deor.* 1.3 and *Fam.* 13.1.2.

[23] Indeed, Cicero was always well aware of the misunderstandings to which a sceptical philosophy could give rise when discussing political issues, as witnessed by *De leg.* 1.39 (this, however, does not mean that we should posit an 'Antiochean' phase in Cicero's philosophical trajectory: against this hypothesis suggested by Glucker 1988, see Görler 1995). On this issue more generally, see Lévy 1992: 495–508.

[24] Cf. Chapter 2, Philo of Larissa and the Moderate Turn, p. 56.

order to take a stand on some of the thorniest political issues of his day. In doing so, via Antiochus, he drew close to Stoicism, and even more so to Plato, who constituted the ultimate point of reference for his reflection and literary output. This may be inferred from three great works he composed between 55 and 51 BC, and which provide a full outline of his political project: *De oratore*, *De republica*, and *De legibus*.

Describing a text which defends rhetoric such as the *De oratore* as a Platonist work might seem surprising, considering Plato's frequently contemptuous treatment of the art of speaking well. Indeed, this text departs in many respects from the Platonic perspective, particularly in Book I, where the author praises the Sophists and Isocrates while instead criticising Socrates, who, unlike the former, sought to separate the study of the truth from that of persuasion. However, the underlying thesis of the dialogue, which compares the two leading orators from the generation before Cicero, namely Licinius Crassus and Marcus Antonius, is actually completely in line with the *Phaedrus'* teaching: the perfect orator has a broad and solid cultural background – of the sort which, of course, can only be achieved through the study of philosophy. The ideal orator is someone capable of combining wisdom and persuasion; it is this capacity that can make a true politician of him, a politician who can effectively lead his community towards the good without giving in to the temptation of using his skills for private profit (a risk of which every reader of the *Gorgias* is well aware: cf. *De or.* 3.55).

The Platonic influence is especially evident in the other two texts, which from their very titles refer to the Athenian philosopher's two major political works.[25] In both cases, Cicero's intention is to treat (*De leg.* 1.37) the tendency to make force, rather than justice and the law, the cornerstone of the political community. Naturally, in the case of a creative thinker like Cicero, influence does not translate into passive repetition.[26] Just as

---

[25] Cicero himself notes this: *De rep.* 1.16; *De leg.* 1.15 and 3.4. On the relationship between the *De republica* and the *De legibus*, see Ferrary 1995.

[26] On Cicero's creativeness and independence, see Gildenhard 2011.

in Plato's *Republic*, the underlying theme of *De republica*[27] is the best form of government; yet unlike Plato, Cicero does not search for a solution in the establishment of an ideal State, existing in some remote time and place, and whose abstract nature is actually criticised (*De rep.* 2.3.21–22, 52, and 66). *Moribus antiquis res stat Romana virisque*, 'Roman power rests on ancient habits and men' (*De rep.* 5.1): drawing upon a verse by the poet Ennius, Cicero defends the thesis according to which the ideal State is ancient Rome, that which existed before the Gracchi's reforms, and which combined the advantages of all forms of government (monarchy, aristocracy, and democracy: *De rep.* 2.42.65 and 69). The problem is to ensure the survival of these institutions by reinforcing the bond between the *mos maiorum* and philosophy (*De rep.* 3.5–6: this is where Scipio's greatness lies). The various books that make up the work thus discuss this State and what makes a good citizen (the second problem addressed by Cicero is precisely the moral education of citizens and especially of the ruling class). The text culminates in a final vision, the famous 'Dream of Scipio', a parallel of the myth of Er which celebrates the need for political engagement: the protagonist, Publius Cornelius Scipio Aemilianus, when 'carried off' into the heavens, is instructed about the nature of the world and the immortality of the soul, and learns that the highest task for man is engagement in politics, which must take the concrete form of the pursuit of the common good.[28]

In *De legibus* too, the borrowing of Platonic themes comes with certain changes: Plato's dialogue was designed to establish

[27] This text, which was famous in antiquity, was lost around the fifth century (only its final section was preserved, the so-called 'Dream of Scipio', which was commented upon by the Neoplatonist Macrobius in the fifth century, and went on to become one of the most widely read texts in the Middle Ages). Only in 1819 did the work start circulating again, after the Prefect of the Vatican Library, Angelo Mai, the 'bold Italian' (*italo ardito*) celebrated by Leopardi, discovered that a manuscript of this text had been erased to make room for a copy of Augustine's commentary on the Psalms. By working on this palimpsest, it was possible to retrieve extensive sections of the first two books and part of the third (out of a total of six).

[28] *De rep.* 6.29, expanding on some points made in the first book. On the importance of the active life (by contrast to the contemplative) according to Cicero, see Joly 1956: 158–65.

a body of laws that would also apply in the absence of a perfect ruler; by contrast, the laws of the *De legibus* are those laid down for the *optimus status* described in the *De republica* (*De leg.* 1.15, 2.23, and 3.12), whose everlasting value is celebrated (as already in *De rep.* 2.34 and 41). Regrettably, the *De legibus* is incomplete (only the first three books have survived in full). Yet what we have is enough to show its importance, particularly with reference to one of the fundamental problems for political Platonism, namely the issue of natural law (*ius naturae*). The underlying thesis of the text is that all positive laws rest on natural law. Cicero had already written about this law in Book 3 of the *De republica*, evoking Carneades' embassy to Rome in 155 BC. Carneades had inverted the order found in Plato's *Republic* by discussing the need for justice in human communities on the first day, and the need for injustice on the second. Cicero re-established the original sequence, and has Laelius affirm the existence of natural law in opposition to Philo's conventionalism:

True law is right reason, consonant with nature, spread through all people. It is constant and eternal; it summons to duty by its orders, it deters from crime by its prohibitions. Its orders and prohibitions to good people are never given in vain; but it does not move the wicked by these orders or prohibitions. It is wrong to pass laws obviating this law; it is not permitted to abrogate any of it; it cannot be totally repealed. [...] There will not be one law at Rome and another at Athens, one now another later; but all nations at all times will be bound by this one eternal and unchangeable law, and the god will be the one common master and general (so to speak) of all people. He is the author, expounder, and mover of this law; and the person who does not obey it will be in exile from himself. Insofar as he scorns his nature as a human being, by this very fact he will pay the greatest penalty, even if he escapes all the other things that are generally recognized as punishments. (*De rep.* 3.33)

The same thesis crops up again in the *De legibus*:

Law is the highest reason, rooted in nature, which commands things that must be done and prohibits the opposite. When this same reason is secured and established in the human mind, it is law. And therefore they think that law is judgment, the effect of which is such as to order people to behave rightly and forbid them to do wrong; they think that its name in Greek is deriving from giving to each his own (*suum cuique*), while I think that in Latin it is derived from choosing (*a legendo*; 1.18–19).

Many scholars believe that this thesis exclusively reflects Stoic philosophy,[29] but this is an overly simplistic assessment: no doubt, a similar thesis was also upheld by the Stoics (and partly reached Cicero via Antiochus).[30] But previously it had already been a cornerstone of Plato's political thought, and Cicero can undoubtedly be credited with having taken it up (as the most genuine expression of the morality underlying Roman institutions) and transmitted it to future centuries.[31]

A second phase in Cicero's philosophical production dates from the years 46–44 BC, when Caesar was seizing power and the avenues for political action were growing increasingly narrower. Cicero's plan was to reproduce the whole body of Greek philosophy in Latin: with remarkable swiftness, according to the typical tripartition of Greek thought, Cicero composed works on epistemology (*Academica*), physics (*De natura deorum, De divinatione, De fato*), and ethics (*De finibus bonorum et malorum, Tusculanae disputationes, De officiis*).[32] Scholars have often questioned Cicero's philosophical competence, accusing him of eclecticism. But these are works written by a sharp mind, capable of clearly presenting frequently complex problems. Without Cicero's valuable testimony, our knowledge of Greek philosophy – particularly Hellenistic philosophy – would be far more limited (nor should we overlook the importance of his translations of Greek technical terms). In this context, what must be stressed are the motivations behind a feat so bold that not even Greek philosophers had ever attempted to undertake it: one might speak of patriotism (the belief that even in the philosophical field Rome was not inferior to Greece: *De nat. deor.* 1.7–8, *De fin.* 1.1–10), and further

---

[29] Cf. e.g. *SVF* 1.162 and 3.4. Particularly close to Stoicism is the emphasis on rationality and the argument underlying this thesis (natural law is identical to right reasoning; reason is common to all human beings; the correct use of reason leads to an understanding of natural law and a desire to obey it). See Zetzel 2013: 192.

[30] Cf. *De leg.* 1.53–56; see Ferrary 1995: 67–8.

[31] A detailed analysis of the relationship between Cicero, Plato, and the Stoics may be found in Neschke-Hentske 1995: 183–202. An interesting, and generally overlooked, parallel that might confirm that the context is Platonic is ps.-Archit. *De lege et iustitia*, 33.20–28.

[32] An equally important, yet lost, work is the *Hortensius*, a philosophical protreptic. Just as interesting, albeit less technical, are *Laelius de amicitia* and *Cato de senectute*. Cicero also translated the *Timaeus* and *Protagoras*.

adduce personal reasons (philosophy as a means to overcome the pain Cicero felt at the death of his beloved daughter Tullia). But the most significant element is, once again, the political factor; the idea of spreading philosophy in Rome – an apparently bizarre endeavour – was motivated by the desire to provide a basis for a moral resurgence capable of saving the Roman State from the crisis that was bringing it to its knees: 'For what greater or better service can I render to the commonwealth than to instruct and train the youth – especially in view of the fact that our young men have gone so far astray because of the present laxity?'[33] In other words, Cicero never ceased thinking of philosophy and politics as indissolubly linked. This trust in the political importance of philosophical education is something that makes Cicero a genuine *Platonis comes* (companion of Plato), as he wrote of himself.[34]

Regrettably, Cicero shares one last feature with Plato: like the latter, he failed to achieve his goals. And the end he met was far more tragic than Plato's, since Mark Antony literally demanded – and obtained – his head from Octavian, which was displayed in the Senate along with the hands that had penned so many speeches against him (the famous *Philippics*).[35]

2. *Julian*. Julian, Emperor from 361 to 363, may be described as the only Platonist philosopher-ruler of antiquity. However, he is in many ways an enigmatic figure, and it cannot automatically be assumed that he envisaged his political activity as the completion and culmination of his adherence to (Neo)Platonist philosophy: several scholars have sought to defend this interpretation, but many others have opposed it.[36]

Doubts and uncertainties clearly emerge in one of the Emperor's first texts, a letter he wrote to Themistius, one of the most authoritative philosophers of his time.[37] A Senator and leading court

---

[33] *De div.* 2.2. More generally, see André 1977: 59–67.
[34] *De rep.* 1.1b. On the political motivations underlying Cicero's philosophical works, see Baraz 2012.
[35] Plut. *Vita Cic.* 48–9.
[36] On Julian's political conceptions, see Athanassiadi 1981, Chiaradonna 2013, and esp. Elm 2012.
[37] Recent analyses of Themistius' political thought, with a special focus on his relationship with Julian and Platonism, are found in Swain 2013 and Schramm 2014; the classic study remains Dagron 1968.

intellectual, Themistius had chosen the literary genre of the letter to address the new Caesar Julian (355),[38] exhorting him to embrace the true philosophical life: a life which coincided with political engagement, according to the mythological example of Dionysus and Heracles. In his letter to Julian, Themistius drew upon themes dear to him, and already widely featured in his orations,[39] outlining a doctrine of kingship that made the latter intrinsically superior to the bond of laws: 'an emperor must be a genuine philosopher-king, a philanthropist, someone fully engaged in governing, a living embodiment of the law, and an image of divine rulership in the world'.[40] This is the model which Julian was encouraged to follow.

The new Caesar's reply, however, was very different in tone. Given his position, Julian could hardly avoid political engagement; yet, he criticised what he regarded as the orator's exclusive emphasis on the earthly dimension, which risked compromising the specific quality of philosophy, namely its capacity to reunite man with divine reality (which is ultimately the reason for its superiority). The model of the true philosophy was not Alexander the Great: it was Socrates, who had saved so many souls through his teaching (*Ad Them.* 10). The rather explicit meaning of these claims is clear, and coincides with faithfulness to a different philosophical tradition of that period: Julian affirms his adherence to the theurgical Neoplatonism of Iamblichus and his pupils from the so-called School of Pergamon, particularly Maximus of Ephesus, who was Julian's teacher. Finally, to the model of the sovereign above the laws, Julian opposes the alternative model of the *basileus* as the 'custodian and guardian of the law', engaged in a mission (*leitourgia*) on the gods' behalf.

Particularly in reference to this last point, it is difficult to grasp the sense of the polemic with Themistius: in other, later texts – not only the *Orations*, but also the two great theological

---

[38] In actual fact, the date of this letter (regrettably lost) and of Julian's (which enables us to reconstruct Themistius') is uncertain: another hypothesis is that this exchange dates back to the end of 361, when Julian was ascending the Imperial throne. See the discussion in Swain 2013: 53–7.

[39] Cf. *Or.* 20, 239a–d on politics as the natural completion of philosophy.

[40] Chiaradonna 2015.

hymns *To the Mother of the Gods* and *To King Helios* – Julian, while still distinguishing between himself and true philosophers, seems more aware of his divinely ordained role and more inclined to accept the idea of himself as a ruler chosen by the gods, the earthly embodiment of the Platonic Demiurge. These ideas partly draw upon commonplaces in the Platonist tradition and Imperial Age political treatises, but Julian combines them with numerous notions typical of Neoplatonism, leading to a highly original universalist conception: the ideal of *romanitas* as a synthesis of Greek and Roman wisdom, as the accomplishment of a universal plan conceived by the gods and destined to have everlasting value. Julian did not live long enough to accomplish his political project. But his universal ideal was soon to influence Christian thinkers, eventually finding its way into the medieval and modern world. This is yet another element proving the importance of the Platonic political tradition.[41]

Christians, Platonism, and Politics: Eusebius and Augustine

As we will show in Appendix 2, the mutual engagement between Platonists and Christians was far richer, more articulated, and more complex than is commonly assumed: behind openly professed rejections, we find highly interesting borrowings and adaptations. Further confirmation of the importance of these interactions is provided by Eusebius, Bishop of Caesarea (c. 260–340), who adapted typically Platonic themes and doctrines to a Christian model, developing a genuine political theology, destined to exercise considerable influence on the political thought of later centuries, particularly in the Eastern-Greek world.

The last heir to the great era of Alexandrian Platonising Christianity represented by Clement and Origen, Eusebius is best known for two remarkable works, the *Preparation for the Gospel* (*Praeparatio Evangelica*) and *Proof of the Gospel* (*Demonstratio Evangelica*), which – among other things – seek to demonstrate that the Christian religion is not just compatible with pagan philosophy, but is superior to it. The former work is a treasure trove

---

[41] This is the (highly original and masterfully defended) thesis of Elm 2012.

of quotes from ancient philosophers, particularly Platonists, and unequivocally shows the bishop's great competence. In other works, this knowledge is applied to the political field with highly significant results. On 25 July 336, Eusebius delivered a public address in honour of Emperor Constantine, to celebrate the thirty years of his reign.[42] The occasion – celebrating the ruling Emperor – was a conventional one, common to many late antique addresses; but the results reached by Eusebius are original and momentous. In sumptuous language, the bishop outlines the model of the Christian Emperor as God's earthly image, via Christ's mediation: God's Kingdom is a monarchy, acknowledged by human beings yet utterly transcendent (ἐπέκεινα τῶν ὅλων, 1.1, p. 196, 18); its transcendence is such that not even the sovereign can approach it: his reign is modelled after God's *logos*, the second person of the Trinity that governs the universe (3.6); and it is by looking at this 'intelligible archetype' (3.5) that the sovereign must govern the world of human beings. Constantine's sovereignty, in other words, is ensured by this faithfulness to the true sovereignty of God: a faithfulness that is unattainable for Greek polytheism (3.6), but which makes the Roman Empire the kingdom providentially willed by God (16). The borrowings from the Greek tradition and from Platonism are evident,[43] and their consequences truly remarkable: this fresh adoption of the model of the philosopher-king and the emphasis on the monarchical model lie at the origin of so-called Caesaropapism, while also – one might say – jarring with the most distinctive trait of Christian theology, namely its trinitarianism, as theologian Erik Petersen noted in a famous book published in 1935.

Eusebius wrote his eulogy of Constantine at a particular moment: when Christians had finally made it to the top of an empire that had repeatedly launched persecutions against them, to no avail. His optimism is therefore perfectly understandable. A different case is that of another thinker equally influenced by the Platonist tradition, yet capable of leading his brand of Christianity

---

[42] Two translations providing plenty of additional information are Maraval 2001 (in French) and Amerisi 2005 (in Italian); more generally on Eusebius and Constantine, see Barnes 1981.

[43] See O'Meara 2003: 147–51, with a further bibliography.

towards new outcomes. In 410, the Empire witnessed the sack of Rome by Alaric's Goths: a shocking event (no army had ever sacked Rome since the Gauls in 390 BC) which soon enough was blamed on the Christians, who were seen as having promoted the betrayal and abandonment of the gods that had made Rome and its Empire great. *The City of God* by Augustine (354–430) is a response to these accusations, and it goes far beyond his specific polemic about pagan gods and demons (attacked in the first ten books, while the second part of the work discusses the origin and nature of the two cities).[44] Augustine's underlying thesis is the existence of two cities, a City of God and a City of Satan, the heavenly Jerusalem and Babylon, which mix and intertwine in the events of this world, only to be forever separated by the Final Judgement. The two cities are distinct; what characterises them are two different kinds of love (love directed towards God in the case of the heavenly city, and self-love, to the point of contempt for God, in the case of the earthly city). This makes the two irreconcilable, ruling out the possibility of a Christian kingdom foreshadowing the Kingdom of God in this world. The true Christian is a pilgrim upon this earth, and his destination is heaven. The dualism underlying this thesis can certainly be compared to the dualism typical of Imperial Platonism. Besides, many theses in this work present evident affinities with Platonic theses (this is particularly the case with the emphasis on justice).[45] However, the way in which Augustine makes use of these entails an attempt on his part to distance himself from and undermine[46] the political model developed by Imperial Platonism (this distance is further increased by the importance assigned to the doctrine of grace: it is divine grace, not asceticism or theurgy, that can save the souls of Adam and Eve's descendants). The State is no doubt essential in order to control the disorder stemming from human passions

---

[44] For an introduction to this fundamental text, see O'Daly 1999. Concerning Augustine's political thought, see Weithman 2001. Previously, Augustine had upheld theses compatible with those of the Platonists or Eusebius; see O'Meara 2003: 151–3.

[45] On Augustine's importance and distinctiveness within the tradition of natural law theory stretching back to Plato, see Neschke-Hentske 1999 (taken up in Neschke-Hentske 2003: 37–67) and Cassi 2013.

[46] See Chiaradonna 2013: 752.

(*De civ. Dei* 19.17) and the Christian does not oppose its authority (provided it does not force him to go against God's will); but
no earthly government can legitimately aspire to represent the
Kingdom of God, nor can a sovereign claim to exercise the salvific mediating function that is proper to Christ alone:

> As far as this mortal life is concerned, which is passed and ended in a few days,
> what difference does it make for a man who is soon to die, under what ruler he
> lives, if only the rulers do not force him to commit unholy and unjust deeds?[47]

In other words, 'Augustine replaces the hierarchical structure,
whereby political life (in Neoplatonism and Eusebius' theocracy)
represents a stage leading to a higher existence, with a dualism
of opposed cities traversing history of all political structures
and even of the Church.'[48] Whereas Eusebius shows the optimism of a faith aligned with politics, Augustine preserves the
memory of Christianity's early stages, which were frequently
marked by an intransigent affirmation of its incompatibility with
Roman power, without thereby slipping into messianic expectations;[49] and whereas Eusebius defines the Caesaropapist model,
Augustine defends the independence of the City of God and lays
the foundations for the medieval affirmation of the superiority of
Church over Empire. Similar tensions also emerge in the relationship with Platonism: the borrowing of themes typical of Imperial
Platonism is evident in Eusebius; but the Augustinian alternative
too finds numerous parallels in some of Plato's more unpolitical
passages (e.g. the philosopher's refusal to return to the cave once
he has beheld the ideas, *Rep.* 517c–e). For Augustine too, then,
Platonism played an important role, offering ideas that were to
lead the Bishop of Hippo to set out on unbeaten tracks.

---

[47] *De civ. Dei* 5.17.
[48] O'Meara 2003: 157.
[49] Let us think of Tatian – 'I scorn your laws' (*Address to the Greeks* 28) – and even more
of Tertullian, an African like Augustine: 'there is nothing more alien to us than politics'
(*Ap.* 38.3). A succinct presentation of Christian political thought in the early centuries
of the Empire may be found in Barbero 1985.

APPENDIX 2

PLATONISM AND CHRISTIANITY

Now while Paul waited for them at Athens, his spirit was provoked within him as he beheld the city full of idols. [...] And certain also of the Epicurean and Stoic philosophers encountered him. And some said 'What would this babbler say?'; others 'He seemeth to be a setter forth of strange gods', because he preached Jesus and the resurrection. And they took hold of him, and brought him unto the Areopagus, saying 'May we know what this new teaching is, which is spoken by thee?'. [...] And Paul stood in the midst of the Areopagus, and said 'Ye men of Athens, in all things, I perceive that ye are very religious. For as I passed along, and observed the objects of your worship, I found also an altar with this inscription, TO AN UNKNOWN GOD. What therefore ye worship in ignorance, this I set forth unto you'. [...] Now when they heard of the resurrection of the dead, some mocked; but others said 'We will hear thee concerning this yet again.' Thus Paul went out from among them. But certain men clave unto him, and believed: among whom also was Dionysius the Areopagite, and a woman named Damaris, and others with them. (*Acts of the Apostles*, 17:16–34)

The first encounter between Greek philosophy and Christianity can hardly be described as a success. Nevertheless, it marked a momentous step in our history, whose importance should not be underestimated. Indeed, the above passage from the *Acts of the Apostles* shows that, behind an apparently inevitable mutual incomprehension, the engagement was far more complex and interesting. Upon closer inspection, the passage in question already reveals a range of attitudes that over the course of the following centuries were to characterise the engagement between Platonists and Christians. To be sure, hostility and contempt are expressed on both sides, but we also find curiosity and interest, culminating in a conversion destined to play a very significant role in the transition from Greek to Christian and medieval philosophy. On a broader scale, things did not go very differently during the centuries of the Roman Empire: on both sides, polemics were frequent and often virulent; but what ultimately prevailed was a spirit of integration which on the one hand translated into the preservation of much

189

of the Platonist tradition (and more generally of the Hellenistic philosophical tradition, insofar as Platonism had also absorbed the other schools),[1] and on the other brought about a profound transformation of Christian thought. Truly, it would be difficult to overestimate the importance of this encounter.

Platonists against Christianism

As we briefly saw in Chapter 3, Platonists were for the most part well disposed towards Eastern traditions, but this only partly applies to the Jews, and not at all to the Christians. Numenius of Apamea, who in a work bearing a markedly Platonic title (*On the Good*) had spoken favourably of Jesus (fr. 10a des Places), represents a significant exception in this regard, since other Platonist philosophers across the centuries were to engage in a polemic against the Christian tradition. Between 160 and 180, Celsus composed *The True Discourse*; around 270 (or, according to other interpretations, just before the last great persecution, launched by Emperor Diocletian in 303), Porphyry wrote *Against the Christians*; Hierocles' *Philalethes* (*Lover of Truth*) also dates from the years before the persecution; then, in 362, just as the Empire was about to become definitely Christian, Julian penned *Against the Galileans*.[2] This kind of polemical output ceased with the triumph of Christianity, yet the hostile attitude endured, as

---

[1] One important point to be clarified right from the start is the connection with Platonism: as Donini 1982: 252–8, has rightly shown, Christians chiefly turned their attention to the theses of the Platonists, who in turn had incorporated numerous Stoic doctrines into their system. Leaving the earliest Christian period aside (and particularly Paul's reflection), it would therefore be incorrect to speak of the Christians as fluctuating between the two philosophies, for many of the Stoic theses had become part of Platonism and reached the Christians through it. Also very useful are the articles collected in Baltes 1999: 454–523.

[2] In a predictable twist of history, these works owe their partial survival precisely to the Christians: despised and condemned to oblivion following the triumph of Christianity, they were preserved thanks to the stream of refutations penned by Christians. In general, on pagan anti-Christian polemics, see now Zambon 2019. On Celsus, see Andresen 1955; M. Frede 1997; and Männlein-Robert 2018. As regards Porphyry, besides the classic editions of von Harnack 1916 and Berchman 2005, interested readers will find an important collection of studies in Morlet 2011 and in the highly informative note by Zambon 2012b: 1419–47. On Julian's polemics, see Smith 1995: 179–218; De Vita 2011; and Elm 2012. To these sources we might also add Plotinus' anti-Gnostic polemic, particularly in treatises 29–32, if it is true – as Tardieu 1992 has compellingly shown – that the Gnostics attending his school were Christians.

may be inferred from the delicate yet clear statements made by many leading Neoplatonists, starting from Proclus.[3] What are the reasons for such hostility, which seems all the more surprising considering the Platonists' positive regard for other Eastern traditions?

Despite their peculiarities, it is easy to find a common ground for these polemics, although it only partly fits modern readers' expectations. One recurrent – and to our eyes predictable – accusation is directed against faith's irrationalism, which, by contrast to rational research, leads to the acceptance of absurd doctrines. As Celsus writes, instead of 'accepting doctrines by following reason and a rational guide', Christians, in their ignorance, have let themselves be deceived and have made this attitude normative: 'not wishing either to give or receive a reason for their belief, they resort to the following claims: "Do not examine, but believe" and "Your faith will save you" [...] "The wisdom of this world is an evil, madness is a good thing"'.[4]

One concrete sign of the Christians' ignorance and irrationalism is to be found in some of their most typical doctrines. This is especially the case with the doctrines of resurrection and the Final Judgement, and the idea of a God (Christ) who has become man and suffers. In the eyes of a Platonist, these are absurd theses, which can only be explained by Christians' ignorance of the nature of true realities: 'What body, once utterly corrupted, could revert to its original nature? [...] Not knowing how to answer, Christians opt for the most absurd way out: "Everything is possible for God!".'[5]

But what is most interesting to note is that these specific polemics do not undermine the background of beliefs, convictions, and

---

[3] See Saffrey 1975.
[4] Orig. *Contra Cels.* 1.9; 'through a procedure that is usual in ancient polemical literature, Celsus echoes certain biblical passages, distorting their meaning: *Mk.* 5:36 and 9:23; *1 Cor* 1:18–19 and 3:18–19': Zambon 2015: 476 note 7. Cf. Alexander of Lycopolis' polemics (I–II, p. 3, 4–7, 19 Brinkmann) against the Manichaeans, regarded as a Christian sect (see van den Horst 1996), or Plotinus' attacks on the Gnostics (2.9[33].10.3–11), who were also Christian. Polemics of this sort extend well beyond Platonic circles: cf. Epictetus *Diss.* 4.7.5–7; Marcus Aurelius 11.3; Galen, *De diff. puls.* 579.10–17; 657.1–5 Kühn [Medic. Graec. op. VIII]); and Lucian, *De morte Per.* 13.
[5] Orig. *Contra Cels.* 5.14.

expectations shared by Christians and Platonists alike: while disagreeing about certain important yet circumscribed questions, Platonists share the same underlying perspective as the Christians, one based on the close identification between philosophy and theology (and religion).[6] Like their Christian opponents, they firmly believe that all research culminates in the knowledge of God, to the extent that human beings have the faculty to acquire it. The polemic against Christianity, then, does not amount to an attack on religion as such or on the centrality of the divine; on the contrary, Platonists fully embrace a 'theological' conception of philosophy. Furthermore, the underlying framework of the Christian doctrine is not all that different from the Platonic one: far from defending polytheism, Platonists too believe in a single divine principle to which other divine beings are subordinated (in this respect, the doctrine of the Trinity is not so different from Middle Platonist or Neoplatonist divine hierarchies and, likewise, significant analogies can be found between the faith in angels and that in demons).[7] Given this underlying approach, Platonists too were willing to acknowledge the importance of 'faith', in the face of the impossibility of gaining full knowledge of the divine principles.[8]

All in all, then, the points of convergence outweigh the discrepancies: the divergences regarding certain doctrinal issues are not enough in themselves to account for such great enmity. The real bone of contention is to be sought elsewhere: it depends not so much on philosophical or theological reasons as on cultural and political ones. The true problem lies in the Christians' 'isolationist' attitude (to some extent the same problem also holds in the case of the Jews, who were also frequently – yet not always – a target for virulent criticism). In the Imperial Age, among Platonic philosophers, as well as in other milieus, the idea took root that the truth was something which belonged to the past, to the earliest stage in the history of mankind, when the first populations – Greek

---

[6] Cf. Chapter 3, The Doctrine of Principles, p. 90.

[7] This problem is part of the broader issue of 'pagan monotheism', which has been the focus of numerous studies in recent years; see esp. the collections of essays Athanassiadi and Frede 1999 and Mitchell and van Nuffelen 2010.

[8] Two revealing testimonies are Plutarch's *Amatorius* (756b) and esp. Proclus' *Platonic Theology* 4.9, which H. D. Saffrey has aptly defined as 'a profession of anti-intellectualistic faith'; for an overview, see Morlet 2014: 183–90.

or barbarian, but in any case still untainted – had been capable of
grasping the true nature of things. The philosophers' duty was to
reconstruct this 'true discourse' (*alethes logos*, to quote the title
of Celsus' work), and Plato's superiority lay precisely in this – not
in having said anything new, but in having been able to express
this primordial truth more fully. The Christians' fault, and the
main reason for the polemic against them, was to have rejected
this shared belief, which all peoples of the Empire agreed on: their
God was the only true God, their scriptures alone were divinely
inspired, and their miracles alone were genuine ones, whereas
all other beliefs were disparaged as examples of idolatry.[9] But in
reality this was not the case at all, because Christianity was merely
the outcome of a seditious and recent schism within Judaism,[10]
which in turn had sprung from Moses' rebellion against Egypt.[11]

It is therefore quite clear what was at stake in these polemics.
Platonist philosophers' criticism was merely a variation on the
theme of the danger posed by Christianity: its success threatened to
bring about the destruction of the very values on which the Graeco-
Roman tradition rested. The well-known charges of misanthropy,
subversion, sexual transgression, and cannibalism often levelled
against the Christians[12] can be explained as a consequence of their
choice to stand outside the civil, ethical, and religious order on
which the Graeco-Roman world was founded – a world capable
of encompassing the most diverse religious and cultural traditions,
and which felt mortally challenged by the new religious movement.

The same concern also drives the Platonists' polemic. The figure of Porphyry here stands out, and arguably provides what is the
most significant testimony with regard to this inclusive ideological tendency.[13] A highly skilled polemicist, capable of buttressing

---

9 See M. Frede 1997: 236–40.
10 Celsus *ap.* Origen. *Contra Cels.* 2.1.4 and 6; 3.5; 5.33.41.
11 Celsus *ap.* Origen. *Contra Cels.* 3.5; 4.31.
12 Levieils 2007.
13 A more detailed analysis of Porphyry's position – and not merely in relation to his anti-
Christian polemic – is provided by Johnson 2013. In the case of the Platonists, who
were members of the upper classes, the problem was further exacerbated by the fact
that Christianity, particularly in its initial stage, had been most warmly received among
the lowest strata of society, 'among craftsmen and shopkeepers' (Origen. *Contra Cels.*
3.44–55; see Donini 1982: 259).

his attacks with subtle philological analyses,[14] Porphyry was the most feared enemy. Nor should we forget Julian, the Emperor who abjured the Christian faith and sought to re-Hellenise the Empire, leading him to be forever branded by Christian propaganda as an apostate, as the turncoat par excellence. Certainly, Julian's position of absolute prominence at the head of the Empire lends a peculiar colouring to his polemic. What is particularly interesting is its political bent – partly common to other authors as well – whereby the charge of isolationism translates into the accusation that the Christians were undermining the Empire's foundations (an argument justifying their persecution).[15] We are not dealing merely with theoretical distinctions, then, because theological-philosophical divergences were concretely expressed in a political programme designed to safeguard all those cults that Christian 'atheism' had sought to abolish. Herein lies the *raison d'être* of the numerous measures taken to exclude Christians from the army, the government, and education. For Julian, the battle against the Christians was not merely a battle of ideas. In his Hellenism and in his attempt to pit the ancient world of Greek values, centred on the philosophy of Plato – a mystical and theurgical Plato – against the new Christian hegemony, the more strictly political element played a key role.

Significantly, however, this clash with Christianity did not fail to produce secondary, and rather curious, results. With regard to several issues, Julian was ultimately influenced by those opponents he so staunchly fought against. For instance, he simplified his theological model in a way that is reminiscent of the Christians' position (let us think of his references to a 'solar

---

[14] In particular, Porphyry had succeeded in showing that the prophecies included in the Book of Daniel had been written *post eventum* (during the reign of Antiochus IV Epiphanes, the ruler of the Seleucid Kingdom of Syria between 175 and 163 BC), see fragments 41 and 43. As further evidence of Porphyry's exegetical and philological effort, we may recall his argument against the authenticity of the Gospel of John (based on its divergence from the three synoptic Gospels), and his emphasis on the doctrinal disagreements between Peter and Paul (frgs. 12.15–16.33).

[15] One thorny and recently much-debated problem concerns the possible role played by Platonist philosophers in the great persecution launched by Diocletian in 303: in support of the thesis of their active involvement (or at any rate of a significant influence on their part), see e.g. Depalma Digeser 2012; conversely, doubts about this have been raised by Zambon 2012b: 1430 and Johnson 2013.

trinity' or celebration of a pagan 'virgin mother').[16] In this regard, one scholar has spoken of an 'unconscious nostalgia'[17] for the religion he had embraced in the earliest years of his life. However, it may be more plausible to see this influence, and this attempt on Julian's part to emulate Christianity, as clear proof of the new Christian faith's success and of its capacity to mark a break with entrenched frameworks.

With Julian's death and the end of his fleeting attempt at a pagan restoration, Christianity triumphed, increasingly reducing the avenues open to the Platonists. In 448, Theodosius II and Valentinian III issued a law, later included in the *Code of Justinian* (1.1.3), decreeing that 'all the works by Porphyry, or by anyone else, against the Christians had to be burned'.

It is hardly surprising, then, that even in Athens, a Platonist and pagan stronghold, figures of Proclus' standing confined themselves to ciphered polemical allusions that only those sharing their ideas could grasp, while invoking the gods' intervention to free the holy soil of Greece from these insolent and ignorant barbarians.[18] Yet in this case, as in many others, the gods paid little heed and, with the closing of the Neoplatonist School in 529, Platonism vanished from Athens for quite some time.

Christian 'Platonisms'

The Christians' response was more complex, and right from the start it is possible to distinguish between two contrasting, yet frequently intertwined, tendencies: opposition on the one hand, and reconciliation and integration on the other.[19] The former position,

---

[16] See de Vita 2011: 49–50. On Julian's possible influence on the Christians, cf. Appendix 1, Two Political Platonists: Marcus Tullius Cicero and Flavius Claudius Julianus, p. 185.

[17] Lacombrade 1964: 94.

[18] A list of these ciphered allusions may be found in Saffrey 1975: 563: among other things, Christians are referred to as the rabble, neighbours incapable of sobriety, people foreign to our (Hellenic) world, atheists, intemperate individuals, and evil people.

[19] Unsurprisingly, the literature on this topic is vast; see Zambon 2012a with a further bibliography. More recently, see also Morlet 2014, Karamanolis 2021, and the essay collections in Riedweg, Horn, and Wyrwa 2018 and Edwards 2020, featuring up-to-date profiles of numerous Christian philosophers. Other studies will be mentioned in the course of this chapter, with no claim to exhaustiveness.

which endorsed the prospect of a head-on collision, finds its earliest champions in Tatian (c. 120–180) in Greece and Tertullian (mid-second century to after 220) in Roman Africa. The idea of radical discontinuity was de facto supported by a number of authoritative statements, given that St Paul had already warned the faithful not to be deceived by philosophy:

> Take heed lest there shall be any one that maketh spoil of you through his philosophy and vain deceit, after the tradition of men, after the rudiments of the world, and not after Christ. (*Col.* 2:8)

More bluntly, Tertulian states:

> What has Athens got to do with Jerusalem? What concord is there between the Academies and the Churches? What between heretics and Christians? We need no inquisitiveness after Jesus Christ, no research after the Gospel. When we believe, we desire nothing more, for first of all we believe this, that there is nothing further which we ought to believe. (*De praescr. Haer.* 7)

However, we must not assume that these intentionally paradoxical statements were the outcome of conscious and complete ignorance: both Tatian and Tertullian were sophisticated writers who had received an excellent education and were perfectly capable of refuting the pagan philosophers' many contradictions (in line with the theme of *irrisio philosophorum*).[20] This polemic and the paradoxical praise of Christian absurdity ('I believe because it is absurd; it is certain because it is impossible')[21] were rather motivated by the need to safeguard the specificity of the faith, in an effort to prevent it becoming entangled in metaphysical speculation. Besides, in Tertullian's case, if we consider some of his corporalist theses (particularly with regard to the soul),[22] it is conceivable that his rejection of Platonism amounted to the rejection of an excessively Platonising version of Christianity (which was nonetheless fated to become predominant).[23] The desire to preserve the purity of Christianity against pagan influences also explains the popularity of the belief that many Christian heresies had arisen due to an interest in Greek philosophy: Tertullian

[20] Cf. e.g. Tat. *Or. ad Graecos*, 31, 36, 110.
[21] Tertull. *De carne Christi* 5.
[22] Cf. e.g. *Hermog.* 35; *De carne Christi* 11; *De an.* 7.3.
[23] See Donini 1982: 255.

described Plato as 'the caterer to all heretics' (*On the Soul* 23.5), while Hippolytus (first half of the third century) claimed that people like Valentinian, Heracleon, and Ptolemaeus (that is, Christian Gnostics) were pupils not of the Gospel, but of Pythagoras and Plato (*Refutation of all Heresies*, 6.29.1).[24]

Nevertheless, in the long run, a different approach was to become predominant. As already anticipated, what was at stake was the thorny issue of the relationship between Christianity and Graeco-Roman culture. In this context, philosophy, and more specifically Platonism, played a crucial connecting role. For the pagans, Plato and philosophy had become part of *paideia*; for the Christians, the identification between philosophy and theology that was typical of Platonism disclosed unexpected possibilities. By showing the convergence between Christianity and Platonism, it was possible to present the former in a different and more favourable light – as the completion rather than subversion of a tradition whose value was acknowledged. Moreover, and just as importantly, the Platonists' sophisticated reflections provided valuable conceptual tools for a system of thought in the making such as the Christian one.[25] It is therefore hardly surprising that most Christian thinkers, both in the Greek East and in the Latin West, held philosophy, and particularly Platonism, in high regard.

The basic framework for this engagement came to be defined in a relatively short time already in the first centuries of the Christian era, through the works of apologists such as Justin – Tatian's teacher, who was martyred between 162 and 168 – and Athenagoras (second century), and even more so through the first generation of great Christian thinkers: the so-called Alexandrian School of Pantaenus (the least known of such thinkers, with Stoic leanings; he would appear to have been active around 180), Clement (c. 150–215), and Origen (180–after 250, when he died as a consequence of Decius' persecution).[26] By stressing the more

---

[24] See e.g. Mansfeld 1992.

[25] 'It is not an exaggeration to say that these early Christian thinkers relied on Greek philosophy to discover what they actually thought about the revelation that they embraced': Gerson 2010b: 234.

[26] On Philo of Alexandria's influence, see Runia 1993. All in all, Origen's case best exemplifies the fascinating yet challenging nature of this encounter: deeply acquainted

rational aspects of the Christian religion, these authors promoted a genuine engagement with Platonic and Greek philosophy.

The Christian response essentially took the thesis of Moses' primacy over Plato as its starting point. In antiquity, anecdotes on Plato's journeys to the East abounded, and the Greeks' fascination with Eastern traditions is well known: as already noted, quite a few Platonists believed that Plato had perfected an ancestral lore common to all – or almost all – peoples. According to the Platonists, this primordial truth was foreign precisely to Jews and Christians. But according to the Christians (and, before them, to the Jews),[27] the opposite was the case: Plato's wisdom was merely an adaptation of Moses', since it was from Moses that Plato had drawn inspiration with regard to his most distinctive doctrines (the unity and transcendence of the first principle as opposed to the aberrations of polytheism; providence as opposed to determinism; the immortality of the soul).[28]

When presented in more polemical terms – for example, by Tatian – this thesis amounted to a charge of theft. Yet the result was still the same: the acknowledgement of this convergence entailed the belief that Christianity was the 'true philosophy';[29]

with philosophy, yet not a champion of its indiscriminate use, Origen was nonetheless attacked, both during his own lifetime and in later centuries, for having allowed himself to be 'blinded by Greek *paideia*' (Epifanius, *Panarion* 64.72.1); (a distorted version of) his teaching was finally condemned by the Second Ecumenical Council of 553, after having influenced a generation of Christian theologians (the Cappadocian Fathers above all). Given the present state of our knowledge, it is impossible to ascertain whether the Christian Origen can be identified with the Origen who attended Ammonius Saccas' school and with whom Plotinus entertained a highly problematic relationship: see Zambon 2011.

[27] One important text, for example, is Flavius Josephus' *Against Apion* (cf. e.g. 1.1.1–2); see also Philo of Alexandria, *De aetern. Mundi* 19, *De spec. Leg.* 4.10.6.

[28] Cf. e.g. Iust. *Apol.* 1.44; Clem. *Str.* 1.15–17; 21–29; 5.5; 14; 90; 102–3; 115–16; Origen. *De princ.* 3.6.1. More specifically, Plato was believed to have familiarised himself with the Pentateuch in Egypt. This idea might seem – and is – absurd to modern eyes, yet it is not all that different from the claim made in relation to pseudo-Pythagorean treatises. The fact that in the *Timaeus* Socrates learns about cosmic deluges from an Egyptian priest offered excellent confirmation of this thesis. It goes without saying that another polemical claim made against the Christians was that Christ had derived his ideas from Plato: see Origen. *Contra Cels.* 5.65–7.68; August. *Ep.* 31.8.

[29] Christianity is presented as the true philosophy not just from a strictly theoretical perspective, but also based on the belief that Christians alone were capable of living a fully philosophical life, according to the ideal of the Greek schools: see e.g. Iust. 1.4.8–9.

as a logical consequence, it enabled an engagement with – and
the use of – the philosophical tradition. Since 'Plato was merely
an Attic Moses' (a quote from the Platonist Numenius, fr.
8 des Places, which Christians were always keen to bring up),[30] it could
be inferred that there was a strong affinity between philosophy
and the Christian religion: against those seeking to clearly distinguish between the two, it was remarked that philosophy too
contained something divine, if only indirectly; therefore, philosophy could rightfully be employed to shed light on theological
issues. This foreshadows the theme of philosophy as 'the hand-
maid of theology':[31] Platonism (and, with it, Greek philosophy)
thus became fully part of the Christian tradition. Indeed, as has
aptly been noted, it would be more correct to speak of 'Christian
Platonisms', in the plural, given the many different appropriation
strategies that were deployed.[32]

Without wishing to make any claim to exhaustiveness with
regard to such a complex topic, I will draw attention to some of the
most notable figures. The fourth century witnessed the triumph of
Christianity, and two episodes emerge as particularly emblematic of
the new power relationships in what remained a difficult context: the
century opened with the great anti-Christian persecution launched by
Diocletian and at least partly fuelled by Platonists, but ended with the
monks (or, rather, the armed mob) led by the Bishop of Alexandria
Cyril ripping Hypatia's body to shreds (415).[33] However, it is once
again the attempts at integration that matter most, and in the context of this engagement, despite some moments of harsh conflict, a
position of absolute pre-eminence must be assigned to Eusebius of

[30] Cf. Clem. *Strom.* 1.22.150.4; Eus. *PE* 9.6.9 and 8.1–2; Theodoret. *Ther.* 2.114.
[31] Cf. e.g. Clem. *Strom.* 1.5.28: philosophy is to the Greeks what the Law is to the Jews;
'it is preparatory work which paves the way for he whom Christ will make perfect'.
Besides, as Origen had noted *Letter to Gregory* 2, the Jews too, in leaving Egypt, had
taken gold and other goods to build God's sanctuary; likewise, Christians could put
philosophy to the service of Scripture.
[32] Another thesis designed to bring philosophy and religion closer is that of the existence
of an innate religion common to all men, 'whereby even those who lived according
to the *Logos* before Christ were Christians, as in the case of the Greek philosophers
Heraclitus, Socrates, and Musonius' (Donini 1982: 251); cf. Iust. *Apol.* 1.46 e *Apol.*
2.13.2–6.
[33] Concerning this figure, who has fascinated many readers, see Dzielska 1996 and Beretta
2014.

Caesarea (265–340)[34] and to the three Cappadocian Fathers: Basil of Caesarea (329–78), his brother Gregory of Nyssa (c. 335–after 386), and Gregory of Nazianzus (c. 326–90). They mark the second stage of close interpenetration and integration.

Broadly speaking, the underlying reasons for this privileged relationship between Platonism and Christianity are easy to identify and must be sought in their shared opposition to materialism, and hence in their need to refer to a transcendent first principle within a universe clearly divided into two different levels of reality (the intelligible realm of being and the sensible one of becoming). With regard to this crucial point and all the issues deriving from it (particularly the need to posit mediating figures, to clarify their nature or *ousia*, and to elucidate the relationship between such entities and man), we find clear structural analogies, which the Christians repeatedly emphasised.[35] This, of course, does not rule out divergences. Particularly important was the epistemological problem of the relationship between faith (*pistis*) and reason (*logos*): an ever-present problem in Christian philosophy that was developed precisely by those authors – the Alexandrians and Cappadocians – who were eager to engage with the philosophers' rational arguments, yet unwilling to abandon the salvific truth of revelation. With respect to this point, despite the Platonist criticism we have examined, Christians were unwilling to make any compromises: the primacy of Scripture and faith was never called into question.[36]

But once we have established this point, we should note that Christian theologians encountered the same difficulties that had beset Platonist philosophers dealing with the first principles. The debates on the relationship between God and Christ reproduced, in a different context, the similar problems which Platonists had

---

[34] On Eusebius, see Appendix 1, Christians, Platonism and Politics: Eusebius and Augustine, p. 185 on politics, since his most important contribution is to be found in his definition of a political theology; in more general terms on his relation to Platonism, see Karamanolis 2014.

[35] One collection of significant testimonies is found in Morlet 2014: 130–41.

[36] With reference to debates in the Early Imperial Age, see Zambon 2015. It must be noted that the debate was made all the more complex by the fact that the Christians also needed to take account of the notion of *gnosis*, or knowledge, which is to say the claim made by certain movements – so-called 'Gnostic' movements – that they could provide true knowledge of God and a genuine experience of union with Him.

found themselves addressing. It is therefore hardly surprising that some Christians resorted to these philosophers' theories (Arianism, for example, emerges as an attempt to structure Christian theology according to the interpretive framework of Platonism, yet just as extensive was the use of Plato made by Arius' leading opponents, namely the Cappadocians). Equally unsurprisingly, other Christians instead rejected such theories precisely in an effort to prevent Christianity from turning into a new version of Platonism.[37]

In the Latin world, the development of these tendencies was slower, but the outcomes no less remarkable. Without forgetting Calcidius' commentary on the *Timaeus* (fourth century), a fundamental impulse was provided by Marius Victorinus (281/291–365; particularly important were his Latin translations of Plotinus and Porphyry, which introduced new terms such as *ens*, *existentia*, *intelligibilis*, and *subsistentia*)[38] and Ambrose (333–97). But the real apex was reached with Augustine of Tagaste. An adequate treatment of Augustine would require far more space than is available here.[39] I will only note that, while imbued with Platonism (his conversion to Christianity occurred via the Platonism he was introduced to by Ambrose), Augustine is the thinker who most radically subverted this tradition: as Thomas Aquinas was to note, Augustine's work may be regarded as an effort to follow the Platonists more than the Christian faith allowed it; yet the resistance he encountered from the Platonists forced him to simultaneously embrace originality, 'in search of an adequate understanding of the historical revelation of the Christian God. His contribution to the history of the Christian rethinking of Platonism has therefore been the most creative and radically critical one with regard to the project of acquiring philosophical knowledge of God'.[40] Augustine's

---

[37] See Köckert 2009. It is also worth noting that over time the consolidation of the bishops' control reduced the role played by philosophy with respect to the definition of dogmas; see also Löhr 2010.

[38] Concerning Victorinus and his relationship with Platonism, it is worth recalling the landmark study of P. Hadot 1968.

[39] For an excellent introduction to his thought, see Catapano 2010; one useful collection of studies is Stump and Kretzmann 2001; as regards Augustine's political thought, cf. Appendix 1, Christians, Platonism and Politics: Eusebius and Augustine, p. 186; on Augustine on Plato, see van Riel 2018.

[40] Zambon 2012a: 147.

reflection on grace (the idea of the gratuitous character of the salvation wrought by God), inspired by Paul's doctrine, is probably the most significant testimony to this profound subversion.

After Augustine, the other leading figure in the Western world is no doubt Severinus Boethius (c. 480–525/526), the author of commentaries on Aristotle which mark a crucial turning point in the transmission of ancient knowledge to the medieval world, as well as of theological treatises on the Trinity and Christology. In the East, among many other authors, we find the Bishop of Cyrene Synesius (c. 370–413), Aeneas of Gaza (430–520), Zacharias of Gaza (465–536),[41] and especially John Philoponus (c. 490–575). Boethius and Synesius are the two thinkers who have gone furthest in the attempt to reconcile Plato's theses with the truth of Scripture: this is best illustrated by Synesius' statements that he could never bring himself to believe that the soul is generated after the body, that the world is destined to perish, and that the common people's opinion about resurrection is acceptable.[42] No less significant is the fact that in his theological treatises and *Consolation of Philosophy*, Boethius resorts not to Scripture, but Plato. Evidently, the monotheistic Platonism in which these authors believed was felt to be fully compatible with Christian truths: their adherence to Christianity would appear to have been informed by the doctrinal framework of Platonism.[43] As far as Philoponus is concerned, the distance between his philosophical and theological writings is such that some scholars have posited a late conversion on his part; the most likely hypothesis, however, is that he was always a Christian, which would show what a close connection thinkers such as he perceived between Plato and Christ.[44] However, it was chiefly through Pseudo-Dionysius the Areopagite that this trajectory ran its full course and the appropriation of (Neo)Platonism

---

[41] The interesting role played by the thinkers from Gaza is emphasised by Champion 2014.

[42] *Ep.* 105: 'Now, I shall never accept that the soul's origin is posterior to that of the soul; I shall never grant that the cosmos and its parts are destined to perish together; and as far as resurrection goes – a much debated topic – I deem it at most something mysterious and ineffable, and am far from conforming to the opinions of the masses.'

[43] Zambon 2012a: 137–8.

[44] Cf. Chapter 4, The Sensible World and the Problem of Evil, p. 152 with regard to the polemics about the eternity of the cosmos. On theological works more generally, see Giardina 2012: 491–8.

reached completion, projecting it into the subsequent centuries.[45] The passage from the *Acts of the Apostles* quoted at the beginning of this chapter mentions a certain Dionysius, who was one of the very few Athenians who believed Paul's words; over the course of the sixth century, a series of treatises started circulating – probably drafted towards the end of the previous century – that were attributed to him, yet were clearly influenced by Proclus' philosophy (consider especially the emphasis on the absolute transcendence of the first principle or the reference to the triadic movement of remaining, procession, and return). Translated into Latin in the Carolingian period, the *corpus areopagiticum* became one of the fundamental channels for the spread of Platonic philosophy in the medieval world. The extensive presence of Neoplatonist doctrines within it presented quite a few difficulties for those who continued to tackle the issue of the genuine Christian faith's uniqueness with respect to the Greek philosophical legacy.

As this succinct overview clearly shows, it is difficult, if not impossible, to draw an overall balance of this history of encounters and clashes, for it means taking a stance with regard to the huge problem of the relationship between reason and faith. Nietzsche's description of Christianity as 'Platonism for the people' is well known, and it is interesting to note that many readers would probably accept this definition without sharing the negative judgement it implies: that there exists a unique relationship between Christian theology and Platonist philosophy is a thesis no less widespread today than it was in the early Imperial centuries. Yet today as much as then, some people fear that this might lead to losing the meaning of the true Judeo-Christian experience.[46] This is not a simple problem, nor is it the task of a book on Platonism to solve it. What must be stressed here is the importance of this encounter for the ancient world. As already noted, the engagement between Christianity and Platonism occurred against the backdrop of an even greater engagement: that between Christianity and the entire Graeco-Roman tradition. It is truly remarkable that the outcome of all this was a gradual Platonising of the Graeco-Roman world,

[45] See Klitenic Wear and Dillon 2007; and Ritter 2018 with a further bibliography.
[46] With reference to antiquity, see the lengthy article de Vogel 1985.

which came to be seen as culminating in philosophy – more specifically, in Plato's philosophy. This striking fact is not without irony, considering what Plato had stood for in his own time: Plato, the rebel; he who had opposed the Greeks' traditional culture, and who had developed philosophy precisely as an alternative to this tradition; he who had gone as far as to suggest banishing Homer from his ideal city – this Plato had now become a bastion and emblem of a centuries-old tradition which the innovation of Christianity threatened to wipe out forever.

BIBLIOGRAPHY

Ademollo, F. (2012). 'The Platonic Origins of Stoic Theology'. *Oxford Studies in Ancient Philosophy* 43: 217–43.

Alesse, F. and Ferrari, F. (eds.) (2012). *Epinomide. Studi sull'opera e la sua ricezione*. Naples.

Algra, K. (1997). 'Chrysippus, Carneades, Cicero: The Ethical Divisiones in Cicero's Lucullus'. In Inwood and Mansfeld 1997: 107–39.

(2017). 'The Academic Origins of the Stoic Cosmo-theology and the Physics of Antiochus of Ascalon: Some Notes on the Evidence'. In Y. Z. Libersohn, I. Ludlam, and A. Edelheit (eds.) *For a Skeptical Peripatetic. Festschrift in Honour of John Glucker*. Sankt Augustin: 156–76.

Algra, K., Barnes, J., Mansfeld, J., and Schofield, M. (eds.) (1999). *The Cambridge History of Hellenistic Philosophy*. Cambridge.

André, J.-M. (1977). *La philosophie à Rome*. Paris.

Amerisi, M. (2005). *Eusebio di Cesarea. Elogio di Costantino ; discorso per il trentennale ; discorso regale*. Milan.

Andresen, C. (1955). *Logos und Nomos. Die Polemik des Kelsos wider das Christentum*. Berlin.

Annas, J. (1999). *Platonic Ethics, Old and New*. Ithaca, NY-London.

(2007). 'Carneades' Classification of Ethical Theories'. In A. M. Ioppolo and D. Sedley (eds.) *Pyrrhonists, Patricians, Platonizers: Hellenistic Philosophy in the Period 155–86 BC*. Naples: 187–223.

Armstrong, A. H. (1960). 'The Background of the Doctrine That the Intelligibles Are Not outside the Intellect'. In *Entretiens de la Fondation Hardt*, vol. 5: *Les sources de Plotin*. Vandœuvres-Geneva: 393–413.

(ed.) (1966). *Plotinus*. Cambridge, MA-London, 6 vols.

(1974). 'Tradition, Reason and Experience in the Thought of Plotinus'. In *Plotino e il neoplatonismo in Oriente e Occidente*. Rome: 171–94.

Arnim, H. von. (1895). 'Arkesilaos von Pitane'. *RE* 2: coll. 1164–8.

Aronadio, F. (ed.) (2013). *[Plato]. Epinomis*. Naples.

Arzhanov, Y. (ed.) (2021). *Porphyry. On Principles and Matter*. Berlin.

Athanassiadi, P. (1981). *Julian and Hellenism: An Intellectual Biography*. Oxford.

(ed.) (1999). *Damascius: The Philosophical History*. Athens.

(2006). *La lutte pour l'orthodoxie dans le platonisme tardif de Numénius à Damascius*. Paris.

Athanassiadi, A. and Frede, M. (eds.) (1999). *Pagan Monotheism in Late Antiquity*. Oxford.

Atkins, E. M. (2000). 'Cicero'. In Rowe and Schofield 2000: 477–516.

Bibliography

Atkins, J. W. and Bénatouïl, T. (eds,) (2021), The Cambridge Companion to Cicero's Philosophy. Cambridge.

Aubry, G. (2006). *Dieu sans la puissance. Dunamis et Energeia chez Aristote et chez Plotin.* Paris.

Babut, D. (1969). *Plutarque et le Stoïcisme.* Paris.

Bakhouche, B. (ed.) (2011). *Calcidius, Commentaire au Timée de Platon.* Paris, 2 vols.

Baltes, M. (1972). *Timaios Lokros. Über die Natur des Kosmos und der Seele.* Leiden.

—— (1976). *Die Weltenstehung des Platonischen Timaios nach den antiken Interpreten*, vol. I. Leiden.

—— (1978). *Die Weltenstehung des Platonischen Timaios nach den antiken Interpreten*, vol. II. Leiden.

—— (1983). 'Zur Philosophie des Platonikers Attikos'. In H. D. Blume and F. Mann (eds.) *Platonismus und Christentum. Festschrift für Heinrich Dörrie.* Münster: 38–57. (=DIANOHMATA. *Kleine Schriften zu Platon und zum Platonismus.* Stuttgart-Leipzig, 1999: 81–111).

—— (1985). 'Ammonios Sakkas', *RAC* suppl. 3: 23–32 (=DIANOHMATA. *Kleine Schriften zu Platon und zum Platonismus.* Stuttgart-Leipzig, 1999: 113–20).

—— (1993). 'Plato's School, the Academy'. *Hermatema* 155: 7–28.

—— (1999). *Dianoemata. Kleine Schriften zu Platon und zum Platonismus.* Stuttgart-Leipzig.

Baltes, M. and Dörrie, H. (1987–2020). *Der Platonismus in der Antike.* Stuttgart-Bad Cannstatt, 8 vols.

Baltussen, H. (2008). *Philosophy and Exegesis in Simplicius: The Methodology of a Commentator.* London.

Baltzly, D. (2004). 'The Virtues and "Becoming Like God": Alcinous to Proclus'. *Oxford Studies in Ancient Philosophy* 26: 297–321.

Baraz, Y. (2012). *A Written Republic: Cicero's Philosophical Politics.* Princeton.

Barbero, G. (1985). 'La patristica'. In L. Firpo (ed.) *Storia delle idee politiche, economiche, sociali*, vol ii.1: *Ebraismo e Cristianesimo.* Turin: 479–540.

Barnes, J. (ed.) (1984). *The Complete Works of Aristotle.* Oxford.

—— (1989). 'Antiochus of Ascalon'. In J. Barnes and M. Griffin (eds.) *Philosophia Togata I: Essays on Philosophy and Roman Society.* Oxford: 51–96.

—— (1997). 'Roman Aristotle'. In Barnes and Griffin 1997: 1–69.

Barnes, J. and Griffin, M. (eds.) (1997). *Philosophia Togata II: Plato and Aristotle at Rome.* Oxford.

Barnes, T. (1981). *Constantine and Eusebius.* Cambridge, MA.

Beierwaltes, W. (1961). 'Plotins Metaphysik des Lichtes'. *Zeitschrift für philosophische Forschung* 15: 334–62.

—— (1979). *Proklos. Grundzüge seiner Metaphysik.* Munich.

Bénatouïl, T. (2007). 'Le débat entre platonisme et stoïcisme sur la vie scholastique: Chrysippe, la Nouvelle Académie et Antiochus'. In Bonazzi and Helmig 2007: 1–21.

—— (2017). 'Speusippe et Xénocrate ont-ils Systématisé la Cosmologie du Timée?' In Gavray and Michalewski 2017: 19–38.

Bibliography

Bénatouïl, T. and Bonazzi, M. (eds.) (2012). *Theoria, Praxis and the Contemplative Life after Plato and Aristotle*. Leiden.

Bénatouïl, T. and El Murr, D. (2010). 'L'Académie et les géometres: usages et limites de la géométrie de Platon à Carnéade'. *Philosophie antique* 10: 41–80.

Berchman, R. B. (2005). *Porphyry against the Christians*. Leiden.

Beretta, G. (2014). *Ipazia d'Alessandria*. Rome.

Berti, E. (2010). *Sumphilosophein. La vita nell'Accademia di Platone*. Rome-Bari.

Bett, R. (1989). 'Carneades' *Pithanon*: A Reappraisal of Its Role and Status'. *Oxford Studies in Ancient Philosophy* 7: 59–75.

(1990). 'Carneades' Distinction between Assent and Approval'. *The Monist* 73: 3–20.

(2000). *Pyrrho, His Antecedents, His Legacy*. Oxford.

Bevan, E. (1913). *Stoics and Sceptics*. Oxford.

Billot, M.-F. (1989). 'Académie (topographie et archéologie)'. In R. Goulet (ed.) *Dictionnaire des Philosophes antiques*. Paris, vol. I: 693–789.

Blank, D. (2010). 'Ammonius Hermeiou and His School'. In Gerson 2010a: 654–66.

Blumenthal, H. (1971). *Plotinus' Psychology*. The Hague.

Bobzien, S. (1998). *Determinism and Freedom in Stoic Philosophy*. Oxford.

Bodnár, I. (2020). 'The Study of Natural Kinds in the Early Academy'. In P. Kalligas *et al.* 2020:153–166.

Bonazzi, M. (2003a). *Academici e Platonici. Il dibattito antico sullo scetticismo di Platone*. Milan.

(2003b). 'Un dibattito tra academici e platonici sull'eredità di Platone. La testimonianza del commentario anonimo al *Teeteto*'. In *Papiri filosofici IV*, Florence: 41–74.

(2009). 'Antiochus' Ethics and the Subordination of Stoicism'. In Bonazzi and Opsomer 2009: 33–54.

(2012a). 'Antiochus and Platonism'. In Sedley 2012: 307–33.

(2012b). 'Theoria and Praxis: On Plutarch's Platonism'. In Bénatouïl and Bonazzi 2012: 139–61.

(2012c). 'Plutarch on the Difference between Academics and Pyrrhonists'. *Oxford Studies in Ancient Philosophy* 43: 271–98.

(2013a). 'Pythagoreanising Aristotle: Eudorus and the Systematisation of Platonism'. In M. Schofield (ed.) *Aristotle, Plato and Pythagoreanism in the First Century BC: New Directions for Philosophy*. Cambridge: 160–86.

(2013b). 'Eudorus of Alexandria and the "Pythagorean" Pseudoepigrapha'. In Cornelli, Macris, and McKirahan 2013: 385–404.

(2015a). *À la recherche des Idées. Platonisme et philosophie hellénistique d'Antiochus à Plotin*. Paris.

(2015b). 'Le commentateur anonyme du *Théétète* et l'invention du platonisme'. In D. El Murr (ed.) *La mesure du savoir. Études sur le Théétète de Platon*. Paris 2013: 309–33.

Bibliography

(2016). 'Platonismo e gnosticismo'. In P. Galand and E. Malaspina (eds.) *Vérité et apparence. Mélanges en l'honneur de Carlos Lévy*, Turnhout: 25–37.

(2017a). 'The Platonist Appropriation of Stoic Epistemology'. In Engberg-Pedersen 2017: 120–41.

(2017b). 'Middle Platonists on the Eternity of the Universe'. In G. Roskam and J. Verheyden (eds.) *Light on Creation: Ancient Commentators in Dialogue and Debate on the Origin of the World*. Tübingen: 3–15.

(2017c). 'Plato Systematized: Doing Philosophy in the Imperial Schools'. *Oxford Studies in Ancient Philosophy* 53: 215–36.

(2020a). 'The End of the Academy'. In P. Kalligas *et al.* 2020: 242–55.

(2020b). 'Daemons in the Cave. Plutarch on Plato and the Limits of Politics'. *Mnemosyne* 73: 63–86.

Bonazzi, M. and Celluprica, V. (eds.) (2005). *L'eredità platonica. Studi sul platonismo da Arcesilao a Proclo*. Naples.

Bonazzi, M. and Helmig, C. (eds.) (2007). *Platonic Stoicism – Stoic Platonism: The Dialogue between Platonism and Stoicism in Antiquity*. Leuven.

Bonazzi, M. and Opsomer, J. (eds.) (2009). *The Origins of the Platonic System: Platonisms in the Early Empire and Their Philosophical Contexts*. Leuven.

Boulogne, J. (2003). *Plutarque dans le miroir d'Épicure. Analyse d'une critique systématique de l'Épicurisme*. Villeneuve d'Asq.

Bowen, A. C. (2013). *Simplicius on the Planets and Their Motions: In Defense of a Heresy*. Leiden.

Boys-Stones, G. (2001). *Post-Hellenistic Philosophy: A Study of Its Development from the Stoics to Origen*. Oxford.

(2005). 'Alcinous, Didaskalikos 4: In Defence of Dogmatism'. In Bonazzi and Celluprica 2005: 201–34.

(2007). 'Middle Platonists on Fate and Human Autonomy'. In R. W. Sharples and R. Sorabji (eds.) *Post-Hellenistic Philosophy 100 BC–200 AD*. London: 431–47.

(2013). 'Seneca against Plato: Letters 58 and 65'. In Long 2013: 128–46.

(2017), 'Are We Nearly There Yet? Eudorus on Aristotle's Categories'. In Engberg-Pedersen 2017: 67–79.

(2018a). *Platonist Philosophy 80 BC to AD 250: An Introduction and Collection of Sources in Translation*. Cambridge.

(2018b). 'Numenius on Intellect, Soul and the Authority of Plato', In J. Bryan, R. Wardy, and J. Warren (eds.) *Authors and Authorities in Ancient Philosophy*. Cambridge: 184–201.

Bowen, A. (1983). 'Menaechmus vs. the Platonists: Two Theories of Science in the Early Academy'. *Ancient Philosophy* 3: 12–29.

Brancacci, A. (ed.) (2000). *La filosofia in età imperiale. Le scuole e le tradizioni filosofiche*. Naples.

Brennan, T. and Brittain, C. (eds.) (2002). *Simplicius: On Epictetus Handbook*. London.

Bibliography

Brisson, L. (1999). 'The Philosophical Background in the Apocalypse of Zostrianos'. In J. J. Cleary (ed.) *Traditions of Platonism: Essays in Honour of John Dillon*. Aldershot: 179–87.

(ed.) (2005). *Porphyre. Sentences*, Paris.

(2010). 'The Fragment of Speusippus in Column I of the Anonymus Commentary on the Parmenides'. In J. D. Turner and K. Corrigan (eds.) *Plato's Parmenides and Its Heritage. Vol 1: History and Interpretation from the Old Academy to Later Platonism and Gnosticism*. Atlanta: 59–68.

Brisson, L. *et al.* (eds.) (1982–92). *Porphyre. La vie de Plotin*. Paris.

Brisson, L. and Patillon, M. (eds.) (2001). *Longin. Fragments – Art rhétorique*. Paris.

Brittain, C. (2001). *Philo of Larissa: The Last of the Academic Sceptics*. Oxford.

(2012). 'Antiochus' Epistemology'. In Sedley 2012: 104–30.

Brochard, V. (2002). *Les sceptiques grecs*. Paris (orig. ed. 1887).

Brunt, P. A. (1993). 'Plato's Academy and Politics'. In Id., *Studies in Greek History and Thought*. Oxford: 282–342.

Burkert, W. (1972a). *Lore and Science in Ancient Pythagoreanism*. Cambridge, MA (orig. ed. 1963).

(1972b). 'Zur geistesgeschichtlichen Ordnung einer Pseudopythagorica'. In *Entretiens de la Fondation Hardt, vol. 18: Pseudoepigrapha I: Pseudopythagorica, Lettres de Platon, Littérature, pseudoépigraphique juive*. Vandœuvres-Geneva: 23–55.

Burns, D. M. (2014). *Apocalypse of the Alien God*. Philadelphia.

Burnyeat, M. (1997). 'Antipater and Self-Refutation: Elusive Arguments in Cicero's Academica'. In Inwood and Mansfeld 1997: 277–310.

(2005). 'Platonism in the Bible: Numenius of Apamea on Exodus and Eternity'. In R. Salles (ed.) *Metaphysics, Soul, and Ethics in Ancient Thought*. Oxford: 143–69.

Cardullo, L. (1995–2000). *Siriano esegeta di Aristotele*. Catania, 2 vols.

(1997). 'La "noera theoria" di Giamblico come chiave di lettura delle Categorie di Aristotele'. *Syllecta classica* 8: 79–94.

Carlini, A. (1972). *Studi sulla tradizione antica e medievale del Fedone*. Rome.

Caruso, A. (2013). *Akademia. Archeologia di una scuola filosofia ad Atene da Platone a Proclo (387 a.C.–485 d.C.)*. Paestum-Athens.

Cassi, A. A. (2013). *La giustizia in Sant'Agostino*. Milano.

Castagnoli, L. (2019). 'Dialectic in the Hellenistic Academy'. In T. Bénatouïl and K. Ierodiakonou (eds.) *Dialectic after Plato and Aristotle*. Cambridge: 168–217.

Catana, L. (2013). 'The Origin of the Division between Middle Platonism and Neoplatonism'. *Apeiron* 46: 166–200.

Catapano, G. (ed.) (2006). *Plotino, Sulle virtù I 2 [19]*. Pisa.

(2010). *Agostino*. Rome.

Bibliography

Centrone, B. (1990). *Pseudopythagorica ethica. I trattati morali di Archita, Metopo, Teage, Eurifamo*. Naples.

(1992). 'The Theory of Principles in the *Pseudopythagorica*'. In K. Boudouris (ed.) *Pythagorean Philosophy*. Athens: 90–7.

(1996). *Introduzione ai Pitagorici*. Rome.

(2000a). 'Platonism and Pythagoreanism in the Early Empire'. In Rowe and Schofield 2000: 559–84.

(2000b). 'Cosa significa essere pitagorico in età imperiale. Per una riconsiderazione della categoria storiografica del neopitagorismo'. In Brancacci 2000: 137–68.

(2012). 'L'esegesi del *Timeo* nell'Accademia antica'. In F. Celia and A. Ulacco (eds.) *Il Timeo. Esegesi Greche, Arabe, Latine*. Pisa: 57–80.

(2014). 'The Pseudo-Pythagorean Writings'. In C. Huffmann (ed.) *A History of Pythagoreanism*. Cambridge: 315–40.

Champion, M. W. (2014). *Explaining the Cosmos: Creation and Cultural Interaction in Late-Antique Gaza*. Oxford.

Cherniss, H. (1974). *L'enigma dell'Accademia antica*. Florence.

Chesnut, G. F. (1978). 'The Ruler and the Logos in Neopythagorean, Middle Platonic and Late Stoic Political Philosophy'. In *ANRW* II 16.2: 1310–31.

Chiaradonna, R. (2002). *Sostanza movimento analogia. Plotino critico di Aristotele*. Naples.

(2005). 'Plotino e la corrente antiaristotelica del platonismo imperiale. Analogie e differenze'. In Bonazzi and Celluprica 2005: 235–74.

(2007). 'Platonismo e Teoria della Conoscenza Stoica tra II e III secolo d.C.'. In Bonazzi and Helmig 2007: 209–41.

(2009). *Plotino*. Rome.

(2012). 'Platonismo e aristotelismo'. In Chiaradonna 2012: 85–102.

(2012) (ed.). *Filosofia tardoantica*. Rome.

(2013). 'Neoplatonismo e politica da Plotino e Proclo'. In *Costantino I. Enciclopedia costantiniana sulla figura e l'immagine dell'imperatore del cosiddetto editto di Milano 313–2013*, Rome, vol. I: 743–55.

(2015). 'La Lettera a Temistio di Giuliano Imperatore e il dibattito filosofico nel IV secolo'. In A. Marcone (ed.) *L'Imperatore Giuliano: Realtà. storica e rappresentazione*. Florence: 149–71.

(2017). 'Théologie et époptique aristotéliciennes dans le médioplatonisme: la réception de Métaphysique Λ'. In F. Baghdassiaran and G. Guyomarc'h (eds.) *Réceptions de la théologie aristotélicienne. D'Aristote à Michel d'Éphèse*. Leuven: 143–57.

(2021). 'Ethics and the Hierarchy of Virtues from Plotinus to Iamblichus'. In S. Xenophontos, A. Marmodoro (eds.) *The Reception of Greek Ethics in Late Antiquity and Byzantium*. Cambridge: 36–51.

Chiaradonna, R. and Trabattoni, F. (eds.) (2009). *Physics and Philosophy of Nature in Greek Neoplatonism*. Leiden.

Chiesara, M. L. (2003). *Storia dello scetticismo greco*. Turin.

Bibliography

Chlup, R. (2012). *Proclus: An Introduction*. Cambridge.

Cooper, J. (ed.) (1997). *Plato: Complete Works*. Indianapolis-Cambridge.

Copenhaver, B. P. (1992). *Hermetica: The Greek Corpus Hermeticum and the Latin Asclepius*. Cambridge.

Cornelli, G., Macris, C., and McKirahan, R. (eds.) (2013). *On Pythagoreanism*. Berlin.

Couissin, P. (1929a). 'L'origine et l'évolution de l'*epoche*'. *Revue d'études grecques* 42: 373–97.

(1929b). 'Le stoïcisme de la Nouvelle Académie'. *Revue d'histoire de la philosophie* 3: 241–76.

(1941). 'Le sorites de Carnéade contre le polythéisme'. *Revue d'études grecques* 54: 43–57.

Courcelle, P. (1943). *Les lettres grecques en Occident: de Macrobe à Cassiodore*. Paris.

Credaro, L. (1889–93). *Lo scetticismo degli Accademici*. Rome-Milan, 2 vols.

Cumont, F. (2006). *Les religions orientales dans le paganisme*. Turin (orig. ed. 1906).

Dagron, G. (1968). *L'empire romain d'Orient au IVe siècle et les traditions politiques de l'hellénisme: le témoignage de Thémistios*. Paris.

Dalsgaard Larsen, B. (1972). *Jambliquede Chalcis exégète et philosophe*. Aarhus, 2 vols.

D'Ancona, C. (1992). 'ΑΜΟΡΦΟΝ ΚΑΙ ΑΝΕΙΔΕΟΝ. Causalité des Formes et causalité de l'Un chez Plotin'. *Revue de Philosophie ancienne* 10: 69–113.

(1996). 'Plotinus and Later Platonic Philosophers on the Causality of the First Principle'. In L. Gerson (ed.) *The Cambridge Companion to Plotinus*. Cambridge: 356–85.

(2005). 'Il neoplatonismo alessandrino: alcune linee della ricerca contemporanea'. *Adamantius* 11: 9–38.

(2006). 'À propos du *De anima* de Jamblique'. *Revue des sciences philosophiques et théologiques* 90: 617–39.

(2012). 'Plotin'. In R. Goulet (ed.) *Dictionnaire des philosophes antiques*. Paris, vol. V A: 853–1036.

Dancy, R. M. (1991). *Two Studies in the Early Academy*. Albany.

(2011). 'Xenocrates'. In E. N. Zalta (ed.) *The Stanford Encyclopedia of Philosophy* (Fall 2011 Edition). http://plato.stanford.edu/archives/fall2011/entries/xenocrates.

(2012). 'Speusippus'. In E. N. Zalta (ed.) *The Stanford Encyclopedia of Philosophy* (Winter 2012 Edition). http://plato.stanford.edu/archives/win2012/entries/speusippus.

Decleva Caizzi, F. (1986). 'Pirroniani e Accademici nel III sec. a.C.'. In *Entretiens de la Fondation Hardt, vol. 32: Aspects de la philosophie hellénistique*. Vandœuvres-Geneva: 147–83.

(1992). 'Aenesidemus and the Academy'. *Classical Quarterly* 42: 176–89.

De Haas, F. (2011). 'Principles, Conversion, and Circular Proof: The Reception of an Academic Debate in Proclus and Philoponus'. In T. Bénatouïl,

Bibliography

E. Maffi, and F. Trabattoni (eds.) *Plato, Aristotle, or Both? Dialogues between Platonism and Aristotelianism in Antiquity.* Hildesheim: 215–40.

Depalma Digeser, E. (2012). *Threat to Public Piety: Christians, Platonists, and the Great Persecution.* Ithaca, NY-London.

De Vita, M. C. (2011). *Giuliano imperatore filosofo neoplatonico.* Milan.

De Vogel, C. (1985). 'Platonism and Christianity: A Mere Antagonism or a Profound Common Ground?' *Vigiliae Christianae* 39: 1–62.

Des Places, E. (ed.) (1971). *Oracles Chaldaïques.* Paris.

(ed.) (1973). *Numénius. Fragments.* Paris.

(ed.) (1977). *Atticus. Fragments.* Paris.

Deuse, W. (1983). *Untersuchungen zur mittelplatonischen und neuplatonischen Seelenlehre.* Wiesbaden.

D'Hoine, P. (2011). 'Les arguments de Proclus contre l'existence d'Idées des maux'. *Etudes Platoniciennes* 8: 75–103.

D'Hoine, P. and Martijn, M. (eds.) (2017). *All from One: A Guide to Proclus.* Oxford.

Di Branco, M. (2006). *La città dei filosofi. Storia di Atene da Marco Aurelio a Giustiniano.* Florence.

Dillon, J. (1973). *Iamblichi Chalcidensis in Platonis dialogos commentariorum fragmenta.* Leiden.

(1993). *Alcinous: The Handbook of Platonism.* Oxford.

(1996). *The Middle Platonists (80 B.C. to A.D. 220).* London (orig. ed. 1977).

(2003). *The Heirs of Plato. A Study of the Old Academy (347–247 BC).* Oxford.

(2005). 'Iamblichus' Criticism of Plotinus' Doctrine of the Undescended Soul'. In R. Chiaradonna (ed.) *Studi sull'anima in Plotino.* Naples: 339–51.

(2010). 'Iamblichus of Chalcis and His School'. In Gerson 2010a: 358–74.

(2011). 'The Ideas as Thoughts of God'. *Études platoniciennes* 8: 31–42.

(2018). 'Theories of Knowledge in the Old Academy'. *Lexicon Philosophicum* 6: 44–51.

Dillon, J. and Finamore, J. (eds.) (2002). *Iamblichus De anima.* Leiden.

Dillon, J. and Morrow, G. R. (eds.) (1987). *Proclus. Commentary on Plato's Parmenides.* Princeton.

Dillon, J. and Polleichter, W. (eds.) (2009). *Iamblichus of Chalcis: The Letters.* Atlanta.

Dodds, E. R. (1928). 'The *Parmenides* of Plato and the Origin of the Neoplatonic One'. *Classical Quarterly* 22: 129–42.

(1951). *The Greeks and the Irrational.* Berkeley.

Donini, P. L. (1980). Motivi filosofici in Galeno'. *La parola del passato* 194: 333–70.

(1982). *Le scuole, l'anima, l'impero. La filosofia antica da Antioco a Plotino.* Turin.

(1986). 'Lo scetticismo academico, Aristotele e l'unità della tradizione platonica secondo Plutarco'. In G. Cambiano (ed.) *Storiografia e dossografia nella filosofia antica.* Turin: 203–26.

Bibliography

(1987). 'Testi e commenti, manuali e insegnamento: la forma sistematica e i metodi della filosofia in età postellenistica'. In *ANRW* 2.36.7: 5027–100 (= *Commentary and Tradition. Aristotelianism, Platonism, and Post-Hellenistic Philosophy*. Berlin 2010: 211–81).

(1990). 'Medioplatonismo e filosofi medioplatonici. Una raccolta di studi'. *Elenchos* 11: 79–93 (= *Commentary and Tradition. Aristotelianism, Platonism, and Post-Hellenistic Philosophy*. Berlin 2010: 283–96).

(1993). 'Il ritorno agli antichi'. In P. Rossi and C. A. Viano (eds.), *Storia della filosofia, I: L'Antichità*, Rome: 362–92.

(ed.) (2011). *Plutarco. Il volto della luna*. Salerno.

Dorandi, T. (1989). 'Assiotea e Lastenia: due donne all'Accademia'. *AATC* 54: 53–66.

(1994). 'Chairon de Pellène'. In R. Goulet (ed.) *Dictionnaire de philosophes antiques*. Paris, vol. II: 286–7.

(1999). 'Chronology'. In Algra *et al.* 1999: 31–54.

Dörrie, H. (1965). 'Emanation. Ein unphilosophisches Wort im spätantiken Denken'. In K. Flasch (ed.) *Parousia. Studien zur Philosophie Platons und zur Problemgschichte des Platonismus*. Frankfurt am Main: 119–41 (= *Platonica Minora*. Munich 1976: 7–88).

Duff, T. (1999). *Plutarch's Lives: Exploring Virtue and Vice*. Oxford.

Dzielska, M. (1996). *Hypathia of Alexandria*. Cambridge, MA.

Edwards, M. (ed.) (2020). *The Routledge Handbook of Early Christian Philosophy*. London.

Eliasson, E. (2008). *The Notion of 'That Which Depends on Us' in Plotinus and Its Background*. Leiden.

(2012). 'L'anima e l'individuo'. In Chiaradonna 2012: 213–31.

Elm, S. (2012). *Sons of Hellenism, Fathers of the Church: Emperor Julian, Gregory of Nazianzus, and the Vision of Rome*. Berkeley.

El Murr, D. (2018). 'The Academy from Plato to Polemo'. In L. Perilli and D. P. Taormina (eds.) *Ancient Philosophy: Textual Paths and Historical Reconstructions*. London: 337–54.

Emilsson, E. (2007). *Plotinus on Intellect*. Oxford.

(2017). *Plotinus*. London.

Engberg-Pedersen, T. (ed.) (2017). *From Stoicism to Platonism: The Development of Philosophy, 100 BCE–100 CE*. Cambridge.

Erler, M., Heßler, J. E., and Petrucci, F. (eds.) (2021). *Authority and Authoritative Texts in the Platonist Tradition*. Cambridge.

Falcon, A. (2000). 'Aristotle, Speusippus, and the Method of Division'. *Classical Quarterly* 50: 402–14.

Ferrari, F. (1995). *Dio, idee e materia. La struttura del cosmo in Plutarco di Cheronea*. Naples.

(1998). 'La collocazione dell'anima e la questione dell'esistenza di idee di individui in Plotino'. *Rivista di storia della filosofia* 53: 629–53.

(2000). 'I commentari specialistici alle sezioni matematiche del *Timeo*'. In Brancacci 2000: 169–224.

Bibliography

(2001). 'Struttura e funzione dell'esegesi testuale nel medioplatonismo: il caso del *Timeo*'. *Athenaeum* 89: 525–74.

(2005). 'Dottrine delle idee nel medioplatonismo'. In F. Fronterotta and W. Leszl (eds.) *Eidos – Idea. Platone, Aristotele e la tradizione platoica*. Sankt Augustin: 233–46.

(2008). 'Moderatismo etico e controllo delle passioni in Plutarco'. In G. Giardina (ed.) *Le emozioni secondo i filosofi antichi*. Catania: 135–62.

(2018). 'Der Begriff "Mittelplatonismus" und die Forschungsgeschichte'. In Riedweg, Horn, and Wyrwa 2018: 5445–555.

Ferrary, J. L. (1995). 'The Statesman and the Law in the Political Philosophy of Cicero'. In A. Laks and M. Schofield (eds.) *Justice and Generosity: Studies in Hellenistic Social and Political Philosophy*. Cambridge: 48–73.

(2007). 'Les philosophes grecs à Rome (155–86 Av. J.-C.)'. In A. M. Ioppolo and D. N. Sedley (eds.) *Pyrrhonists, Patricians, Platonizers: Hellenistic Philosophy in the Period 155–86 BC*. Naples: 17–46.

Festugière, A.-J. (1968). 'Contemplation philosophique et art théurgique chez Proclus'. In U. Bianchi (ed.) *Studi di storia religiosa della tarda antichità*. Messina: 7–18 (= *Études de philosophie grecque*. Paris 1971: 575–84).

Finamore, J. and Iles Johnston, S. (2010). 'The Chaldean Oracles'. In Gerson 2010a: 161–73.

Fleischer, K. (2016). 'New Readings in Philodemus' *Index Academicorum*: Dio of Alexandria (*P. Herc.* 1021, col. XXXV, 17–19)'. In *Proceedings of the 27th International Congress of Papyrology (Warsaw/2013)*. Warsaw: 459–70.

Fletcher, R. (2014). *Apuleius' Platonism: The Impersonification of Philosophy*. Cambridge.

Fortenbaugh, W. W., and Pender, E. (eds.) (2009). *Heraclides of Pontus: Discussion*. New Brunswick, NJ.

Fowden, G. (1982). 'The Pagan Holy Man in Late Antiquity'. *Journal of Hellenic Studies* 102: 33–59.

Fowler, H. N. (ed.) (1960). *Plutarch's Moralia, vol. X*. Cambridge, MA-London.

Fraser, P. (1972). *Ptolemaic Alexandria*. Oxford, 2 vols.

Frede, D. (2018). 'A Superannuated Student: Aristotle and Authority in the Academy'. In J. Bryan, R. Wardy, and J. Warren (eds.) *Authors and Authorities in Ancient Philosophy*. Cambridge: 78–101.

Frede, D., and Laks, A. (eds.) (2002). *Traditions of Theology: Studies in Hellenistic Theology, Its Background and Aftermath*. Leiden.

Frede, M. (1984). 'The Skeptic's Two Kinds of Assent and the Question of the Possibility of Knowledge'. In R. Rorty, J. Schneewind, and Q. Skinner (eds.) *Philosophy in History*. Cambridge: 255–78 (= *Essays in Ancient Philosophy*. Minneapolis 1987: 201–22).

(1987). 'Numenius'. In *ANRW* II 36.2: 1034–75.

(1990). 'La teoría de las ideas en Longino'. *Méthexis* 3: 85–98.

(1994). 'The Stoic Conception of Reason'. In K. Boudouris (ed.) *Hellenistic Philosophy*. Athens: 50–63.

Bibliography

(1997). 'Celsus' Attack on the Christians'. In Barnes and Griffin 1997: 218–40.

(1999a). 'Stoic Epistemology'. In Algra *et al.* 1999: 295–322.

(1999b). 'Epilogue'. in Algra *et al.* 1999: 771–97.

Fronterotta, F. (2018). 'Eudoxe et Speusippe sur le Plaisir (Selon Aristote): un Débat dans l'Ancienne Académie'. *Revue de Philosophie Ancienne* 36: 39–72.

Fuentes Gonzáles, P. B. (2005). 'Ménaichmos'. In R. Goulet (ed.) *Dictionnaire des philosophes antiques*. Paris, vol. IV: 401–7.

Gaiser, K. (1980). *Das Philosophenmosaik in Neapel. Eine Darstellung der platonischen Akademie*. Heidelberg.

Gavray, M. A. (2007). *Simplicius lecteur du Sophiste*. Langres.

Gavray, M. A. and Michalewski, A. (eds.) (2017). *Les principes cosmologiques du Platonisme*. Turnhout.

Gawlick, G. and Görler, W. (1994). 'Cicero'. In H. Flashar (ed.) *Die Philosophie der Antike, vol. 4: Die hellenistische Philosophie*. Basel: 991–1168.

Gersh, S. (1986). *Middle Platonism and Neoplatonism: The Latin Tradition*. Notre Dame, 2 vols.

(2019). 'Introduction'. In S. Gersh (ed.) *Plotinus' Legacy*. Cambridge: 1–15.

Gerson, L. P. (ed.) (1996). *The Cambridge Companion to Plotinus*. Cambridge.

(2005). *Aristotle and Other Platonists*. Ithaca, NY.

(ed.) (2010a). *The Cambridge History of Philosophy in Late Antiquity*. Cambridge, 2 vols.

(2010b). 'The First Encounter of Judaism and Christianity with Ancient Greek Philosophy'. In L. Gerson (ed.) *The Cambridge History of Philosophy in Late Antiquity*. Cambridge: 233–4, 2 vols.

(2013). *From Plato to Platonism*. Ithaca, NY.

Gerson, L. P. and Wilberding, J. (eds.) (2022), The Cambridge Companion to Plotinus. Cambridge.

Giardina, G. (2012). 'Jean Philopon'. In R. Goulet (ed.) *Dictionnaire des philosophes antiques*. Paris, vol. V A: 455–503.

Gigante, G. (1976). 'Polemonis Academici fragmenta'. *Rendiconti dell'Accademia di Archeologia, Lettere e Belle Arti* 51: 91–144.

Gigon, O. (1944). 'Zur Geschichte der sogenannten Neuen Akademie'. *Musaeum Helveticum* 1: 47–64.

(1958). 'Die Erneuerung der Philosophie in der Zeit Ciceros'. In *Entretiens de la Fondation Hardt*, vol. 3: *Recherches sur la tradition platonicienne*. Vandœuvres-Geneva: 25–59.

Gildenhard, I. (2011). *Creative Eloquence: The Construction of Reality in Cicero's Speeches*. Oxford.

Gioé, A. (ed.) (2002). *Filosofi medioplatonici del II secolo d.C.* Naples.

Glucker, J. (1978). *Antiochus and the Late Academy*. Göttingen.

(1988). 'Cicero's Philosophical Affiliations'. In J. Dillon and A. A. Long (eds.) *The Question of Eclecticism*. Berkeley: 34–69.

(1995). 'Probabile, Veri simile and Related Terms'. In Powell 1995: 115–43.

(2004). 'The Philonian/Metrodorians: Problems of Method in Ancient Philosophy'. *Elenchos* 25: 99–153.

Bibliography

Görler, W. (1994). 'Ältere Pyrrhonismus, Jüngere Akademie, Antiochos aus Askalon'. In H. Flashar (ed.) *Die Philosophie der Antike*, vol. 4: *Die hellenistiche Philosophie*. Basel: 719–989.

(1995). 'Silencing the Troublemaker: De legibus I 39 and the Continuity of Cicero's Scepticism'. In Powell 1995: 85–113.

Gottschalk, H. B. (1980). *Heraclides of Pontus*. Oxford.

Goulet, R. (2001). *Études sur les vies des philosophes de l'Antiquité tardive. Diogène Laërce, Porphyre de Tyr, Eunape de Sardes*. Paris.

Granieri, R. (2021). 'Xenocrates and the Two-Category Scheme'. *Apeiron* 54: 261–85.

Greig, J. (2021). *The First Principle in Late Neoplatonism: A Study of the One's Causality in Proclus and Damascius*. Leiden.

Haake, M. (2007). *Der Philosoph in der Stadt. Untersuchungen zur öffentlichen Rede über Philosophen und Philosophie in den hellenistischen Poleis*. Munich.

(2008). 'Das "Gesetz des Sophokles" und die Schliessung der Philosophenschulen in Athen unter Demetrios Poliorketes'. In H. Hugonnard-Roche (ed.) *L'enseignement supérieur dans les mondes antiques et médiévaux*. Paris: 89–111.

(2020). 'The Academy in Athenian Politics and Society. Between Disintegration and Integration: The First Eighty Years (387/6–306/5)'. In Kalligas *et al.* 2020: 65–88.

Habicht, C. (1994). 'Hellenistic Athens and Her Philosophers'. In Id. *Athen in hellenistischer Zeit*. Munich: 231–47.

Hadot, I. (1978). *Le problème du néoplatonisme alexandrine: Hiéroclès et Simplicius*. Paris.

(ed.) (1987). *Simplicius. Sa vie, son œuvre, sa survie*. Berlin.

(ed.) (1990). *Simplicius. Commentaire sur les Catégories*. Leiden.

Hadot, I. and Hadot, P. (2004). *Apprendre à philosopher dans l'Antiquité. L'enseignement du 'Manuel d'Épictete' et son commentaire néoplatonicien*. Paris.

Hadot, P. (1957). '*De lectis non lecta componere* (Marius Victorinus, *adv. Ar.* ii, 7). Raisonnement théologique et raisonnement juridique'. *Studia Patristica* 1: 209–20 (= Id., *Études de philosophie ancienne*. Paris 2010: 13–25).

(1968). *Porphyre et Victorinus*. Paris.

(1981). *Exercices et philosophie antique*. Paris.

(1987). 'Théologie, exégèse, révélation, écriture dans la philosophie grecque'. In M. Tardieu (ed.) *Les règles de l'intérpretation*. Paris: 13–34 (=*Études de philosophie ancienne*. Paris 2010: 27–58).

Halfwassen, J. (1993). 'Speusipp und die metaphysische Deutung von Platons *Parmenides*'. In L. Hagemann and R. Glei (eds.) *En kai Plethos. Festschrift für Karl Bormann*. Würzburg: 339–73.

Hankinson, J. (1999). 'Determinism and Indeterminism'. In Algra *et al.* 1999: 513–41.

Bibliography

Harnack, A. von (1916). 'Porphyrios "Gegen die Christen"'. In *Philosophische und historische Abhandlungen der königlichen Akademie der Wissenschaften zu Berlin*. Berlin: 3–115.

Hatzimichali, M. (2011). *Potamo of Alexandria and the Emergence of Eclecticism in Late Hellenistic Philosophy*. Cambridge.

(2018). 'Pseudo-Archytas and the *Categories*'. In J. Bryan, R. Wardy, and J. Warren (eds.) *Authors and Authorities in Ancient Philosophy*. Cambridge: 162–83.

(2020). 'The Academy through Epicurean Eyes: Some Lives of Academic Philosophers in Philodemus' Syntaxis'. In Kalligas *et al.* 2020: 256–75.

Heinze, R. (1892). *Xenocrates. Darstellung der Lehre und Sammlung der Fragmente*. Leipzig.

Hoffmann, P. (1987). 'Sur quelques aspects de la polémique de Simplicius contre Jean Philopone: de l'invective à la réaffirmation de la transcendance du Ciel'. In I. Hadot 1987: 183–221.

(1994). 'Damascius'. In R. Gulet (ed.) *Dictionnaire des philosophes antiques*. Paris, vol. II: 541–93.

(2000). 'La triade Chaldaïque erôs, alêtheia, pistis: de Proclus à Simplicius'. In Segonds and Steel 2000: 459–89.

Horky, P. S. (2009). 'Persian Cosmos and Greek Philosophy: Plato's Associates and the Zoroastrian Magoi'. *Oxford Studies in Ancient Philosophy* 37: 47–103.

(2013). 'Theophrastus on Platonic and "Pythagorean" Imitation'. *Classical Quarterly* 63: 686–712.

(2018). 'Speusippus and Xenocrates on the Pursuit and Ends of Philosophy'. In H. Tarrant, F. Renaud, D. Baltzly, and D. A. Layne (eds.) *Brill's Companion to the Reception of Plato in Antiquity*. Leiden: 29–45.

Horn, C. and Wilberding, J. (eds.) (2012). *Neoplatonism and the Philosophy of Nature*. Oxford.

Howald, E. (1921). *Die platonische Akademie und die moderne Universitas Litterarum. Eine Akademische Rede*. Zürich.

Huffman, C. (2005). *Archytas of Tarentum: Pythagorean, Philosopher and Mathematician King*. Cambridge.

Inwood, B. (2007). 'Seneca, Plato and Platonism: The Case of Letter 65'. In Bonazzi and Helmig 2007: 149–67.

(2012). 'Antiochus on Physics'. In Sedley 2012: 188–219.

Inwood, B. and Mansfeld, J. (eds.) (1997). *Assent and Argument: Studies in Cicero's Academic Books*. Leiden.

Ioppolo, A. M. (1986). *Opinione e scienza. Il dibattito tra Stoici e Accademici nel III e nel II secolo a.C.* Naples.

(1993). 'The Academic Position of Favorinus of Arelate'. *Phronesis* 38: 183–213.

(2007). 'L'assenso nella filosofia di Clitomaco: un problema di linguaggio?' In A. M. Ioppolo and D. Sedley (eds.) *Pyrrhonists, Patricians, Platonizers: Hellenistic Philosophy in the Period 155–86 BC*, Rome: 225–67.

Bibliography

(2009). *La testimonianza di Sesto Empirico sull'Academia ellenistica*. Naples.

Isnardi Parente, M. (1979). *Studi sull'Accademia antica*. Florence.

(ed.) (1980). *Speusippo. Testimonianze e frammenti*. Naples. Available at: http://rmcisadu.let.uniroma1.it/isnardi/fronte.htm.

(ed.) (1982a). *Senocrate e Ermodoro. Testimonianze e frammenti*. Naples (new edition by T. Dorandi, Pisa 2012).

(1982b). 'Un Fragment de Xénocrate et le Problème de la Connaissance Sensible'. *Revue Philosophique de la France et de l'Étranger* 107: 293–305.

(1989). *L'eredità di Platone nell'Accademia antica*. Milan.

(1998). 'L'Accademia antica e le sue vicende filosofiche'. *Rivista di storia della filosofia* 53: 215–34.

Johnson, A. P. (2013). *Religion and Identity in Porphyry of Tyre: The Limits of Hellenism in Late Antiquity*. Cambridge.

Joly, R. (1956). *Le thème philosophique des genres de vie dans l'antiquité Classique*. Brussels.

Joosse, A. (ed.) (2021). *Olympiodorus of Alexandria: Exegete, Teacher, Platonic Philosopher*. Leiden.

Jourdan, F. (2013). 'La matère à l'origine du mal chez Numénius. Un enseigne-ment explicité chez Macrobe'. *Revue de philosophie ancienne* 31: 41–87, 149–78.

Kaklamanou, E. (2010). 'Speusippus on Cognitive Sense Perception: Sextus Empiricus M 7.145–6'. *British Journal for the History of Philosophy* 20: 1183–93.

Kalligas, P. (1997). 'Forms of Individuals in Plotinus: A Re-examination'. *Phronesis* 42: 206–27.

(2014). *The Enneads of Plotinus: A Commentary*. Princeton.

Kalligas, P., Balla, C., Baziotopoulou-Valavani, E., and Karasmanis, V. (eds.) (2020). *Plato's Academy: Its Workings and Its History*. Cambridge.

Karamanolis, G. (2006). *Plato and Aristotle in Agreement? Platonists on Aristotle from Antiochus to Porphyry*. Oxford.

(2014). 'The Platonism of Eusebius of Caesarea'. In R. C. Fowler (ed.) *Plato in the Third Sophistic*. Berlin: 193–210.

(2018). 'Why Did Porphyry Write Aristotelian Commentaries?' In B. Strobel (ed.) *Die Kunst der philosophischen Exegese bei den spätantiken Platon- und Aristoteles- Kommentatoren*. Berlin: 9–44.

(2021). *The Philosophy of Early Christianity*. Abingdon.

Kechagia, E. (2011). *Plutarch against Colotes: A Lesson in History of Philosophy*. Oxford.

Klitenic Wear, S. and Dillon, J. (2007). *Despoiling the Hellenes: Dionysius the Areopagite and the Neoplatonist Tradition*. Aldershot-Burlington, VT.

Köckert, C. (2009). *Christlichle Kosmologie und kaiserzeitliche Philosophie. Die Auslegung des Schöpfungsberichtes bei Origenes, Basilius und Gregor von Nyssa vor dem Hintergrund kaiserzeitlicher Timaeus-Interpretationen*. Tübingen.

Bibliography

Krämer, H. J. (1964). *Der Ursprung der Geistmetaphysik.* Amsterdam.

(1971). *Platonismus und Hellenistische Philosophie.* Berlin.

(1983). 'Ältere Akademie'. In H. Flashar (ed.) *Die Philosophie der Antike,* vol. 3: *Ältere Akademie – Aristoteles – Peripatos.* Basel: 1–174.

Kristeller, P. O. (1929). *Der Begriff der Seele in der Ethik Plotins.* Tübingen.

Kupreeva, I. (2010). 'Themistius'. In Gerson 2010a: 397–416.

Lacombrade, C. (1964). *L'empereur Julien. Œuvres complètes.* Paris.

Lakmann, M. L. (2017). *Platonici minores. 1Jh.n.Chr. – 2.Jr.n.Chr. Prosopographie. Fragmente und Testimonien mit deutscher Übersetzung.* Leiden.

Lamberton, R. (1986). *Homer the Theologian. Neoplatonist Allegorical Reading and the Growth of the Epic Tradition.* Berkeley-Los Angeles.

Lasserre, F. (1966). *Die Fragmente des Eudoxos von Knidos.* Berlin.

(1987). *De Léodamas de Thasos à Philippe d'Opunte. Témoignages et fragments.* Naples.

Lauwers, J. (2015). *Philosophy, Rhetoric, and Sophistry in the High Roman Empire: Maximus of Tyre and Twelve Other Intellectuals.* Leiden.

Lavaud, L. (2008). *D'une métaphysique à l'autre. Figures de l'altérité dans la philosophie de Plotin.* Paris.

Levieils, X. (2007). *Contra Christianos. La critique sociale et religieuse du christianisme des origines au concile de Nicée (45–325).* Berlin.

Levin, F. R. L. (2009). *Greek Reflections on the Nature of Music.* Cambridge.

Lévy, C. (1978). 'Scepticisme et dogmatisme dans l'Académie: "l'ésotérisme" d'Arcésilas'. *Revue d'études latines* 56: 335–48.

(1986). 'Le "scepticisme" de Philon d'Alexandrie: une influence de la Nouvelle Acadèmie?' In A. Caquot, M. Hadas-Lebel, and J. Riaud (eds.) *Hellenica et Judaica. Hommage à Valentin Nikiprowtzky.* Paris: 29–41.

(1992). *Cicero Academicus. Recherches sur les Académiques et sur la philosophie cicéronienne.* Rome.

(1993). 'La Nouvelle Académie a-t-elle été antiplatonicienne?' In M. Dixsaut (ed.) *Contre Platon 1. Le platonisme dévoilé,* Paris: 139–56.

(1997). *Les philosophies hellénistiques.* Paris.

(2000). 'Academy'. In J. Brunschwig and G. E. R. Lloyd (eds) *Greek Thought: A Guide to Classical Knowledge.* Cambridge, MA: 799–821.

(2005). 'Les petits Académiciens: Lacyde, Charmadas, Métrodore de Stratonice'. In Bonazzi and Celluprica 2005: 51–77.

(2008). 'Cicéron, le moyen platonisme et la philosophie romaine: à propos de la naissance du concept latin de *qualitas*'. *Revue de Métaphysique et de Morale* 57: 5–20.

(2016). 'Philon d'Alexandrie fondateur du fidéisme?' In A. I. Bouton-Touboulic and C. Lévy (eds.) *Scepticisme et religion. Constantes et évolutions de la philosophie hellénistique à la philosophie médiévale.* Turnhout: 57–73.

Lewy, H. (1978). *Chaldean Oracles and Theurgy.* Paris.

Bibliography

Linguiti, A. (1988). 'Giamblico, Proclo e Damascio sul principio anteriore all'Uno'. *Elenchos* 9: 97–106.

(1990). *L'ultimo platonismo greco*. Florence.

(1995). 'Commentarium in Platonis Parmenidem'. In *Corpus dei papiri filosofici greci e latini*, Florence, vol. 3: 63–202.

(2012a). 'Il primo principio'. In Chiaradonna 2012: 193–212.

(2012b). 'Etica'. In Chiaradonna 2012: 233–52.

(2015). 'L'etica medioplatonica'. *Rivista di storia della filosofia* 70: 359–80.

Lloyd, A. C. (1990). *The Anatomy of Neoplatonism*. Oxford.

Löhr, W. H. (2010). 'Chrstianity as Philosophy: Problems and Perspectives of an Ancient Intellectual Project'. *Vigiliae Christianae* 64: 160–88.

Long, A. A. (1974). *Hellenistic Philosophy: Stoics, Epicureans, Sceptics*. London.

(1978). 'Timon of Phlius, Pyrrhonist and Satirist'. *Proceedings of the Cambridge Philological Society* 24: 68–91.

(1986). 'Diogenes Laertius, Life of Arcesilaus'. *Elenchos* 7: 429–49.

(1988). 'Socrates in Hellenistic Philosophy'. *Classical Quarterly* 38: 150–71.

(1990). 'Scepticism about Gods in Hellenistic Philosophy'. In M. Griffith and D. Mastronarde (eds.) *Cabinet of the Muses*. Atlanta: 279–91.

Long, A. A. and Sedley, D. (eds.). (1987). *The Hellenistic Philosophers*. Cambridge, 2 vols.

Long. A. G. (ed.) (2013). *Plato and the Stoics*. Cambridge.

Longo, A. (ed.) (2009). *Syrianus et la métaphysique de l'antiquité tardive*. Naples.

(2010). 'Syrianus'. In Gerson 2010a: 616–29.

Lucarini, C. (2010–11). 'Osservazioni sulla prima circolazione delle opere di Platone e sulle trilogie di Aristofane di Bisanzio'. *Hyperboreus* 16/17: 346–361.

Luna, C. (2001). 'Review of R. Thiel, Simplikios und das Ende der neuplatonischen Schule in Athen'. *Mnemosyne* 54: 482–504.

Lynch, P. (1972). *Aristotle's School: A Study of a Greek Educational Institution*. Berkeley.

Majercik, R. (ed.) (1989). *The Chaldean Oracles: Text, Translation, and Commentary*. Leiden.

Männlein-Robert, I. (2001). *Longin. Philologe und Philosoph. Eine Interpretation der erhaltenen Zeugnisse*. Munich-Leipzig.

(2018). 'Kelsos'. In Riedweg, Horn, and Wyrwa 2018: 665–72.

Mansfeld, J. (1992). *Heresiography in Context: Hippolytus' Elenchos as a Source for Greek Philosophy*. Leiden.

(1994). *Prolegomena: Questions to Be Settled before the Study of an Author, or a Text*. Leiden.

(1995). 'Aenesidemus and the Academics'. In L. Ayres (ed.) *The Passionate Intellect: Essays for I. Kidd*. New Brunswick, NJ-London: 235–48.

(1999). 'Theology'. In Algra *et al.* 1999: 452–78.

Bibliography

Maraval, P. (2001). *Eusèbe de Césarée. La théologie politique de l'Empire chrétien. Louanges de Constantin*. Paris.

Martijn, M. (2010). *Proclus on Nature: Philosophy of Nature and Its Methods in Proclus' Commentary on Plato's Timaeus*. Leiden.

Mazzarelli, C. (ed.) (1985). 'Raccolta e interpretazione dei frammenti del medioplatonico Eudoro di Alessandria'. *Rivista di Filosofia Neoscolastica* 77: 197–209, 535–555.

Maso, S. (2014). *Cicerone, Il fato*. Rome.

McCracken, G. E. (ed.) (1957). *Augustine: City of God*. Cambridge, MA-London.

Merki, H. (1952). *Homoisis Theo. Von der platonischen Angleichung an Gott zur Gottähnlichkeit bei Gregor von Nyssa*. Fribourg.

Metry-Tresson, C. (2012). *L'aporie ou l'expérience des limites de la pensés dans le Peri archon de Damascius*. Leiden.

Mette, H. J. (1984). 'Zwei Akademiker heute: Krantor von Soli und Arkesilaos von Pitane'. *Lustrum* 21: 7–94.

(1986/1987). 'Philon von Larissa und Antiochos von Askalon'. *Lustrum* 28/29: 9–63.

Michalewski, A. (2012). 'Le premier de Numenius et l'Un de Plotin'. *Archives de philosophie* 75: 29–48.

(2014). *La puissance de l'intelligible. La théorie plotinienne des Formes au miroir de l'héritage médioplatonicien*. Leuven.

(2017). 'Atticus et le nombre des principles. Nouvel examen de quelques problèmes textuels du fragment DP 26 (= Proclus, In Tim., I, 391, 6–12)'. In Gavray and Michalewsky 2017: 119–41.

(2020). 'Les principes cosmologiques selon Atticus dans le *Candélabre du Sanctuaire* de Bar Hebraeus'. *Documenti e studi sulla tradizione filosofica medievale* 31: 203–33.

Mitchell, S. and van Nuffelen, P. (eds.) (2010). *One God: Pagan Monotheism in the Roman Empire*. Cambridge.

Moore, E. and Turner, J. D. (2010). 'Gnosticism'. In Gerson 2010a: 174–96.

Moraux, P. (1973–2001). *Der Aristotelismus bei den Griechen von Andronikos bis Alexander von Aphrodisias*. Berlin, 3 vols.

Moreschini, C. (1978). *Apuleio e il platonismo*. Florence.

Morlet, S. (ed.) (2011). *Le traité de Porphyre contre les Chrétiens. Un siècle de recherches, nouvelles questions*. Paris.

(2014). *Christianisme et philosophie. Les premières confrontations (Ier-VIe siècle)*. Paris.

Napoli, V. (2008). *Epekeina tou henos. Il principio totalmente ineffabile tra dialettica ed esegesi in Damascio*. Catania.

Neschke-Hentske, A. (1995). *Platonisme politique et théorie du droit naturel*. Louvain-Paris, vol. I.

(1999). 'La cité n'est pas à nous. *Res publica* et *civitas* dans le XIXème livre du *De civitate Dei* d'Augustin d'Hippone'. In M. Abate and M. Vegetti (eds.) *La Repubblica di Platone nella tradizione antica*. Naples: 219–44.

Bibliography

(2003). *Platonisme politique et théorie du droit naturel.* Louvain-Paris, vol. II.

O'Brien, D. (1992). 'Origène et Plotin sur le roi de l'universe'. In M.-O. Goulet-Cazé, G. Madec, and D. O'Brien (eds.) *ΣΟΦΙΗΣ ΜΑΙΗΤΟΡΕΣ. 'Chercheurs de sagesse'. Hommage à Jean Pépin.* Paris: 317–42.

(1999). 'La matière chez Plotin: son origine, sa nature'. *Phronesis* 44: 45–71.

O'Daly, G. (1999). *Augustine's City of God: A Reader's Guide.* Oxford.

O'Meara, D. (1989). *Pythagoras Revived: Mathematics and Philosophy in Late Antiquity.* Oxford.

(1993). *Plotinus: An Introduction to the Enneads.* Oxford.

(ed.) (1999). *Plotin. Traité 51 (I, 8).* Paris.

(2003). *Platonopolis: Platonic Political Philosophy in Late Antiquity.* Oxford.

(2006). 'Patterns of Perfection in Damascius' Life of Isidore'. *Phronesis* 51: 74–90.

Opsomer, J. (1994). 'L'âme du monde et l'âme de l'homme chez Plutarque'. In M. García Valdés (ed.) *Estudios sobre Plutarco: ideas religiosas.* Madrid: 33–49.

(1998). *In Search of the Truth: Academic Tendencies in Middle Platonism.* Brussels.

(2001). 'Proclus vs. Plotinus on Matter (*De mal. Subs.* 30–7)'. *Phronesis* 46: 154–88.

(2005). 'Demiurges in Early Imperial Platonism'. In R. Hirsch-Luipold (ed.) *Gott und Götter bei Plutarch. Götterbilder – Gottesbilder – Weltbilder.* Berlin: 51–99.

(2007). 'Some Problems with Plotinus' Theory of Matter/Evil: An Ancient Debate Continued'. *Quaestio* 7: 165–89.

(2014a). 'The Middle Platonic Doctrine of Conditional Fate'. In P. D'Hoine and G. van Riel (eds.) *Fate, Providence and Moral Responsability in Ancient, Medieval and Early Modern Thought.* Levuen: 137–67.

(2014b). 'Plutarch and the Stoics'. In M. Beck (ed.) *A Companion to Plutarch.* Oxford. 88–103.

(2017). 'Is Plutarch Really Hostile to the Stoics?' In Engberg-Pedersen 2017: 296–321.

Opsomer, J. and Ulacco, A. (2014). 'Elements and Elemental Properties in Timaeus Locrus'. *Rheinisches Museum* 157: 154–206.

Opsomer, J. and Steel, C. (eds.) (2003). *Proclus: On the Existence of Evil.* London.

Pease, A. S. (ed.) (1955–1958). *M. Tulli Ciceronis De natura deorum.* Cambridge, Mass., 2 vols.

Pelling, C. (2004). 'Do Plutarch's Politicians Never Learn?' In L. De Blois *et al.* (eds.) *The Statesman in Plutarch's Works*, vol. I: Plutarch's Statesman and His Aftermath: Political, Philosophical, and Literary Aspects. Leiden: 87–103.

Perkams, M. (2006). 'An Innovation by Proclus: The Theory of the Substantial Diversity of the Human Soul'. In M. Perkams and R. M. Piccione (eds.) *Proklos. Methode, Seelenlehre, Metaphysik.* Leiden: 167–85.

Bibliography

Perrin, B. (ed.) (1917). *Plutarch's Lives*, vol. V: *Agesialus and Pompey, Pelopidas and Marcellus*. Cambridge, MA-London.

Petrucci, F. M. (ed.) (2012). *Teone di Smirne*. *Expositio rerum mathematicarum ad legendum Platonem utilium*. Sankt Augustin.

(2016). 'Argumentative Strategies in the "Platonic Section" of Plutarch' s *De Iside et Osiride*. *Mnemonsyne* 69: 226–48.

(2018a). *Taurus of Beirut: The Other Side of Middle Platonism*. London.

(2018b). 'Wave-Like Commentaries: The Structure and Philosophical Orientation of Middle Platonist Commentaries'. *Journal of Hellenic Studies* 138: 209–26.

(2018c). 'Wie man eine Platonstelle deutet: Exegetische Strukturen im Mittelplatonismus'. *Philologus* 162: 55–91.

(2019). 'Ascoltare l'anima cosmica: riargomentazione ed esegesi tecnica κατὰ ζητήματα della divisio animae platonica'. In C. Helmig (ed.) *World Soul – Anima Mundi: On the Origins and Fortune of a Fundamental Idea*. Berlin: 91–134.

(2021). 'Authority beyond Doctrines in the First Century bc: Antiochus' Model for Plato's Authority'. In Erler, Heßler, and Petrucci 2021: 89–114.

Pietsch, C. (ed.) (2013). *Ethik des antiken Platonismus*. Stuttgart.

Pottle, D. (1978). 'The Platonic Element in the *Metapmorphoses* of Apuleius'. Dissertation, Ann Arbor.

Powell, J. G. F. (ed.) (1995). *Cicero the Philosopher*. Oxford.

Praechter, C. (1910). 'Richtungen und Schulen im Neuplatonismus'. In *Genethliakon. Carl Robert zum 8 Mär 1910*. Berlin: 103–56.

Puech, B. (2000). 'Eudoxe de Cnide'. In R. Goulet (ed.) *Dictionnaire des philosophes antiques*. Paris, vol. III: 293–303.

Puech, H.-C. (1934). 'Numénius d'Apamée et les théologies orientales au second siècle'. *EQG*: 25–54.

Radice, R. (1991). 'Observations on the Theory of Ideas as the Thoughts of God in Philo of Alexandria'. *The Studia Philonica Annual* 3: 126–34.

Rappe, S. (ed.) (2010). *Damascius. Problems and Solutions Concerning First Principles*. Oxford.

Rashed, M. (2012). 'La mosaïque des philosophes de Naples: une représentation de l'Académie platonicienne et son commanditaire'. In C. Noirot and N. Ordine (eds.) *Omnia in Uno, Hommage à Alain-Philippe Segonds*. Paris: 27–49.

Rashed, M. and Auffret, T. (2014). 'Aristote. *Métaphysique* A 6, 988a7–14, Eudore d'Alexandrie et l'histoire ancienne du texte de la *Métaphysique*'. In C. Brockmann, D. Deckers, L. Koch, and S. Valente (eds.) *Handschriften und Textforschung heute. Zur Überlieferung der griechischen Literatur*. Wiesbaden: 55–84.

Remes, P. (2007). *Plotinus on Self: The Philosophy of the 'We'*. Cambridge.

(2008). *Neoplatonism*. Stocksfield.

Remes, P. and Slaveva-Griffin, S. (eds.) (2014). *The Routledge Handbook of Neoplatonism*. Oxford.

Bibliography

Reydams-Schils, G. (1999). *Demiurge and Providence: Stoic and Platonist Readings of Plato's Timaeus*. Turnhout.

(2013). 'The Academy, the Stoics and Cicero on Plato's Timaeus'. In Long 2013: 29–58.

(2017). '"Becoming Like God" in Platonism and Stoicism'. In Engberg-Pedersen 2017: 142–58.

(2020). *Calcidius on Plato's Timaeus. Greek Philosophy, Latin Reception, and Christian Contexts*. Cambridge.

Riedweg, C. (2018). 'Das Origens-Problem aus der Sicht eines Klassischen Philologen'. In B. Bäbler and H. G. Nesselrath (eds.) *Origenes der Christ und Origenes der Platoniker*. Tübingen: 13–39.

Riedweg, C., Horn, C., and Wyrwa, E. (eds.) (2018). *Die Philosophie der Antike*, vol. 5: *Philosophie der Kaiserzeit und der Spätantike*. Basel.

Ritter, A. M. (2018). 'Dionysios Areopagites und die Kontroverse um sin Werk'. In Riedweg, Horn, and Wyrwa 2018: 2220–36, 2305–10.

Rowe, C. and Schofield, M. (eds.) (2000). *The Cambridge History of Greek and Roman Political Thought*. Cambridge.

Runia, D. (1986). *Philo of Alexandria and the Timaeus of Plato*. Leiden.

(1993). *Philo in Early Christian Literature: A Survey*. Assen.

(1995). 'Why Does Clement of Alexandria Call Philo "the Pythagorean"?' *Vigiliae Christianae* 49: 1–22.

(2002), 'The Beginning of the End: Philo of Alexandria and Hellenistic Theology'. In Frede and Laks 2002: 281–316.

Runia, D. and Share, M. (eds.) (2008). *Proclus. Commentary on Plato's Timaeus*, vol. II: *Proclus on the Causes of the Cosmos and Its Creation*. Cambridge.

Saffrey, H. D. (1968). 'ΑΓΕΩΜΕΤΡΗΤΟΣ ΜΗΔΕΙΣ ΕΙΣΙΤΩ. Une inscription legendaire'. *Revue des Études grecques* 81: 67–87 (= *Recherches sur le néoplatonisme après Plotin*. Paris 1990: 251–71).

(1975). 'Allusions anti-chrétiennes chez Proclus, le diadoque platonicien'. *Revue des sciences philosophiques et théologiques* 59: 553–63 (=*Recherches sur le néoplatonisme après Plotin*. Paris 1990: 201–12).

(1987). 'Comment Syrianus, le maître de l'école néoplatonicienne d'Athènes considérait-il Aristote?' In J. Wiesner (ed.) *Aristoteles Werk und Wirkung. Paul Moraux gewidmet*. Berlin vol. II, 205–14 (= *Recherches sur le néoplatonisme après Plotin*. Paris 1990: 131–40).

(1988). 'Connaissance et inconnaissance de Dieu: Porphyre et la Théosophie de Tübingen'. In J. Duffy and J. Peradotto (eds.) *Gonimos: Neoplatonic and Byzantine Studies Presented to Leendert G. Westerink at 75*. Buffalo: 3–20 (= *Recherches sur le néoplatonisme après Plotin*. Paris 1990: 11–30).

(1992). 'Accorder entre elles les traditions théologiques: une caractéristique du néoplatonisme athénienne'. In P. Bos and P. A. Mejer (eds.) *Proclus and His Influence in Medieval Philosophy*, Leiden: 35–50 (=*Le Néoplatonisme après Plotin*. Paris 2000: 143–58).

(2000). *Le Néoplatonisme après Plotin*. Paris.

Bibliography

Saffrey, H. D. and Segonds, A. P. (eds.) (2001). *Marinus. Proclus ou Sur la bonheur.* Paris.

(2013). *Jamblique. Réponse à Porphyre. De mysteriis.* Paris.

Saffrey, H. D. and Westerink, L. G. (1978). *Proclus. Théologie platonicienne,* Paris, vol. III.

Schibli, H. (1993). 'Xenocrates' Daemons and the Irrational Soul'. *Classical Quarterly* 43: 143–67.

(2002). *Hierocles of Alexandria.* Oxford.

Schniewind, A. (2003). *L'éthique du sage chez Plotin. Le paradigme du spoudaios.* Paris.

Schofield, M. (2021). *Cicero.* Oxford.

Schramm, M. (2014). 'Platonic Ethics and Politics in Themistius and Julian'. In R. C. Fowler (ed.) *Plato in the Third Sophistic.* Berlin: 131–44.

Schroeder, F. M. (1987). 'Ammonius Saccas'. In *ANRW* II 36.1: 493–526.

Schrenk, L. (1991a). 'A Middle Platonic Reading of Plato's Theory of Recollection'. *Ancient Philosophy* 11: 103–10.

(1991b). 'Faculties of Judgment in the *Didaskalikos*'. *Mnemosyne* 44: 347–63.

Schütrumpf, E. (ed.) (2008). *Heraclides of Pontus: Texts and Translation.* New Brunswick, NJ-London.

Schwyzer, H.-R. (1983). *Ammonios Sakkas, der Lehrer Plotins.* Opladen.

Sedley, D. (1977). 'Diodorus Cronus and Hellenistic Philosophy'. *Proceedings of the Cambridge Philosophical Society* 23: 74–120.

(1996). 'Alcinous' Epistemology'. In K. Algra, P. W. van der Horst, and D. T. Runia (eds.). *Polyhistor: Studies in the History and Historiography of Ancient Philosophy. Presented to Jaap Mansfeld on His Sixtieth Birthday.* Leiden: 300–12.

(1997). 'Plato's *Auctoritas* and the Rebirth of the Commentary Tradition'. In Barnes and Griffin 1997: 110–29.

(2002). 'The Origins of the Stoic God'. In Frede and Laks 2002: 41–83.

(2003). 'Philodemus and the Decentralisation of Philosophy'. *Cronache ercolanesi* 33: 31–41.

(ed.) (2012). *The Philosophy of Antiochus.* Cambridge.

(2020). 'Carneades' Theological Arguments'. In Kalligas *et al.* 2020: 220–41.

(2021a). 'Xenocrates' Invention of Platonism'. In Erler, Heßler, and Petrucci 2021: 12–37.

(2021b). 'An Iconography of Xenocrates' Platonism'. In Erler, Heßler, and Petrucci 2021: 38–63.

Sedley, D. and Bastianini, G. (ed.) (1995). 'Commentarium in Platonis *Theaetetum*'. In *Corpus dei papiri filosofici greci e latini, parte III: Commentari,* Florence: 227–562.

Segonds, A. P. and Steel, C. (eds.) (2000). *Proclus et la théologie platonicienne.* Leuven-Paris.

Seng, H. and Tardieu, M. (eds.) (2010). *Die Chaldaeischen Orakel. Kontext – Interpretation – Rezeption.* Heidelberg.

Bibliography

Sharples, R. W. (2003). 'Threefold Providence: The History and Background of a Doctrine'. In R. W. Sharples and A. Sheppard (eds.) *Ancient Approaches to Plato's Timaeus*. London: 107–27.

(2010). *Peripatetic Philosophy 200 BC to AD 200: An Introduction and Collection of Sources in Translation*. Cambridge.

Smith, A. (ed.) (1993). *Porphyri Philosophy Fragmenta*. Leipzig.

(2010). 'Porphyry and His School'. In Gerson 2010a: 325–57.

Smith, R. (1995). *Julian's Gods: Religion and Philosophy in the Thought and Action of Julian the Apostate*. London-New York.

Sorabji, R. (2004). *The Philosophy of the Commentators 200–600 AD*. Ithaca, 3 vols.

Spinelli, E. (2000). 'Sextus Empiricus, the Neighbouring Philosophies and the Sceptical Tradition'. In J. Sihvola (ed.) *Ancient Scepticism and the Sceptical Tradition*. Helsinki: 35–61.

Steel, C. (1978). *The Changing Self*. Brussels.

(1998). Proclus on the Existence of Evil'. *Proceedings of the Boston Area Colloquium in Ancient Philosophy* 14: 83–102.

(2002a). 'A Neoplatonic Speusippus?' In M. Barbanti, G. Giardina, and P. Mangano (eds.) *Henosis kai Philia. Unione e amicizia. Omaggio a Francesco Romano*. Catania: 469–76.

(2002b). 'Une histoire de l'interprétation du Parménide dans l'antiquité'. In M. Barbanti and F. Romano (eds.) *Il Parmenide di Platone e la sua tradizione*, Catania: 11–40.

(2006). 'Appendice. Dopo trent'anni ... uno sguardo retrospettivo'. In *Il Sé che cambia. L'anima nel tardo Neoplatonismo: Giamblico, Damascio e Prisciano*. Bari (Italian translation of Steel 1978).

(ed.) (2007). *Proclus: On Providence*. London.

(2010). 'Proclus'. In Gerson 2010a: 630–53.

(ed.) (2013). *The Cambridge Companion to Cicero*. Cambridge.

Stern-Gillet, S. (2014). 'Plotinus on Metaphysics and Morality'. In P. Remes and S. Slaveva-Griffin (eds.) *The Routledge Handbook of Neoplatonism*. Oxford: 396–420.

Stover, J. A. (ed.) (2016). *A New Work by Apuleius: The Lost Third Book of the De Platone*. Oxford.

Striker, G. (1980). 'Sceptical Strategies'. In M. Schofield, M. F. Burnyeat, and J. Barnes (eds.) *Doubt and Dogmatism: Studies in Hellenistic Epistemology*. Oxford: 54–83 (= *Essays on Hellenistic Epistemology and Ethics*. Cambridge 1996: 92–115).

(1981). 'Über den Unterschied zwischen den Pyrrhoneern und den Akademikern'. *Phronesis* 26: 153–71 (English translation: 'On the Difference between the Phyrrhonists and the Academics'. In *Essays on Hellenistic Epistemology and Ethics*. Cambridge 1996: 135–49).

(1997). 'Academics Fighting Academics'. In Inwood and Mansfeld 1997: 257–76.

Bibliography

Stroh, W. (2008). *Cicero*. Munich.

Stump, E. and Kretzmann, N. (eds.) (2001). *The Cambridge Companion to Augustine*. Cambridge.

Swain, S. (2013). *Themistius, Julian, and Greek Political Theory under Rome*. Cambridge.

Szlezák, T. A. (ed.). (1972). *Pseudo-Archytas über die Kategorien*. Berlin.

(1979). *Platon und Aristoteles in der Nuslehre Plotins*. Basel.

Tanaseanu-Döbler, I. (2008). *Konversion zur Philosophie in der Spatantike: Kaiser Julian und Synesios von Kyrene*. Stuttgart.

(2013). *Theurgy in Late Antiquity: The Invention of a Ritual Tradition*. Göttingen.

Taormina, D. P. (1999). *Jamblique critique de Plotin et de Porphyre. Quatre études*. Paris.

(2012). 'Platonismo e pitagorismo'. In Chiaradonna 2012: 103–27.

Taormina, D. P. and Piccione, R. M. (eds.) (2010). *Giamblico. I frammenti dalle Epistole*. Naples.

Tarán, L. (1981). *Speusippus of Athens: A Critical Study with a Collection of the Related Texts and Commentary*. Leiden.

(1987). 'Proclus on the Old Academy'. In J. Pépin and H. D. Saffrey (eds.) *Proclus lecteur et inteprète des anciens*. Paris: 227–76.

Tardieu, M. (1987). 'Les calendriers en usage à Harrân d'après les sources arabes et le commentaire de Simplicius à la *Physique* d'Aristote'. In I. Hadot 1987: 40–57.

(1992). 'Les gnostiques dans la Vie de Plotin, analyse du chapitre 16'. In L. Brisson *et al.*, *Porphyre. Vie de Plotin*, Paris: 503–63.

(1996). 'Recherches sur la formation de l'*Apocalypse* de Zostrien et les sources de Marius Victorinus'. *Res Orientales* 9: 1–114.

Tarrant, H. (1985). *Scepticism or Platonism? The Philosophy of the Fourth Academy*. Cambridge.

(1993). *Thrasyllan Platonism*. Ithaca, NY.

(2005). *Recollecting Plato's Meno*. London.

(2020). 'One Academy? The Transition from Polemo and Crates to Arcesilaus'. In Kalligas *et al.* 2020: 200–19.

Theiler, W. (1930). *Die Vorbereitung des Neuplatonismus*. Berlin.

Thesleff, H. (1965). *The Pythagorean Texts of the Hellenistic Period*. Åbo.

Thiel, D. (2006). *Die Philosophie des Xenocrates im Kontext der alten Akademie*. Leipzig.

Thiel, R. von (1999). *Simplikios und das Ende der neuplatonischen Schule in Athen*. Mainz.

Timotin, A. (2018). *La prière dans la tradition platonicienne. De Platon à Proclus*. Turnhout.

Todd, R. B. and Bowen, A. C. (2009). 'Heraclides on the Rotation of the Earth: Texts, Contexts and Continuities'. In W. W. Fortenbaugh and E. E. Pender (eds.) *Heraclides of Pontus: Discussion*. New Brunswick, NJ: 155–84.

Bibliography

Tornau, C. (2000). 'Die Prinzipienlehre des Moderatos von Gades'. *RhM* 143: 197–220.

(2009). 'Qu'est-ce qu'un individu? Unité, individualité et conscience de soi dans la métaphysique plotinienne de l'âme'. *Les études philosophiques* 90: 333–60.

(2015). 'Happiness in this Life? Augustine on the Principle that Virtue is Self-Sufficient for Happiness'. In Ø. Rabbås, E. K. Emilsson, H. Fossheim, and M. Tuominen (eds.) *The Quest for the Good Life: Ancient Philosophers on Happiness*. Oxford: 265–80.

Trabattoni, F. (1987). 'Il frammento 4 di Attico'. *Rivista di storia della filosofia* 42: 421–38.

(2005). 'Arcesilao platonico?' In Bonazzi and Celluprica 2005: 13–50.

(2010). 'Y a-t-il une onto-théologie dans le platonisme antérieur à Plotin?' *Études platoniciennes* 7: 201–15.

(2011). 'Le "silence de Platon", ou le renversement du dicours dialectique chez Damascius'. In A. Longo (ed.) *Argument from Hypothesis in Ancient Philosophy*. Naples: 413–35.

(2016). 'L'accademia antica'. In F. Trabattoni and M. Vegetti (eds.) *Storia della filosofia antica*, vol. 2: *Platone e Aristotele*. Rome: 143–64.

Trampedach, K. (1994). *Platon, die Akademie und die zeitgenössische Politik*. Stuttgart.

Trapp, M. (ed.) (1997). *Maximus of Tyre: The Philosophical Orations*. Oxford.

(2004). 'Statesmanship in a Minor Key?' In L. De Blois *et al.* (eds.) *The Statesman in Plutarch's Works*, vol. I: *Plutarch's Statesman and His Aftermath: Political, Philosophical, and Literary Aspects*. Leiden: 189–200.

(2007a). *Philosophy in the Roman Empire: Ethics, Politics and Society*. London.

(2007b). 'Apuleius of Madauros and Maximus of Tyre'. In R. Sharples and R. Sorabji (eds.) *Greek and Roman Philosophy. 100 BC–200 AD*. London, vol. 2: 467–82.

Tsouni, G. (2019). *Antiochus and Peripatetic Ethics*. Cambridge.

Tuominen, M. (2009). *The Ancient Commentators on Plato and Aristotle*. Berkeley.

Turcan, R. (1975). *Mithras Platonicus. Recherches sur l'hellénisation philosophique de Mithra*. Leiden.

Turner, J. D. (2001). *Sethian Gnosticism and the Platonic Tradition*. Québec-Paris.

Ueberweg, F. and Prächter, K. (1926). *Grundriss der Geschichte der Philosophie*. Berlin.

Ulacco, A. (ed.) (2017). *Pseudopytagorica Dorica. I trattati di argomento metafisico, logico ed epistemologico attribuiti ad Archita e Brotino*. Berlin.

Van den Berg, R. (2000). 'Towards the Paternal Harbour. Proclean Theurgy and the Contemplation of th Forms'. In Segonds and Steel 2000: 425–43.

Van den Horst, P. (1996). '"A Simple Philosophy": Alexander of Lycopolis on Christianity'. In K. Algra, P. W. van der Horst, and D. T. Runia

Bibliography

(eds.) *Polyhistor: Studies in the History and Historiography of Ancient Philosophy. Presented to Jaap Mansfeld on His Sixtieth Birthday*, Leiden: 313–29.

Van Hoof, L. (2010). *Plutarch's Practical Ethics: The Social Dynamics of Philosophy*. Oxford.

Van Nuffelen, P. (2011). *Rethinking the Gods: Philosophical Readings of Religion in the Post-Hellenistic Period*. Cambridge.

Van Riel, G. (2000). *Pleasure and the Good Life: Plato, Aristotle, and the Neoplatonists*. Leiden.

(2001). 'Horizontalism or verticalism? Proclus vs Plotinus on the Procession of Matter'. *Phronesis* 46: 129–53.

(2010). 'Damascius'. In Gerson 2010a: 667–696.

(2018). 'Augustine's Plato'. In H. Tarrant, D. Layne, D. Baltzly, and F. Renaud (eds.) *Brill's Companion to the Reception of Plato in Antiquity*. Leiden: 448–69.

Vegetti, M. (2003). 'I filosofi a scuola e la scuola dei filosofi'. In M. Vegetti (ed.) *Platone. La repubblica*, vol. V: *Libro VI–VII*. Naples: 603–24.

(2015). 'Galeno, il "divinissimo" Platone e i platonici'. *Rivista di storia della filosofia* 70: 447–72.

Verde, F. (2014). 'Review of Caruso 2013'. *Elenchos* 35: 387–95.

Verrycken, K. (2010). 'John Philoponus'. In Gerson 2010a: 733–55.

Vezzoli, S. (2016). *Arcesilao di Pitane*. Turnhout.

Von Wilamowitz Möllendorf, U. (1881). *Antigonos von Karystos*. Berlin.

Wallis, R. T. (1972). *Neoplatonism*. London.

Warren, J. (2009). 'Aristotle on Speusippus on Eudoxus on Pleasure'. *Oxford Studies in Ancient Philosophy* 36: 249–81.

Waszink, J. H. (ed.) (1962). *Timaeus a Calcidio translatus*. Leiden.

Watts, E. (2007). 'Creating the Academy: Historical Discourse and the Shape of Community in the Old Academy'. *Journal of Hellenic Studies* 127: 106–22.

Wehrli, F. (1969). *Die Schule des Aristoteles, Heft VII: Herakleides Pontikos*. Basel.

Weische, A. (1961). *Cicero und die Neue Akademie*. Münster.

Weithman, P. (2001). 'Augustine's Political Philosophy'. In E. Stump and N. Kretzmann (eds.) *The Cambridge Companion to Augustine*. Cambridge: 234–52.

White, S. (ed.) (2021). *Diogenes Laertius: Lives of the Eminent Philosophers*. Cambridge.

Whittaker, J. (1973). 'Neopyhtagoreanism and the Transcendent Absolute'. *Symbolae Osloenses* 48: 77–86.

(ed.) (1990). *Alcinoos. Enseignement des doctrines de Platon*. Paris.

Wilberding, J. (2006). *Plotinus' Cosmology: A Study of Ennead II.1 (40)*. Oxford.

Wildberg, C. (2005). 'Philosophy in the Age of Justinian'. In M. Maas (ed.) *The Cambridge Companion to the Age of Justinian*. Cambridge: 316–40.

Bibliography

Wilson, M. C. (1997). 'Speusippus on Knowledge and Division'. In W. Kullmann and S. Föllinger (eds.) *Aristotelische Biologie: Intentionen, Methoden, Ergebnisse.* Stuttgart: 13–25.

Yavetz, I. (1998). 'On the Homocentric Spheres of Eudoxus'. *Archive for History of Exact Sciences* 52: 221–78.

Zambon, M. (2002). *Poprhyre et le Moyen-Platonisme.* Paris.

(2011). 'Porfirio e Origene'. In S. Morlet (ed.) *Le traité de Porphyre contre les Chrétiens. Un siècle de recherches, nouvelles questions.* Paris: 107–64.

(2012a). 'Platonismo e cristianesimo'. In Chiaradonna 2012: 129–51.

(2012b). 'Poprhyre de Tyre. *Contra Christianos'.* In R. Goulet (ed.) *Dictionnaire des philosophes antiques.* Paris, vol. V B: 1419–47.

(2015). 'Il confronto tra cristiani e platonici nel II–III secolo'. *Rivista di storia della filosofia* 70: 473–88.

(2019. *'Nessun dio è mai sceso quaggiù'. La polemica anticristiana dei filosofi antichi.* Rome.

Zanker, P. (1996). *The Mask of Socrates: The Image of the Intellectual in Antiquity.* Berkeley-Los Angeles-Oxford.

Zetzel, J. E. G. (ed.) (1999). *Cicero: On the Commonwealth and on the Laws.* Cambridge.

(2013). 'Political Philosophy'. In C. Steel (ed.) *The Cambridge Companion to Cicero.* Cambridge: 181–95.

Zhmud, L. (1998). 'Plato as "Architect of Science"'. *Phronesis* 43: 211–44.

(2005). '"Saving the Phenomena" between Eudoxus and Eudemus'. In G. Wolters and M. Carrier (eds.) *Homo Sapiens und Homo Faber: epistemische und technische Rationalität in Antike und Gegenwart: Festschrift für Jürgen Mittelstrass.* Berlin: 17–24.

(2006). *The Origin of the History of Science in Classical Antiquity.* Berlin.

(2013). 'Pythagorean Number Doctrine in the Academy'. In Cornelli, Macris, and McKirahan 2013: 343–44.

(2016). 'Greek Arithmology: Pythagoras or Plato?' In A.-B. Renger and A. Stavru (eds.) *Pythagorean Knowledge from the Ancient to the Modern World: Askesis, Religion.* Wiesbaden: 321–46.

Zumpt, K. G. (1843). 'Über den Bestand der philosophischen Schulen in Athen und die Succession der Scholarchen'. *Abhandlungen der königlichen Akademie der Wissenschaften zu Berlin*: 27–119.

INDEX

Index

Eudoxus of Cnidus, 7
  on forms, 20
  on the movements of the planets, 25
  on pleasure, 30
eulabeia. See Plutarch of Chaeronea
Eusebius of Caesarea, 185, 200
Exegetical principles, 83–5, 124

Gnosticism, 111–2

Hadot, Ilsetraut, 129
Henads, 138, 147
Heraclides of Pontus, 6, 7
Hierocles, 190
Hypatia of Alexandria, 199

Iamblichus of Chalcis, 122–5, 147
  canon of Plato's dialogues, 124
  on the One, 138
  school of, 125
  on the Soul, 158
  and theurgy, 166
interpretation of the Hellenistic Academy
  Aenesidemus, 59
  Antiochus, 67–8
  Numenius, 106–7
  Philo, 63–4
  Plutarch and the anonymous commentator
    on the *Theaetetus*, 79, 99
  Proclus, 39, 127

John Philoponus, 130, 131, 152, 202
Julian, Flavius Claudius, 183–5, 190
  and Christianism, 194
Justin, 197

Krämer, Hans Joachim, 37

Longinus, 81, 119, 144
  On Forms, 93
Lucius, 81, 100

mathematics, 26, 105
Maximus of Ephesus, 184
Maximus of Tyre, 114
Menaechmus, 27
Menedemus of Pyrrha, 6
metaphysical scepticism, 99
metriopatheia, 35, 101

Metrodorus of Stratonicea, 42, 57
Middle Platonists
  and assimilation to God, 101
  and Christianism, 191–2
  on the eternity of the universe, 95–6
  on Fate, 102–3
  on the first principles, 91–2, 108
  on Forms, 92–4, 98, 144
  On the human soul, 101
  on Matter, 94
  theory of knowledge, 97–9
Moderatus of Gades, 82, 104

Nag Hammadi, 111
negative theology, 134
Neoplatonists
  and Christianism, 191–2
  on the sensible world, 150
Nicomachus of Gerasa, 82, 104
Nicostratus, 81, 100
Nigidius Figulus, 103
Numenius of Apamea, 82, 91, 105–10,
  122, 199

Oriental wisdom, 108
Origen, 119, 197

paideia, 114, 197
Pantaenus of Alexandria, 197
Peripatetics on Plato, 78
Philip of Opus, 7
Philo of Larissa, 42, 178
  and Plato, 63–4
  Roman Books, 58–9
  theory of knowledge, 57
pistis, 200
Plato
  Parmenides, 125, 127, 135, 146
  Republic, 26, 135
  Sophist, 144
  Theaetetus, 161
  Timaeus, 21, 22, 84, 87–9, 95, 125,
    147, 152
platonikos, 3
Platonism
  and Aristotle, 80–2, 88, 90, 124, 148
  and Pythagoreanism, 87, 89,
    103–5, 124
  and Stoicism, 80, 147

Index